THE ROUTLEDGE INTRODUCTION TO AFRICAN AMERICAN LITERATURE

The Routledge Introduction to African American Literature considers the key literary, political, historical, and intellectual contexts of African American literature from its origins to the present, and also provides students with an analysis of the most up-to-date literary trends and debates in this field. This accessible and engaging guide covers a variety of essential topics such as:

- The origins of African American literature
- The emergence of slave narratives
- The Harlem Renaissance
- Mid-twentieth-century black American literature
- Literature of the Civil Rights and Black Power eras
- Contemporary African American writing
- Key theoretical debates within the field

Examining the relationship between the literature and its sociopolitical contexts, Quentin Miller covers key authors and works as well as less canonical writers and themes, including literature and music, female authors, queer writing and transnational black writing.

D. Quentin Miller is Professor of English at Suffolk University, USA.

ROUTLEDGE INTRODUCTIONS TO AMERICAN LITERATURE

Series Editors: D. Quentin Miller and Wendy Martin

Routledge Introductions to American Literature provide a comprehensive overview of the most important topics in American literature in its historical, cultural, and intellectual contexts. They present the most up-to-date trends, debates, and exciting new directions in the field, opening the way for further study.

The volumes in the series examine the ways in which both canonical and lesser known writers from diverse cultural backgrounds have shaped American literary traditions. In addition to providing insight into contemporary and theoretical debates and giving attention to a range of voices and experiences as a vital part of American life, these comprehensive volumes offer clear, cohesive narratives of the development of American literature.

The American literary tradition has always been flexible and mutable. Every attempt to define American literature as a static body has been thwarted by the nature of the subject, which is – like its nation's ideals – pluralistic, diverse, democratic, and inventive. Our goal in this series is to provide fresh perspectives on many dimensions of the American literary tradition while offering a solid overview for readers encountering it for the first time.

D. Quentin Miller and Wendy Martin

Available in this series:

The Routledge Introduction to African American Literature
D. Quentin Miller

The Routledge Introduction to American Modernism
Linda Wagner-Martin

The Routledge Introduction to American Women Writers
Wendy Martin and Sharone Williams

THE ROUTLEDGE INTRODUCTION TO AFRICAN AMERICAN LITERATURE

D. Quentin Miller

 Routledge
Taylor & Francis Group

LONDON AND NEW YORK

First published 2016
by Routledge
2 Park Square, Milton Park, Abingdon, Oxon OX14 4RN

and by Routledge
711 Third Avenue, New York, NY 10017

Routledge is an imprint of the Taylor & Francis Group, an informa business

British Library Cataloguing in Publication Data
A catalogue record for this book is available from the British Library

Library of Congress Cataloging in Publication Data
  Names: Miller, D. Quentin (Daniel Quentin), 1967-
  Title: The Routledge introduction to African American literature /
  D. Quentin Miller.
  Description: New York : Routledge, 2016. | Series: Routledge introductions
  to American literature | Includes bibliographical references and index.
  Identifiers: LCCN 2015030103| ISBN 9780415839648
  (hardback : alk. paper) | ISBN 9780415839655 (pbk. : alk. paper) |
  ISBN 9780203771013 (ebook)
  Subjects: LCSH: American literature--African American authors--History
  and criticism.
  Classification: LCC PS153.N5 M5 2016 | DDC 810.9/896073--dc23
  LC record available at http://lccn.loc.gov/2015030103

ISBN: 978-0-415-83964-8 (hbk)
ISBN: 978-0-415-83965-5 (pbk)
ISBN: 978-0-203-77101-3 (ebk)

Typeset in Bembo
by Taylor & Francis Books

CONTENTS

ACKNOWLEDGEMENT

This small book about a big subject started as a collaborative project with Doug Field, who realized early on that he had too much on his plate and backed out, reluctantly and politely. I'd like to begin by thanking him for getting the ball rolling. I would also like to thank my series co-editor, Wendy Martin, for all of her patience and goodwill throughout the process. At Routledge, a big shout-out to Polly Dodson for developing the series with us and to Liz Levine for filling in while Polly was on parental leave.

During the summer of 2012 I was fortunate enough to spend three weeks at the Pennsylvania State University for an NEH Summer Fellowship on contemporary African American literature. Lovalerie King organized a stellar group of scholars, led by Trudier Harris, Maryemma Graham, and Dana Nelson, who guided our discussions for three memorable, valuable weeks. I'd like to thank all of them and also all of my fellow institute scholars: space prevents me from listing everyone here, but you know who you are and how much I value your insights and friendship.

I would also like to thank Claudine Raynaud of the Université Paul-Valéry in Montpellier, France for arranging a visiting professorship for me in the summer of 2013 where I was able to make substantial progress on this volume. Un million de merci!

At Suffolk University I appreciate, as ever, the support of Dean Ken Greenberg, in many tangible and intangible ways. One of the tangible ways was through providing the funding for an extraordinary research assistant in 2013–2014, Mary Boutet, whose attention to detail, organizational skills, and eye for editing are tremendous. I owe a world of gratitude to Professor Emeritus Ed Clark for initiating and maintaining the Clark Collection of African American literature at the Sawyer library. This resource allowed Mary and me to conduct most of the research we needed without leaving campus. Finally, Kelly Hoarty provided her trademark cheery clerical support whenever I asked for it, both for this volume and for the James Baldwin conference Claudine and I hosted in France while I was completing it.

I dedicate this book to my students at Suffolk University, past, present, and future.

1

INTRODUCTION AND OVERVIEW

The Stories of African American Literature

We younger Negro artists who create now intend to express our individual dark-skinned selves without fear or shame. If white people are pleased we are glad. If they are not, it doesn't matter. We know we are beautiful. And ugly too.... If colored people are pleased we are glad. If they are not, their displeasure doesn't matter either.
Langston Hughes, "The Negro Artist and the Racial Mountain," 1926

The Negro writer who seeks to function within his race as a purposeful agent has a serious responsibility. In order to do justice to his subject matter, in order to depict Negro life in all of its manifold and intricate relationships, a deep, informed, and complex consciousness is necessary; a consciousness which draws for its strength upon the fluid lore of a great people, and moulds this lore with the concepts that move and direct the forces of history today.
Richard Wright, "Blueprint for Negro Writing," 1937

I would like to write novels that were unmistakably mine, but nevertheless fit first into African American traditions and second of all, this whole thing called literature.
Toni Morrison, interview, 1993

These days I find myself wanting to avoid being pigeon-holed, ghettoized, held in a different category [from] other authors. And when people ask me if I'm a black writer, or just a writer who happens to be black, I tend to say that it's either a dumb question or a question which happens to be dumb. I'm an African-American writer, I'm a lazy writer, I'm a writer who likes to watch *The Wire*, I'm a writer who likes to eat a lot of steak.
Colson Whitehead, interview, 2013

These pronouncements about the nature and function of African American literature by some of the most prominent black writers over the past hundred years indicate some crucial differences of opinion. There are some easily discernible patterns based on history: in moments of crisis, such as the racially segregated Great Depression during which Richard Wright wrote his "blueprint," there is an intensity and sharpness to his message as he uses phrases like "purposeful agent," "serious responsibility," and "complex consciousness" to describe the situation of the black writer. Colson Whitehead, writing in our contemporary world which seems much more prosperous and less fraught by racial antagonism than Wright's did, can joke about how the fact that he likes steak is nearly as important as his race. Regardless of their historical context, all four of these quotations raise important questions that cannot be answered easily, especially about audience and about the responsibilities of the black writer. There is always a tension between an African American writer's individual impulses and a perceived duty to respond to a tradition defined in racial terms. Note that Morrison's *first* obligation is to write works that complement that tradition, and that Wright is conscious of "the fluid lore of a great people." Both Hughes and Whitehead seem to want to rise above their audience's expectations, but both begin their responses heavily conscious of what those expectations are.

Hughes's 1926 essay "The Negro Artist and the Racial Mountain" is often read as a cogent definition of the goals of the Harlem Renaissance (or "New Negro Renaissance"). This brief period during the 1920s marks a significant moment in African American literary history, as it was the first time black authors had articulated their hopes and goals as a collective group of artists. Hughes celebrates black American life and acknowledges that it is different from white American life: not inferior, but different. The quotation above is a clarion call not only to black artists, but also to all African Americans. Hughes hopes for a celebration of black culture and identity. But the words "fear" and "shame" at the beginning of it are significant. Why are fear and shame associated with blackness in America? Why does it take an exhortation like this one from Hughes to rally black artists to express themselves honestly? Why did some black readers in 1926 favor what Hughes called "ordinary" (read "dull") white books over the exuberant expressions of their own culture? Why did they need art to teach them how to appreciate their own beauty?

These are questions that had to be raised with some urgency in the 1920s, and they reverberate thereafter. Hughes and his contemporaries were conscious that there was a body of African American literature that preceded them, but also that the historical and social circumstances that produced that literature was fraught with injustice and immorality. Bluntly, the horrors of the system of chattel slavery in the United States are impossible to overcome, even for those who were born after slavery was abolished. Although the era of slavery is now a century and a half in the past, its long-term effects live on. The goal of racial equality and harmony remains an elusive one. African American writers respond to these basic facts, but they do so in a variety of ways broad enough to produce a rich literary tradition.

The Nature of *The Routledge Introduction to African American Literature*

With the idea in mind that the African American literary tradition is neither stable nor complete, I offer a short meditation on the nature of this book, to distinguish it from a host of other books on this subject that are also available. The chapters that follow constitute a literary history of a fairly traditional kind: a chronological arrangement of some of the most significant works written by people of African descent living in the nation that is now the United States. This book is very much an *overview* of this tradition, an *introduction* intended to provide context for readers who are approaching the body of African American literature for the first time. The works, authors, and movements or periods discussed here are ones that the student of African American literature should become acquainted with. Ideally, this book will deepen the experience of anyone coming to African American literature with little previous exposure to it. It is not a book for experts: its primary intent is to provide an accurate and informative overview of the main works in the tradition, their basic relationship to one another, and their connection to the historical circumstances in which they were produced. I refer to more works and authors here than one could study in a semester or two, but that is the nature of an overview. My hope is to provide readers with a cursory familiarity with the traditions surrounding the literary works they will read and discuss closely, as well as brief summaries of the central works in the tradition so they are better equipped to situate and contextualize those works.

Even though the amount of literature discussed in these pages may seem overwhelming to a student encountering the African American literary tradition for the first time, teachers or advanced scholars might be aghast by all this book leaves out. The African American literary tradition is vast. There are significant African American authors, individual works, and even movements that are not represented in this study in the interest of brevity. Also, any literary history is more a narrative than an encyclopedia. In constructing this narrative, I have had to cope with questions of not only what to include and what to leave out, but also what to emphasize. Some literary historians try to avoid distinguishing between authors who are important (or "major") from those whose works have traditionally been marginal or ancillary to the mainstream of the tradition. Insofar as it is possible, I have tried to sidestep the fallout from the so-called "canon wars" of the late twentieth century, when scholars bickered over the politics behind critics' and educators' decisions about which works constitute "required reading" for students. These debates (still ongoing) are important, as they encourage scholars and students to examine the reasons why some works have been considered "great" while others have been forgotten, but for the purpose of this book, without sounding too naïve, I have merely tried to include at least a glimpse of the works of African American literature that *are* required reading, or once were, or should be for a variety of reasons. My hope is that this volume will inspire its readers to read every work and author it references, then go on to discover those many other worthy works and authors I couldn't include. The "Suggestions for Further Reading" at the end of each chapter are good starting points for anyone wanting to deepen their appreciation and understanding of the field.

Historical and Literary Overview

Since it is organized chronologically, this book progresses against the background of history. African American history begins with the importation of African slaves by European colonizers into the "New World" beginning in the seventeenth century. The story continues through the abolition of slavery into an unstable period toward the end of the nineteenth century when black Americans no longer had slave status, yet faced abhorrent discrimination (some of it legally sanctioned, through the practice of segregation and Jim Crow laws, some of it deeply felt through social ostracism, discrimination in the workplace, and hate speech). The early twentieth century saw the Great Migration of more than a million African Americans from the agrarian South to cities in the industrial North. Following the two world wars, black Americans concentrated on attaining what came to be known as civil rights, and the passage of anti-segregation legislation in 1954 and voting rights legislation in the mid-1960s were steps in the direction of long overdue racial equality. Still, there was considerable turbulence in the 1960s as is evident in the assassinations of prominent black leaders Malcolm X and Martin Luther King, Jr., as well as race riots in many major cities.

The 1970s and 1980s saw less violent and less urgent demonstrations arising from the desire for harmony, yet despite the prominence of high-profile black politicians (such as National Security Advisor Colin Powell, who later became Secretary of State) and presidential candidates (Shirley Chisholm in 1972 and Jesse Jackson in 1984), the main focus during those decades in the popular imagination was on the alarming rise of black-on-black homicide, the rise of gang culture, and an unprecedented spike in the rate of incarceration of black people. The 1992 Los Angeles riots following the acquittal of police officers accused of beating a black motorist named Rodney King indicated that a great deal of racial animosity remained just below the surface of American life.

The election of Barack Obama as America's first black president in 2009 indicates a level of racial cooperation unimaginable even a half-century earlier, and the extraordinary success and media exposure of certain black figures – from Oprah Winfrey and Jay-Z at the popular end of the spectrum to bell hooks and Cornel West at the academic end – reinforces the widespread perception that the worst horrors of racism are largely behind us. Yet many Americans remain skeptical that these success stories tell the whole tale, especially as gaps continue to widen between whites and blacks in terms of income, education, and rates of incarceration. In recent years, demonstrations and sometimes violence over incidents involving the deaths of black citizens at the hands of white police officers and rogue racists bearing arms have stirred up dormant racial unrest.

Against the background of that brief history, one might describe African American literary history as follows. Most of the earliest works of African American literature were slave narratives: non-fiction works by slaves about the slave experience. As the genre evolved in the early nineteenth century, virtually all of these narratives shared a few common features: they were framed by the testimonies of white authors about the veracity and character of the author; they were overtly committed to the cause of abolition and often spoke directly to their intended audiences who were presumed to be sympathetic whites; and they did not end at the moment of the slave's escape, but went beyond to tell how the free ex-slave discovered commitment and purpose in the North, generally in the service of the abolitionist cause. In short, these works, though powerful and inspirational, are somewhat formulaic. While fighting for their literal freedom, the earliest African American writers were hampered by a lack of creative freedom. Toward the end of the era of slavery, black writers started to branch out into imaginative forms of literature (fiction, poetry, and a smattering of drama), and by the end of the nineteenth century, there were a handful of black writers who made a living from writing.

Still, in most critics' estimations, African American literature of the eighteenth and nineteenth centuries did not produce the finest or most fully realized works of the tradition, even if it produced some important foundational ones. The horrors of slavery and the traumatic aftershocks of segregation, lynching, and general widespread discrimination in the late nineteenth and early twentieth centuries (including limited publication opportunities) continued to inhibit the black literary imagination. Black writers arrived at a new level of artistic freedom in the early decades of the twentieth century, especially in the 1920s when the Harlem Renaissance marked an out-pouring of creative expression and a flourishing of artistic spirit that had not occurred earlier. As the epigraph to this chapter by Langston Hughes (the central figure of the Renaissance) makes clear, it was a time of tremendous positive energy, and the sheer number of enduring novels, poems, plays, and works of non-fiction by African Americans from the 1920s is astounding. The diversity and depth of these works is even more important than their number, and the achievements of this period laid the groundwork for many works that came after.

This is not to say that the works of the Harlem Renaissance were uniformly optimistic, nor that the optimism was deeply felt. There remained serious issues of racial inequality during the 1920s (legal segregation and voting disenfranchisement being the most obvious), as well as nagging self-doubt or even racial self-loathing. Black writers in the decades which followed explored some of the contradictions, discontentment, and rage that might have been buried below the surface of some Renaissance works. Richard Wright in the 1930s and 1940s expressed that rage in no uncertain terms, and his works, along with those of Ralph Ellison, Ann Petry, James Baldwin, Gwendolyn Brooks, Margaret Walker, and Lorraine Hansberry, made the 1940s and 1950s a time of intense literary examination of the psychology as well as the sociology of black life in America.

As riots erupted on the streets in 1960s America, there was also a riot going on in the literary world. The Black Arts Movement, led by Larry Neal, Amiri Baraka, Addison Gayle, Jr., Sonia Sanchez, and Askia Touré, sought to settle once and for all what black literature should be, and what it should do. The architects of this movement had little patience for literature that did not catalyze social change, or did not seek to alter the consciousness of its readers who were, for the most part, assumed to be black. Black Arts Movement authors built on the assassination of the Nation of Islam leader Malcolm X to infuse their works with a new mandate for radical change, and their impassioned writings were difficult to ignore. At the same time, their cries for solidarity carried with them a tendency to reinforce traditional gender roles, which pushed aside the voices of some women. Those voices, inspired not only by the Black Arts Movement of the 1960s but by the feminist movement flourishing at the same time, began to be heard in the 1970s and 1980s in a major way. African American literature in those decades was dominated for the first time by female voices, culminating in Toni Morrison's Pulitzer Prize-winning novel *Beloved* (1987), the publication of which contributed heavily to her glorious achievement as the first African American recipient of the Nobel Prize in Literature in 1993.

Morrison and her contemporaries demonstrated finally that black writers had burst through the barriers that had once held them back in terms of widespread acknowledgement of their contributions. These writers turned their attention largely to history, which became an enduring topic for black writers of the late twentieth century. Revising and revisiting history has remained a prominent subject in African American literature, but it is not necessarily the central subject in recent writing. In fact, there is little consensus about what the central subject of contemporary black literature *is*, or whether there is a central subject. The direction of this tradition in the twenty-first century involves a dispersal of subject matter, and also of style. The radical experimentalism of the Black Arts Movement, with its emphasis on black vernacular traditions such as the blues, has given way to an array of styles and subjects so diverse that the authors of contemporary African American literature do not necessarily seem to form a coherent group. Black literature may no longer be "about" any one thing, including, even, a generic umbrella category like "black identity." Depending upon one's perspective, this development can be seen as a triumph (because black artists are no longer obligated to write about racial themes exclusively) or as a failure (because black artists might feel less compelled to work collectively to improve the circumstances of their race).

The historical and literary–historical scope of the African American literary tradition is covered in greater detail over the next seven chapters. These chapters provide a narrative timeline of some of the key movements and shifts that students of African American literature should know about as they encounter any work from the tradition, no matter where they enter. But the pleasure of learning about this tradition lies in the rich motifs and themes that occur along the timeline, the issues that continually arise for critics, the ongoing debates that will never be resolved, and the themes that emerge through all of these points of productive tension. What follows are some of these points that are likely to occur and recur throughout any sustained engagement with African American literature.

What Makes Black Literature "Black"?

It is easy enough in the abstract to say that everything written by black Americans constitutes African American literature, but literary traditions are not simply collections of all available texts. The epigraph to this chapter by Hughes acknowledges a difference between literature by black Americans and white Americans circa 1926. An assumption was firmly in place at that time: black writers wrote about black experiences, black themes, black history, etc. James Baldwin raised eyebrows in 1956 when he published his second novel, *Giovanni's Room*, in which virtually all of the characters were white. (The novel's treatment of homosexuality was admittedly part of its ability to shock, and Baldwin deliberately wrote about white characters so that the novel didn't get muddled with multiple "issues"). A decade later, the white novelist William Styron – a friend of Baldwin's – met with strong resistance from black readers, writers, and critics for daring to write from the slave's per-spective in his novel *The Confessions of Nat Turner* (1967). This resistance is born of a long history of white authors' stereotyping and/or ignorance of the realities of the African American experience: see Sterling Brown's 1933 essay "Negro Characters as Seen By White Authors" or Toni Morrison's 1992 study *Playing in the Dark: Whiteness and the American Literary Imagination*. As Carolyn F. Gerald wrote in 1969, "we must reject white attempts at portraying black reality....They are valid only in terms of the white man's projection of himself. They have no place in the definition of blackness, for they reveal the white writer's attempt to work through his own cultural guilt, fascination with blackness, or sense of spiritual emptiness" (133). Clearly many readers throughout history have expected black and white writers to stay on their side of the color line. At least, that has been the case at certain moments in history. In the last two epigraphs to this chapter we see Toni Morrison affirming her commitment to African American traditions and Colson Whitehead expressing skepticism about the label "African American writer." The narrator of Percival Everett's novel *erasure* (2001), a black novelist, is mystified that his works are shelved in the African American Studies section of the bookstore, claiming that they are not recognizable within that category: "the only thing ostensibly African American [about them] was my jacket photograph" (28). What are the presumed acceptable subjects for black writers, though? And should writers feel a strong obligation to write about those subjects only or should they rebel against expectations?

It is reasonable to expect that writers during the era of slavery would have written about that experience, and we read their work partly to understand what slavery was like from the perspective of the slaves themselves. But many writers in the last half-century have also written about slavery: Ishmael Reed, Ernest J. Gaines, Alex Haley, Toni Morrison, Octavia Butler, Edward P. Jones, Thylias Moss, and many more. Slavery is the ignoble aspect of the American story – and the fact of African American history – that must not be forgotten. A century and a half after the Emancipation Proclamation and the Thirteenth Amendment to the Constitution abolished slavery, this fact of history remains a source of pain in the national psyche. Contemporary Americans may prefer to move on rather than to dwell on the sins of previous generations, but in this case the past is too strong and its wounds too deep to treat this way. The story of slavery must be told repeatedly, in all of its ugliness, if the nation and individuals within it are to heal properly.

It is not uncommon for black writers to be sensitive to post-slavery injustices, such as racial discrimination, segregation, hate crimes, and the preponderance of crime and poverty in black communities, particularly urban ones, even if these subjects are not necessarily features of these writers' lives. There is more than the usual amount of pressure on these works to frame and comment on social issues. Are these subjects *necessary* to black writing, though? Over time, some black authors have argued that black literature need not be solely a grim catalog of oppression. Hughes's pronouncement at the beginning of this chapter calls for a celebration of black life and its expressions – both the beautiful and the ugly, in his words. As the tradition approaches our contemporary moment, black writers approach black experiences in a variety of ways. There is a great deal at stake when black writers decide on their topics and how to approach them. At the same time, when writers like Richard Wright in his epigraph to this chapter define black writing, they run the risk of limiting its range. If the expectations for black writers are too rigid, the tradition will not evolve; if the expectations are completely eliminated, the distinction between African American literature and American literature in general will cease to exist.

The question "what makes black literature black?" is impossible to answer succinctly or with any consistency in the abstract. There is no critical consensus or "litmus test" that can be applied over the course of the tradition to determine whether or not an author has contributed significantly to it, either in terms of subject matter or the language or idiom in which that subject matter is framed. The fact of the matter is that there is no single "story" of African American literature. There are, though, a cluster of related stories that link history to African American culture. As critic Henry Louis Gates, Jr. writes, "Black literature…can no longer simply name the 'margin.' Close readings are increasingly naming the specificity of black texts, revealing the depth and range of cultural details far beyond the economic exploitation of blacks by whites. This increased focus on the specificity of the text has enabled us to begin to chart the patterns of repetition and revision among texts by black authors" (*Loose*, 101). This repetition and revision – also known as theme and variation, or call and response – is the salient feature of the African American literary tradition. There are patterns, clusters, a nearly infinite web of interconnection. There are moments of explosive breakthrough that set new paradigms for future works. In sum, there is finally a tradition, but even while acknowledging it and defining it, we should be aware that the tradition is always growing and changing shape. Put differently, the story or stories we tell about African American literature change over time, and will continue to change.

The Oral/Vernacular Tradition

The word "vernacular" is a broad term often used in discussions about African American cultural production to refer to many expressions that are not strictly literary (that is, written and published) in nature. Henry Louis Gates, Jr. and Nelly McKay, in their introduction to "The Vernacular Tradition" section of their edited volume *The Norton Anthology of African American Literature*, write, "What, then, is the African American vernacular? It consists of forms sacred – songs, prayers, and sermons – and secular – work songs, secular rhymes and songs, blues, jazz, and stories of many kinds. It also consists of dances, wordless musical performances, stage shows, and visual art forms of many sorts" (6). By including "the vernacular" in a discussion of African American literature, critics like Gates and McKay clearly want to stress the importance of these forms to an understanding of this literature, considerably expanding not only our sense of what might be considered "literature," but also refocusing our attention on what might be especially important within that literature.

In his highly influential study *The Signifying Monkey* (1988) Gates draws on both African and African American myths "to show how the vernacular informs and becomes the foundation for formal black literature" (xxii). Gates's complex theory is original and intriguing for any student of African American literature, but his emphasis on the vernacular is not his alone. Amiri Baraka in *Blues People* (1963) writes, "I cite the beginning of blues as one beginning of American Negroes" (*Blues*, xii). In her memoir *I Know Why the Caged Bird Sings* (1970) Maya Angelou tells of a mentor who instructed her "to listen carefully to what country people called mother wit. That in those homely sayings was couched the collective wisdom of generations" (83). Houston Baker in his 1984 study *Blues, Ideology, and Afro-American Literature* subtitles his work "A Vernacular Theory" and attempts "to demonstrate that a blues matrix…possesses enormous force for the study of literature, criticism, and culture" (14). Richard J. Powell in 1989 writes, "if one is knowledgeable about Afro-America – its history, its traditions, its geography, its verbal and visual codes, its heroes, its demons, its ever changing styles, and its spiritual dimensions – then one knows the blues" (291). In their introduction to *The Cambridge History of African American Literature*, Maryemma Graham and Jerry Ward write, "[African American] literature comprises orature (oral literature) and printed texts simultaneously….The role of utterance or speech is not necessarily secondary to the role of writing or inscription. Speaking and writing are interlocked frequencies of a single formal phenomenon" (2).

Although Gates names many extra-literary expressions as part of the vernacular tradition, two in particular recur in many discussions of black literature: storytelling and the blues. To connect oral literature and the blues may seem to conflate two distinct modes of expression (speech and music), but in fact the black vernacular does not draw a hard line between them. Virtually all critics agree that the blues are integral to an understanding of what black literature is. Many of them have analyzed the lyrics of blues songs as a key to the structure of many black literary works. Blues lyrics state a theme, restate it, and provide a clever variant of it that often comments on and ironically reverses the meaning of the original lyric, indicating the ambiguity of the African American experience. As Ralph Ellison (author of *Invisible Man* (1952), one of the central novels in the black literary canon) writes, "The blues speak to us simultaneously of the tragic and the comic aspects of the human condition and they express a profound sense of life shared by many Negro Americans precisely because their lives have combined these modes" (*Shadow*, 256). Others speak of the nature of the blues, the origins of which include the "sorrow songs" of slaves, Negro spirituals, and jazz.

The "blue note" that technically defines the blues is a means of individual expression, achieved by "bending" a note so that it stretches beyond its tonal range: guitar players push a string upwards within a fret, trumpet players tighten their lips and depress the valves of their instrument slowly, singers subtly adjust their diaphragms, and so forth. These are all ways of manipulating a tune, of turning something familiar into something distinctive, which is the same relationship the blues have to other musical forms. The parallels in African American literature are clear: the most acclaimed African American literature is distinctive because it is familiar within a broader tradition of American literature, yet identifiable as something unique and expressive.

The blues operates as more than a musical form when we consider it as an inroad into black literature. Some writers make us aware of the blues as a theme through even the titles of their works: Langston Hughes titles a story "The Blues I'm Playing" and a famous poem "The Weary Blues;" James Baldwin's most famous story is "Sonny's Blues," and he titled his poetry collection *Jimmy's Blues* (1983) and a play *Blues For Mister Charlie* (1964); the poet Sterling Brown published poems with titles like "Memphis Blues" and "Tin Roof Blues;" Elizabeth Alexander, who read a poem at Barack Obama's first inauguration, has a poem entitled "Blues," and so on. These are just the most overt statements of the influence of the blues on black writing, though. The blues itself is an expansive, fluid term, capable of signifying much more than the popular musical form that has given birth to a host of other popular music forms in America.

One form of the blues is the so-called "talking blues," which is one of the early ancestors of contemporary rap music. There have been variations on the oral/vernacular tradition as long as something like African American literature has existed. As will be discussed in Chapter Two, most slaves in the American colonies in the eighteenth and nineteenth centuries were kept illiterate on purpose, so speech carried extra weight as the means to preserve culture, as well as to communicate. Zora Neale Hurston, a towering figure in the African American literary canon, worked as a folklorist, and her celebrated novel *Their Eyes Were Watching God* (1937) depends heavily on storytelling. Toni Morrison, another towering figure, makes storytelling a central theme of her two most renowned novels, *Song of Solomon* (1977) and *Beloved*. Meaning in these works can only be constructed by those willing to pay attention to told stories, which frequently unfold differently than written stories. Trudier Harris argues that "the interactive dynamics of audience and narrator inform many African American literary texts" (452). Moreover, storytelling showcases the crucial development of a unique *voice* in African American literature. As Morrison writes, one of "the major characteristics" of black writing is "to be both print and oral literature: to combine those two aspects so that the stories can be read in silence, of course, but one should be able to hear them as well" ("Rootedness," 199).

This is too brief a space to discuss fully the crucial importance of the vernacular to the African American literary tradition. Suffice it to say that students who encounter folk tales, evocations of music, and instances of storytelling within this literature would do well to mark them as potentially important.

Popular v. High Art

The prominence of the vernacular isn't the only complicating factor in defining African American literature. "Literature," in addition to referring to written texts, generally connotes writing of some enduring social or cultural value. Literature is often associated with complexity, and its texts embody multiple meanings. The poet Ezra Pound defined it as "news that stays news;" in other words, its relevance endures over time. As a subject of study in academic settings, literature is often presented as a form of cultural production that is challenging to understand due to complex layering and obscure allusions. This line of thinking suggests that literature is something not everyone can appreciate: it requires of its readers a level of sophistication that comes with experience, education, and training.

Yet within every tradition there are works of literature deemed "popular," or works that might fit into certain genre categories (such as "crime," "romance," or "science fiction" within the broader category of fiction). Our discussion of "the vernacular" brings with it the question of what makes a work worthy of the name *literature*. Must literature be high art in the sense of being sophisticated, intellectual, and informed by a long tradition of other literary works? These questions pertain to all bodies of literature, but they are especially poignant in terms of nineteenth-century African American literature because of the context of its production and the nature of its audience. Many early works of African American literature had a specific rhetorical intent: to persuade the (white, educated) reader of the moral repugnancy of slavery and to expose readers to the physical, mental, and spiritual degradation suffered by slaves. These works are relatively straightforward, and their central intent can be gleaned by readers without much experience or training, as well as by more sophisticated readers. Yet one of the earliest works of African American literature is Phillis Wheatley's poetry collection, *Poems on Various Subjects, Religious and Moral* (1773), and it is consistent with the most erudite poetry of the eighteenth century: highly formal in terms of its strict meter and rhyme, allusive to classical literature, marked by learned diction, etc.

Holding up Wheatley's poetry alongside some of the early slave narratives, one sees a superficial contrast between "high" and "low" works of literature. The questions such a comparison raises are profound. Poetry is generally the most rarified of literary forms, so it is not surprising that it reads very differently from prose works like the early slave narratives, but the comparison also reveals divergent intents within the African American literary tradition, as well as divergent voices. This divergence continues throughout the tradition. One can compare Booker T. Washington's very accessible narrative *Up From Slavery* (1901) with W.E.B. DuBois's intellectual cultural analysis in *The Souls of Black Folk* (1903). (There was a lively debate spawned by this contrast, which is discussed in Chapter Three). One can do the same with the folksy jazz poetry of Langston Hughes and the formal poetry of Countee Cullen (discussed in Chapter Four); the gritty, plot-driven novels of Richard Wright and the ideas-laden fiction of Ralph Ellison (Chapter Five); or the nearly overtly stated theme of Alice Walker's novel *The Color Purple* (1982) and the dizzying narrative challenges of a novel like Toni Morrison's novel *Paradise* (1994), and so forth.

There are many factors at play here, not just the divergence of rhetorical intent that we see during the era of slavery when black readers were rare, and thus rarely the intended audience. The question of audience endures, though: is any given work of African American literature written for the masses or for the elite? Would it be interpreted differently by those two sets of readers? And who writes it: the purveyors of folk wisdom or the highly educated (which might, obviously, be a false distinction)? Scholars of this particular body of literature are especially sensitive to reinforcing hierarchies of any kind, and the distinction between high and low art, or literature and popular writing, can exacerbate this subject.

Is the Personal Necessarily Political?

Zora Neale Hurston's famous essay "How It Feels to Be Colored Me" (1928) contains in its title a paradox: the "me" is individual, but the "colored" (now an antiquated term) indicates that the individual speaks as a representative of the race. James Baldwin's essays play creatively with pronouns as he, too, attempts both to speak from personal experience and to project a voice that includes other black people: when he says "I," he often means "we." Langston Hughes, in many of his early poems, creates the persona of a black individual who is really more a racial representative, as in "The Negro Sings of Rivers," "I, Too," "American Heart-break," or "Negro." In the last of these poems, the speaker declares "I am a Negro" (1). He goes on to describe his experiences and characteristics, but it is clear that he is not describing an individual: "The Belgians cut off my hands in the Congo / They lynch me still in Mississippi" (15–16). He embodies the history of African Americans, and might have begun the poem collectively rather than individually (that is, "We are Negroes"). But not every black character or speaker feels the obligation to speak on behalf of an entire race.

A popular slogan of the second-wave feminist movement in the 1960s and 1970s was "The personal is political," meaning an incident of oppression against an individual is a powerful testimony to the larger oppression of groups. There has never been any critical agreement about whether or not African American litera-ture has a greater duty than other American literature to be "political," or socially conscious, or anything besides carefully constructed and self-expressive. Literature has different pressures, obligations, and functions over time, and even within a given time period there are great variations regarding what is seen as an appropriate balance of individual expression and social consciousness. Yet with its origins in the era of slavery, African American literature has often felt the pressure to be political to some degree: to tell the truth about society's injustices as a way of spurring action. At the same time, literary authors are wary of becoming "pamphleteers," as Baldwin discussed in his notorious critique of Richard Wright's novel *Native Son* (1940). Baldwin believed that the best literary forms of social protest were subtle.

Slave narratives were intensely personal, even while political. Even though they share common structural and thematic features, each one is the story of an individual life. Frederick Douglass, author of the most prominent slave narrative, spends roughly an equal amount of time discussing his own experiences as a slave and the experiences of other slaves whose lives (and sometimes deaths) he witnesses. The narrative is about his life, but also about the lives of others. Baldwin writes, "One writes out of one thing only: one's own experience," yet "experience" involves more than what actually happens to an individual (*Notes*, 9). Like Douglass, Baldwin writes both about himself and about characters derived partly from his direct experience and partly from his creative imagination. Ellison's *Invisible Man* is a long study of an individual who insists on his individuality at every possible turn, but who is also expected to represent his race in all social situations. The tension between these two positions fuels the novel, and nearly drives the protagonist crazy. This concept is best articulated in 1903 by W.E.B. DuBois, who speaks of black "double-consciousness," a psychological condition that forces black Americans to look at themselves through the distorting eyes of the white other. I discuss double-consciousness at length in Chapter Three, and in virtually all chapters thereafter, as it became an enduring concept for black writers.

The Black Arts Movement in the 1960s and 1970s insisted that political action be the primary outcome of African American writing. It is not clear, though, whether the personal always fulfills that function. A memoir like Maya Angelou's *I Know Why the Caged Bird Sings* (1970) is clearly political in that it situates the author's life against a background of injustices that affected many African American women during the time of Angelou's youth. A novel like Colson Whitehead's *Sag Harbor* (2009), by contrast, is obviously derived from personal experience, yet it would not pass any sniff test that insisted upon the political power of African American writing because the experiences it speaks about are limited to a small number of black people: upper middle-class adolescents summering in a mostly white resort community. Race presents itself in Whitehead's novel mostly in speech, fashion, and musical taste, and its central dramatic elements involve non-racial conflicts like the narrator Benji's accident involving a BB gun or his father's drinking problem. And yet, race is not a subject the narrator Benji can simply ignore; he muses, "According to the world, we were the definition of paradox: black boys with beach houses…you could embrace the contradiction, say, what you call paradox, I call *myself*. In theory" (57, 58). The final two words of this declaration of selfhood indicates that Whitehead's protagonist doubts his own ability to separate the individual from race so easily, and is still plagued by double-consciousness a century after DuBois named it.

Does Race Trump Class?

The main reason Whitehead's novel does not seem to speak for the vast majority of African Americans is that it focuses on a relatively affluent protagonist. Many of the issues framed by the most recognized works of African American literature highlight poverty regardless of whether they also document slavery or examine African diasporic identity. Both black people and poor people in the United States have faced throughout history grotesque discrimination that has hindered them from advancing toward any number of American dreams. The majority of black Americans have historically belonged to an underclass whose status is determined both by the color of their skin and by the impoverished circumstances into which they were born. Thus the autobiographical writings of a number of prominent black writers – Booker T. Washington, Richard Wright, James Baldwin, Malcolm X, Maya Angelou – emphasize the extreme poverty of their youth. The miserable economic circumstances that have affected black Americans throughout history have caused a number of prominent black writers, such as DuBois, Hughes, Wright, and Baraka, to turn to Marxism as a way of understanding the plight of African Americans in economic terms.

Such a perspective allows for interconnections between African American writers and oppressed groups globally, a perspective Baraka embraced as he shifted his focus from black nationalism to Third World Marxism toward the middle of his career. We can see connections between black people and other racial or ethnic minorities in the United States. But there is also a recurrent strain of thought amongst African American writers that forges global connections, specifically through the African diaspora, that is, the spreading of people of African descent across the globe. The concept of "Négritude" arose in France in the early to mid-twentieth century. It celebrates "blackness" and urges writers of the African diaspora to become ever more conscious of their racial heritage primarily, rather than their material circumstances. The place of Africa within African American literature – either its presence or its absence – is an issue that arises with some regularity.

Phillis Wheatley, discussed in Chapter Two, has a strained relationship with Africa, where she was born. In one infamous poem, "On Being Brought from Africa to America," she posits that her conversion to Christianity from Pagan thought is a form of "Mercy" (line 1). Africa is the "pagan land" of her youth, and she appears untroubled that slavery is the price she has to pay for religious conversion (1). Countee Cullen, in his 1925 poem "Heritage," wonders aloud, "What is Africa to me?" (1, 10, 63). Since he is cut off from his heritage and removed from the African continent by centuries, he initially dismisses it: "Africa? A book one thumbs / Listlessly, till slumber comes" (31–32). He is especially wary of African gods since he is a Christian, and yet he admits that there is something African deep inside him struggling for release: "the unremittant beat / Made by cruel padded feet / Walking through my body's street" (65–67). He feels Africa deep inside him, in other words, even if his mind dismisses it. Writers in the 1960s and 1970s participated in various imaginative and literal pilgrimages to Africa to confront Cullen's question first-hand. It was not uncommon during those decades for black Americans to rename themselves with African names (as Amiri Baraka did), or to dress in African dashikis or head wraps, or to learn African languages. Famous works like Alex Haley's *Roots* (1976) and Walker's *The Color Purple* document this return to Africa as a way of deepening racial connections.

Improvisation, Play, Tricksters, and Conjurers

Improvisation is the heart of jazz music, one of the most essential African American cultural expressions, and is also evident in freestyling, a contemporary parallel in rap music. It is the ability to express one's individual impulses freely in the context of performance. It involves confidence and risk as well as the spirit of freedom. African American literature tends to prefer instances of improvisation, intuition, and flexibility over rigidity and careful planning. The narrator of Ellison's *Invisible Man* must learn the lesson repeatedly as his plans are consistently thwarted, and he only makes progress when he breaks from his prepared script. Milkman Dead, the protagonist of Toni Morrison's *Song of Solomon*, takes a journey south to establish his identity and is not served well by his plans, his material comforts, or his preconceived notions of the way things are going to be. Both men learn to value their impulses and intuition over their rational minds and the accepted wisdom of Western civilization.

This theme and variations on it are common in black American literature. It is reflected in traditional African American folk tales, some of which were imported from Africa. In the era of slavery, such tales (such as the familiar tale of Br'er Rabbit) demonstrated how wit and the clever manipulation of language could provide power to the powerless. Thus the trickster becomes a recurrent figure in African American literature. With their origins in African stories, tricksters originally took the form of somewhat lowly animals (such as rabbits, spiders, or monkeys) who gained power through outwitting larger, fiercer animals. These tales serve as metaphors for the actions of slaves who relied on their wits in order to gain power under the monolith of slavery. Tricksters could be gods as well as animals, for example, the Yoruba trickster deity Eshu-Elegba whose ability to manipulate rendered him the keeper of the crossroads, a symbol of choice and destiny. Although virtually all folklore traditions include tricksters, they are well suited to the African American vernacular tradition not only because of their potential to undermine slavery, but because they connote survival more generally.

Trickster characteristics can be transferred to humans, and it is easy to find instances of trickster behavior in works by prominent African American writers like Charles Chesnutt ("The Goophered Grapevine" [1899]), Zora Neale Hurston (*Mules and Men* [1935]), Ralph Ellison (Rinehart in *Invisible Man*), Toni Morrison (*Tar Baby* [1981]), or Ishmael Reed (*Flight to Canada* [1976]). Ellison "see[s] a danger" in overemphasizing the connection between the archetype of the trickster in his own tradition without paying attention to its unique features: "From a proper distance *all* archetypes would appear to be tricksters and confidence men; part-God, part-man, no one seems to know he-she-its true name, because he-she-it is protean with changes of pace, location, and identity...if we are to discuss *Negro* American folklore, let us not be led astray by interlopers" (*Shadow*, 47). One particular feature of tricksters that he may be alluding to is their ability to manipulate language, which is consistent with a number of black oral traditions, as Gates discusses in *The Signifying Monkey*. To signify is to improvise verbally, using free play to achieve irony and perhaps power. Practices like toasts (recited narratives involving wit) and "the dozens" (traded insults, often more clever than truly mean-spirited) turn signifying into a kind of informal verbal duel, and rap lyrics, with their emphasis on double-entendre, bravado, and punning, grow out of this tradition.

A somewhat related motif that recurs throughout the tradition is conjuring: the practice of summoning spirits and casting spells. Like folktales and their archetypes, conjuring arises from African belief systems, and enters African American literature in a number of ways, beginning again during the era of slavery. In general, conjuring is a supernatural belief system emphasizing spiritual communication and non-Western healing practices that allowed slaves to gain some measure of control over their environment. For instance, in Frederick Douglass's famous slave narrative, one of the older slaves gives him a special root and instructs him to carry it on his right side as a kind of protective amulet. Many of the same writers listed above who employ trickster figures also examine conjuring in their post-slavery works, Charles Chesnutt, Zora Neale Hurston, Ishmael Reed, and Toni Morrison in particular. As with trickster tales, stories of conjuring initially had the effect of empowering a disenfranchised people, giving them a belief system that they could honor and call their own, thus solidifying the black community. More current explorations of conjuring and its variants honor it as a valid expression of cultural heritage and as an alternative to the accepted wisdom and beliefs of the majority (white) culture.

Religion

The subject of religion is of supreme importance throughout African American literature. During the era of slavery, even though the question about whether or not slaves should be converted to Christianity was controversial, virtually all black authors were steeped in Christianity, and used Christian values to address the consciences of their presumably Christian readers. Many, such as Phillis Wheatley, Olaudah Equiano, Sojourner Truth, and Harriet Jacobs, allude frequently to the Bible. Frederick Douglass uses imagery associated with Christ's crucifixion to describe his own tribulations, and also writes a lengthy poetic parody about the hypocrisy of any slave owner who claims to be a Christian.

Throughout the twentieth century Christianity became a more fraught subject in African American letters. In the story "Big Meeting" (1926) Langston Hughes's narrator and his friend watch from a distance as their mothers take part in a passionate religious revival. When some white spectators arrive to ridicule this particular means of spiritual expression, the narrator and his friend question their own scorn for their elder relatives' expression of their faith, and realize that their own arrogance has created a rift in the black community. The narrator of Ernest J. Gaines's novel *A Lesson Before Dying* (1993) is a highly educated non-believer who has been charged with restoring dignity to a young black man on death row. Despite his atheism, he feels considerable guilt for forsaking the faith that gives his community's elders a sense of purpose. In both cases, the main characters realize how Christian faith binds their people, even if they remain at a distance from it.

James Baldwin began life as a boy preacher in a storefront Harlem church, and describes his conversion experience in a number of works, including his debut novel *Go Tell It on the Mountain* (1953). Although Baldwin gave up this role and left the church early on, and in fact became quite critical of it in later works, the influence of the church on him was profound and makes its presence felt in a number of ways in his fiction, such as through the lyrics of gospel songs and spirituals. The ascendancy of the Nation of Islam in the mid- to late twentieth century provided an alternative to Christianity in the form of a code and set of beliefs defined by black people. Baldwin, in his landmark essay *The Fire Next Time* (1963), questions whether the replacement of one structured religion with another truly helped black people at that point in history and memorably wrote, "If the concept of God has any validity or any use, it can only be to make us larger, freer, and more loving. If God cannot do this, then it is time we got rid of Him" (314). Baldwin was speaking in broad terms for a certain rhetorical effect here, but there is no doubt that religion has been such a deep and abiding presence in African American literature (and culture more generally) that it is impossible to imagine one without the other. Although Baldwin was speaking specifically about Christianity and the Nation of Islam, the issue becomes even more complex as one sees the way other practices, such as Vodun or Obeah from the Caribbean islands, have combined with (and resisted) more mainstream religions over time.

Assimilation and its Discontents

The black church, like other bastions of cultural expression, evolved historically in distinct ways that differentiate it from the white church. The same could be said for black music, language, fashion, or cuisine, to name a few. As we seek to understand the nature of the differences between the minority (black) and majority (white) forms of expression, it is important to bear in mind the social and psychological costs and benefits of assimilation: the process of adopting the customs of the majority population. Adopting or adapting to any culture necessarily involves the abandonment or diminishing of one's native culture. To assimilate is to make oneself less vulnerable in a potentially hostile environment. At the same time, the circumstances under which black people were brought to the New World were born of the immoral behavior of those who brought them. It is possible to say that adopting the customs of a people who support slavery is a form of condoning that behavior.

There is plenty of debate throughout the African American literary tradition about this subject. In the first decades of the twentieth century, there were a host of narratives about "passing:" that is, the practice of light-skinned African Americans trying to "pass" for white in social situations, denying their racial heritage as a way of gaining social advantages. Passing is a prevalent topic during the Harlem Renaissance, notably in the famous novellas of Nella Larsen, but it even persists into more recent times in a novel like Danzy Senna's *Caucasia* (1998) and Mat Johnson's graphic narrative *Incognegro* (2009). The title alone of James Weldon Johnson's *The Autobiography of an Ex-Colored Man* (1912) indicates the sacrifices that must be made if one is to forsake one's race: where does one begin to build an authentic identity after forsaking one's racial heritage? But passing is not always as literal as it is treated in these works. It is possible to remain black in appearance while attempting to fit into white society by co-opting white values and tastes, as Milkman Dead in Toni Morrison's *Song of Solomon* or the narrator of Ellison's *Invisible Man* do. The Youngers in Lorraine Hansberry's play *A Raisin in the Sun* (1959) desire to demonstrate their success by moving into a white neighborhood where they are not welcome. Such literary characters are generally poised to learn difficult lessons.

The alternative to assimilation is cultural resistance, or the firm insistence that black heritage must be preserved and celebrated rather than absorbed into American culture and watered down in the process. Moments of this preservation and celebration are easy to find throughout the African American literary tradition. Hurston celebrates herself in the essay "How It Feels to Be Colored Me:" "I am not tragically colored....I do not mind at all. I do not belong to the sobbing school of Negrohood who hold that nature somehow has given them a lowdown dirty deal and whose feelings are all hurt about it" (1031). Alice Walker, whose work was inspired by Hurston's, also includes moments of such celebration, and takes care to preserve moments of black cultural expression and achievements that might have been overlooked, including the domestic folkways of poor black women from rural areas. The Black Arts Movement of the 1960s combined such celebration with black defiance in the attempt to forge black nationhood. They were not the first group to do so: Marcus Garvey in the 1920s led a "back to Africa" movement, encouraging African Americans to simply abandon the United States rather than try to find their place in it.

The separation of black and white members of American society is both artificial (since the phenomenon of miscegenation has made the notion of an absolute separation of the races a fantasy) and a violation of the American belief in a harmonious society where all people are created equal and entitled to free self-expression. This separation is a historical fact, though, born in slavery and reared during the era of legal segregation. African American literature frequently scrutinizes the psychological damage caused by this separation. A good example is in Wright's *Native Son*, in which the anti-hero, Bigger Thomas, buries within him the rage he feels as a scorned member of black America. He cannot bury it forever, though, and it is released in a horrifying murder spree. The flip side of characters who either try to fit into the white world or who celebrate black identity, Bigger is a character who has learned self-hatred through a lifetime of mistreatment and sub-servience, who feels he has no access to the promises of a better life given to white people, and who lashes out at his family, friends, and lover instead of cultivating respect for them. Abraham Lincoln in 1858 proclaimed of slavery, "A house divided against itself cannot stand." The racial divisions created in the era of slavery seriously weakened American society, and the subject has manifested itself in African American literature in a multitude of ways ever since.

Family Trees: Roots, Branches, and Severed Limbs

One of the most poignant moments in any slave narrative occurs in Harriet Jacobs's *Incidents in the Life of a Slave Girl* (1861). In order to escape the abuse and sexual harassment of her master, she fakes her escape and hides in a tiny compartment above her mother's house. It is a mere nine feet by seven feet, and only three feet high. She endures extreme heat and cold, biting ants and rats, and complete isolation from society. Why? So she can catch a glimpse of her children through a one-inch hole she has drilled. She avoids letting them know she's there, for fear of being caught. She writes, "At last I heard the merry laugh of children, and presently two sweet little faces were looking up at me, as though they knew I was there, and were conscious of the joy they imparted. How I longed to *tell* them I was there!" (861). She remained in this hovel for seven years, unseen and unable to speak. In another famous work, Baldwin's short story "Sonny's Blues" (1957), the narrator is a respectable math teacher whose brother has been arrested for heroin use. The narrator distances himself from his anguished brother in his moment of need, but recalls his mother's advice when they were younger: "You may not be able to stop nothing from happening. But you got to let him know you's *there*" (119). The visible or invisible presence of family is crucial throughout African American history as well as literature.

Family is an especially important motif in African American literature, the significance of which is indicated even in the titles of some of its classic works: Wright's *Native Son* or *Uncle Tom's Children* (1938), John Edgar Wideman's *Brothers and Keepers* (1984) or *Fatheralong* (1995), or Gloria Naylor's *Mama Day* (1988). Not coincidentally, all of these works are about family ties that have been broken. Slaves were frequently separated from their families, either at the moment of their forced importation or during the auctioning and reselling of slaves. Jacobs's desperate measures to stay close to her children while in hiding testify to the strong desire to maintain family connections despite all attempts to destroy them. Charles Chesnutt's powerful story "The Wife of His Youth" (1899) tells of a slave woman who searches for more than twenty years for her slave husband. Even well after slavery, the separation of families is traumatic, as in Walker's *The Color Purple* or Senna's *Caucasia*. An affecting scene in Baldwin's "Sonny's Blues" depicts the two brothers staring out of taxi windows in search of something they've lost. The feeling is compared to the phantom pain of an amputated limb. What they've lost, without fully realizing it, is their connection to one another.

Often, the connection to family reaches back to previous generations. Frederick Douglass opens his famous *Narrative of the Life of Frederick Douglass, An American Slave* (1845) by observing that he and his mother were separated when he was an infant, and that the only knowledge he has of his father is that he was a white man. He moves on from his story of orphanage quickly and without much sentimentality, but it is evident that many writers thereafter attempt to fill in these gaps on Douglass's behalf. Alex Haley's *Roots* and Lucille Clifton's *Generations*, both published in 1976, signal a turn toward genealogy within African American literature that has endured through the works of John Edgar Wideman, Toni Morrison, and many more. Rita Dove's award-winning poetry collection *Thomas and Beulah* (1987) chronicles her grandparents' relationship, and more recent poets such as Natasha Trethewey have followed her lead in this regard.

One of the links between individuals and families is a name, and naming is yet another motif of primary importance in this body of literature. Douglass (like many slaves) renames himself. Malcolm X replaces his last name ("Little") with X partly to deny the validity of the family name of the slave-owning Littles from his ancestral past. There are plenty of instances of black authors who changed their birth names for a variety of reasons (Sojourner Truth, Amiri Baraka, Maya Angelou, Toni Morrison) and of literary characters who do the same (in works by Lorraine Hansberry and Alice Walker for instance). Anonymity – namelessness – is also important (as in Johnson's *The Autobiography of an Ex-Colored Man* or Ellison's *Invisible Man*) and instances of creative naming saturate African American literature, especially in Morrison's novels. The unique nature of individual or collective black identity is symbolized by all of these examples of naming or counter-naming. Readers of African American literature should never assume that a name does not bear a weighty meaning, or that it does not tell an important story.

Conclusion

It matters less how we label or classify works of African American literature than that we learn to recognize recurrent patterns and identify important motifs within them. For a people whose history begins with unspeakable crimes, literature can be a vital redemptive force, an opportunity to express the inexpressible, to make the invisible visible, or to clear an important space for necessary reflection. Its very existence is miraculous, given the oppressive circumstances in which it began, and readers of it must approach it as they approach any miracle: with curiosity, wonder, and awe.

2

THE ERA OF SLAVERY

In 1619 the first African slaves were brought to the recently established British colonies in the "New World." This chapter covers the period from that date until the end of the Civil War in 1865. Later chapters in this book cover a decade or two in the same amount of space. The fact that this chapter can cover 250 years of literature indicates that there is relatively little of it. This is no coincidence. The practice of teaching slaves in the colonies to read and write was discouraged, and even outlawed in 1740. Slave owners regarded literacy – and education more generally – as powerful tools, which indeed they were. An educated slave would inevitably understand the injustice of his or her condition, and literacy also allowed for widespread communication (and possibly rebellion) amongst a people who had been deliberately separated from their communities and families. Moreover, slaves did not have access to publication venues. Thus any publication by a black writer prior to the Civil War is something of a wonder, and contemporary readers should bear in mind the number of obstacles that stood in the way of any enslaved writer.

The black literary voice was systematically suppressed during the era of slavery not only through legislation, but at every conceivable level. Racial prejudice was instilled in daily conversation and reinforced by those in power, including clergy and politicians. Take, for example, Thomas Jefferson in Query XIV of his 1787 book *Notes on the State of Virginia*: "never yet could I find that a black had uttered a thought above the level of plain narration….Among the blacks is misery enough, but no poetry" (163–164). In this same chapter, full of disturbing generalizations, he proclaims that "[blacks] astonish you with strokes of the most sublime oratory" and even says "In music they are generally more gifted than the whites" (163, 164). Jefferson purportedly uses his own observations to make such claims, but he is speaking on behalf of a vast number of people and about a vast number of people as he does so. Jefferson's generalizations not only indulge in ridiculous bombast, but they also uphold the false system of logic that made slavery possible. The binary oppositions that inform his perspective are striking: between white and black, European and African, free and slave, we and they, etc. Jefferson blends his literary opinions here with the practice of racial stereotyping. His authority as a "founding father" who drafted the Declaration of Independence and went on to become the young nation's third president is incontrovertible, and he attempts to use legalistic logic to further substantiate it.

It might be possible to read Jefferson's pronouncement as a challenge to black people to do what white people claim they cannot do. But it's also possible to question the very nature of this dynamic: who has the right to dictate the terms of African American literary expression? Should the standards of literary taste Jefferson employs be in any way honored since they come from the perspective of a slave owner who bases his judgment on a repugnant ideology of racial difference? Rather than seeing it as a challenge, would-be writers in the era of slavery (and afterward) might have seen Jefferson's query as a signpost pointing in the wrong direction: African American literature had to originate and evolve on its own terms, and in spite of the appalling circumstances in which its authors lived.

The era of slavery produced the genre that many critics believe is the first – and perhaps the only – literary form indigenous to the United States: the slave narrative. Most authors of slave narratives wrote little or nothing else: very few African American authors before 1865 could be considered professional writers who earned a living at their craft. Toward the end of the period, however, a few black authors emerged as authors of multiple works, and one, William Wells Brown, wrote the first novel by an African American and became relatively prolific in multiple genres, including drama. The subject matter of early African American literature certainly was bounded by slavery, but the treatments of this subject vary widely enough to make it a fascinating and essential period.

Earliest Works

The enslavement and importation of Africans into the eastern coast of what was to become the United States lasted from 1619 through the beginning of the nineteenth century. An estimated 600,000 slaves were brought to the colonies during that period – a small percentage of the total number brought to the "New World" including present-day South America, Central America, and the Caribbean – and an extraordinary number of others died at sea during what is known as the "middle passage" (what the poet Robert Hayden described as a "voyage through death / to life upon these shores" [48]). The United States officially outlawed the further importation of slaves in 1808, though the practice continued, especially in South Carolina, for another twelve years. Vermont was the first state to outlaw slavery (in 1777), and other northern states followed thereafter, yet states below the Mason–Dixon line – the southern border of Pennsylvania – preserved slavery until the end of the Civil War in 1865 and the passage of the Thirteenth Amendment to the Constitution that same year.

Literature certainly contributed in powerful ways to the abolition of slavery, but readers who suppose that the period between the origins of African American literature and the Civil War focuses consistently on the horrors of slavery and calls for its abolition will discover otherwise in the earliest works of the first few African American authors. These works do not provide as strong a repudiation of slavery as some of the more famous writings published during the latter part of this period, yet they do pave the way for these later writings.

Even with an understanding of the difficult circumstances surrounding the production of slavery-era literature, first-time readers of the period covered in this chapter tend to be less inspired by its earliest practitioners than by later ones. The reasons for this common response are several: (1) the earliest works are influenced to a great degree by Christian teachings, to the point that they seem at least slightly doctrinaire in our more secular era; (2) slavery isn't uniformly condemned in these works, or at least isn't the cause for immediate insurrection; and (3) the conventions of eighteenth-century literature allow for less individual free expression than the conventions of later centuries. As Vincent Carretta writes, few of the earliest texts in the tradition are "considered literary, in the sense of being works whose form and style were intended to be at least as significant as their content" (52). Put differently, there wasn't much space in which to innovate. Actual freedom was the goal: literary freedom would develop later.

It isn't just "literature" that makes the very term "African American literature" fraught when we regard its earliest examples. Calling James Albert Ukawsaw Gronniosaw, Phillis Wheatley, and Olaudah Equiano "African American" is in some ways inaccurate because the United States was not a nation until late in their lifetimes. Even aside from the question of citizenship as it pertained to slaves (who were counted as three-fifths of a person in a 1787 "Compromise" agreement by the Constitutional Convention), American nationhood had not been established. Gronniosaw and Equiano ended up in England; yet having lived part of their lives as slaves in the New World, they are still associated with the origins of the tradition.

Gronniosaw's *Narrative of the Most Remarkable Particulars in the Life of James Albert Ukawsaw Gronniosaw* (1772), from its title on, resembles other slave narratives in a few superficial ways. The title names him and emphasizes the actual events of his life, following in the tradition of the eighteenth century's emphasis on reason and known evidence, or "truth." Though the subtitle of the book includes the common claim "as related by himself," the slender book begins with a preface by a white author (William Shirley), reinforcing the fact that the work was not written by Gronniosaw, but "taken from his own Mouth and committed to Paper by the elegant Pen of a young LADY of the Town Of LEOMINSTER" (3). This "elegant Pen" should make readers suspicious right away of the role of an editor who is really a writer. Such suspicion raises questions about rhetorical purpose: Who is the work for? What shape is given to this life by its white author, and what are readers supposed to learn from it?

Shirley's preface frames the narrative not in terms of abolition, but rather of Christian salvation. He identifies a "Christian reader" as the intended audience and asks, "In what Manner will God deal with those benighted Parts of the World where the Gospel of Jesus Christ hath never reach'd?" (3). It would seem that the preface's intent is to inspire Christian missionaries to carry on their work. That intent is borne out by the text itself. It is important to understand the subtleties of the Christian context for this work and others discussed in this chapter. Dickson D. Bruce, Jr. points out that Christian conversion itself was a controversial topic in the New World in the eighteenth century, that some slave owners were for it and others against it; he writes, "Such divisions emphasized, at the simplest level, the extent to which slavery was not a wholly monolithic system and that there was, at least potentially, room for maneuvering and even self-assertion within the system" (10). While works like those of Gronniosaw, Equiano, and Wheatley might closely replicate the teachings of their Christian educators, readers should also look for signs of this self-assertion when evaluating these works. Abolition may not be as robust a topic in these early works as it is in later works by slaves, but Christianity might also be seen as a platform on which the authors begin to establish an identity in a society that has otherwise disparaged and dehumanized them.

Another dimension of this story is that Africans forced into slavery had their own customs, including religion, which were discouraged or suppressed in the New World. Christianity might be seen as a thin covering, or palimpsest, over an author's other concerns. Gronniosaw, born into a royal family, describes himself as an outcast in his birth city of Bournou in Nigeria because of his suspicion that there is a God "above the sun, moon and stars, the objects of our worship" (5). His belief in something resembling the Judeo-Christian God causes him great consternation because his polytheistic tribe does not understand or support it. His parents reject his questions, his peers ostracize him, and, he writes, "even my servants slighted me, and disregarded all I said to them" (8). His ostracism for a curiosity that turns into Christian belief causes him to take refuge on a merchant's ship to the Gold Coast (Guinea). There he is nearly beheaded because the King believes him to be a spy. When a Dutch ship comes into the harbor looking for slaves to buy, Gronniosaw writes, "as soon as ever I saw the Dutch Captain, I ran to him, and put my arms round him, and said, 'father, save me'" (11). Twenty-first-century readers might be aghast by the protagonist's running headlong into the arms of the slaver and treating him as father and savior. Worse, Gronniosaw sees his master praying to the Bible and imagines it talks back to him. When he tries the same thing, of course, the book is silent; Gronniosaw concludes, "when I found it would not speak, this thought immediately presented itself to me, that every body and every thing despis'd me because I was black" (12). The racial self-loathing that arises upon Gronniosaw's arrival in the Western world is testimony to the inferiority that the slave feels instinctively, even when he considers himself well-treated, as Gronniosaw does.

Yet the *Narrative* did not seem like a tale of self-loathing either to its author or to its original readers. It emphasizes two things equally: the extreme power of religious salvation and the subject's tireless desire to learn skills necessary for employment. Gronniosaw moves to New York, where he learns the doctrines of Christian religion gradually, as well as a variety of skills. He even undergoes a full conversion experience: "I was so drawn out of myself, and so fill'd and awed by the Presence of God that I saw (or thought I saw) light inexpressible dart down from heaven upon me" (17). His life from that point on expresses faith in heaven as its ultimate attribute: his mistreatment in New England and England, which generally takes the form of financial exploitation, cannot dissuade him from the path to his concluding belief that "the LORD shall deliver us out of the evils of this present world and bring us to the EVERLASTING GLORIES of the world to come" (34). The "us" in that sentence does not refer to people of African descent, but to all Christians.

Since Gronniosaw dictated his narrative, it is regarded as an important precursor to the slave narrative genre, but not necessarily as the first written work in the African American tradition. That distinction is given to the 1760 text of Briton Hammon "A Narrative of the Uncommon Sufferings and Surprizing Deliverance of Briton Hammon, a Negro Man", a very brief account of thirteen years of the author's life. Hammon leaves his master in Boston in 1747 on a sea journey that involves becoming lost at sea, captured by Native Americans, imprisoned, and enslaved by Spanish colonists, among other tribulations. By coincidence, he encounters his "good Master," now a general, on board a ship and he is overjoyed: "in a few Days Time the Truth was joyfully verify'd by a happy Sight of his Person, which so overcome me, that I could not speak to him for some Time" (13). The narrative ends with a passionate exultation: "That in the Providence of that GOD...I am freed from a long and dreadful captivity" (14). His former master is associated with joy and even salvation: there is no sense of irony in Hammon's work that his initial enslavement was the primary cause of his period of "uncommon sufferings."

Even more surprising than Hammon's "Narrative" was a volume of poetry by a young woman whose first name was taken from the slave ship that brought her to Boston. Phillis Wheatley was a domestic slave whose *Poems on Various Subjects, Religious and Moral* (1773) caused a stir in the publishing world. Her poems are allusive and erudite, consistent with the rigid poetic conventions of that era. They were so surprising coming from a young slave that a council of eight prominent statesmen and religious elders held a trial in 1772 to ascertain whether her writings were authentically hers. The book begins with a written testimony by these eight, plus the governor and lieutenant governor of Massachusetts, and a number of other dignitaries as well as Wheatley's master, John Wheatley, swearing that the poems are authentic. Phillis Wheatley did not appear troubled by this insulting trial. Her poetry in general is not only consistent with the conventions of the time – some detractors would say dull and imitative – but also deferential to figures of authority.

There is relatively little outrage in Wheatley's work, nothing to support our modern conviction that rebellion is the only understandable response to the condition of enslavement. Contemporary readers tend to be less interested in Wheatley's occasional poems – those dedicated to General Washington and various other dignitaries – because they do not indicate the author's racial identity or slave status. The poems in which she mentions herself, or Africa, tend to garner the most attention.

One such poem in particular has become infamous for its suggestion that Christian salvation is preferable to African Paganism, and that slavery is a small price to pay for this salvation. "On Being Brought from Africa to America" is the briefest poem in her first collection and the one most frequently anthologized. The poem is subtler than it might appear at first. It emphasizes mercy, redemption, and refinement; its conclusion clearly indicates that heaven is for black people as well as white. The poem directly addresses hypocritical Christians who would discriminate against Africans, thinking that their color is "diabolic" (evil). As such, the young poet empowers herself to speak righteously to those who would discriminate against her. The controversy is that this discrimination distracts from the more fundamental issue of the ethics of enslavement: the author does not appear disturbed that she has to be "brought" from her "*Pagan* land" in order to reach her current level of understanding (1). *Readers* have tended to be disturbed, though, which is why Henry Louis Gates, Jr. describes "On Being Brought from Africa to America" as "the most reviled poem in African-American literature," yet goes on to say that other critics have effectively argued that "Wheatley elsewhere in her poems complained bitterly about the human costs of the slave trade" (*Trials*, 71). Such examples exist, but all critics would agree that they are not the dominant note of this foundational work. Still, the subject of enslavement and the comparison of Africa and America, coupled with the confidence to directly address white Christians as she does here, or white Harvard students as she does in her poem "To the University of Cambridge, in New-England" with a chiding tone and authoritative voice, make this collection remarkable given the circumstances of Wheatley's life. To recall Bruce's point, the subject of whether or not to convert Africans was a debate rather than an agreed-upon principle in colonial America, and Wheatley manages to make her voice heard within it. And yet, Jefferson singles her out in Query XIV of his 1787 book *Notes on the State of Virginia* and even misspells her name when doing so: "Religion, indeed, has produced a Phyllis Whately; but it could not produce a poet" (164). Questioned in her time and variously ignored or scorned in subsequent centuries, Wheatley's legacy has been unstable, but recent scholars have begun to place her work in new contexts that have yielded fresh readings.

Slave Narratives

As a genre, the slave narrative is fairly coherent, and yet the variations between individual texts are significant. Still, James Olney in a 1984 article delineates the common characteristics of slave narratives in a clear and persuasive way, and suggests that anyone who reads a significant number of slave narratives will be "dazed by the mere repetitiveness of it all" (46). He describes a "master outline" shared by virtually all slave narratives beginning with paratextual elements such as a signed portrait of the author or narrator, a title page including the claim "Written by Himself/Herself" or some variant of this, a series of testimonials by white abolitionists, and a poetic epigraph (50). He then goes on to list twelve characteristics of virtually all narratives, some of which are quite specific: "1. a first sentence beginning 'I was born...,' then specifying a place but not a date of birth.... 4. an account of one extraordinarily strong, hardworking slave – often 'pure African' – who, because there is no reason for it, refuses to be whipped....11. taking of a new last name (frequently one suggested by a white abolitionist) to accord with new social identity as a free man, but retention of first name as a mark of continuity of individual identity" (50–51). The fact that these conventions can be articulated so convincingly indicates the theme-and-variation principle in African American literature more generally: these works are not all the same, but there are enough common features in them to constitute a strong tradition. Individuality can then be woven into this form comfortably. Olney points out how the assertion "I was born…" at the beginning of most slave narratives manages both to signal the individual self ("I") and the existence of slavery through the assertion of the existence of the slave, a convention further underscored by the insistence "written by himself," the testimonies, the photographs, and so forth. If the slave proclaims his or her existence, then the existence of slavery (and the need for its abolition) is firmly established in the reader's mind (53).

Olaudah Equiano's *The Interesting Narrative of the Life of Olaudah Equiano, or Gustavus Vassa, The African. Written By Himself* (1789) carries the genre of the slave narrative a long way toward its representative texts (by Douglass and Jacobs, discussed below). There is some disagreement about whether or not to classify it as American literature, for while Equiano (like Hammon) spends some time in the colonies that become the United States in his lifetime, he also spends a good deal of time in the Caribbean and Europe, and even goes on an excursion to the North Pole. Much of the narrative takes place on various ships rather than on plantations. The fact that one of those ships is the one that carried him into slavery in the New World makes his narrative an important corollary to slave narratives that begin in the United States, for it adds a first-hand account of the so-called "middle passage" that brought slaves to the New World.

Equiano's *Narrative* draws from the conventions of autobiography that were being established around the time of its publication. Like Benjamin Franklin, whose 1791 *Autobiography* is considered the early standard of the genre, Equiano apologizes in the introduction and the conclusion for any faults, dearth of literary merit, or even dullness that might ensue over the course of the narrative. Such an apology became the norm in an era when rhetoric was driven by the desire for balance: anyone vain enough to write about his own life must express humility to counter that vanity. He identifies British politicians overtly as his audience and states his purpose: "to excite in your august assemblies a sense of compassion for the miseries which the Slave-Trade has entailed on my unfortunate countrymen" (37). He goes on to praise both Christianity and the nation of England for advancing human dignity as a way of questioning how either could condone the slave trade. He intends his *Narrative* to be brought to bear "on that important day when the question of Abolition is to be discussed" (37). The emphasis on religion in Equiano has a slightly different rhetorical purpose than it did in Gronniosaw or Wheatley. Equiano discusses his own religious convictions in detail, not to demonstrate his own capacity for forgiveness and supplication to a racial hierarchy, but to argue for his own right to freedom.

Equiano's plea vis-à-vis Christianity is for equality in the eyes of God. In one passage, slightly anomalous for its emotional appeal, he writes, "O, ye nominal Christians! might not an African ask you, learned you this from your God, who says unto you, Do unto all men as you would men should do unto you? Is it not enough that we are torn from our country and friends to toil for your luxury and lust of gain?" (79). He learns at one point, "I could not go to Heaven unless I was baptized" (95). His baptism, he hopes, will be an amulet against mistreatment; he even argues against the legality of enslavement once he has been baptized. Yet following his confident pronouncement of this fact, he is susceptible to mistreatment, especially on the sea, where the laws of the land do not obtain. The *Narrative* carries in it the tension between Equiano's belief in God's providence and ability to determine fate on one hand and humanity's ability to exercise free will, including the perpetuation of slavery, on the other.

Equiano's abolitionist sensibility appeals to the law and to the Christian doctrine of equality and fairness. While establishing his case, though, he does not shy away from describing the emotional, psychological, and physical torments of slavery. There is a visceral quality to his descriptions, including the stench of the lower quarters of a slave ship. He also dwells on the devastation he felt upon being separated from his sister, as well as the extreme isolation he experienced in various situations when he knew no one and had no common language with which to make human contact. His physical descriptions offer scenes of bloody brutality as well as other degradations such as the practice of branding slaves' flesh or weighing them publicly and literally selling them by the pound. He largely backs away from such descriptions roughly halfway through the narrative, stating, "were I to enumerate them all, the catalogue would be tedious and disgusting. The punishments of the slaves on every trifling occasion are so frequent, and so well known, together with the different instruments with which they are tortured, that it cannot any longer afford novelty to recite them" (129). Such descriptions do not completely disappear from his narrative at this moment, but they do diminish.

The features that rise to the forefront at this point in the *Narrative* are Equiano's travels, which give him an astounding global perspective, and the strength of his faith and his character, which enable him to persevere through his trials. Readers are likely to be impressed with Equiano's experiences and achievements as well as moved by his *Narrative*. The work concludes with a strong appeal to British lawmakers, including the Queen, to abolish slavery. His grounds are moral, but he also appeals, as he had in the beginning, to the strength of the British character. Moreover, he calls for the establishment of new industries in Africa so that Europe and the New World can continue to profit from that continent, but through the trade of goods rather than the slave trade.

The next major slave narrative, *Confessions of Nat Turner* (1831), differs from Equiano's in a number of significant ways. Whereas Equiano's narrative is presented in his own eloquent, mannered, carefully arranged prose, Turner's *Confessions* is an almost conversational account of the infamous rebellion he led: an expression of rage, but told in a factual, calm manner. Equiano's much longer narrative describes a varied life over a range of settings, whereas Turner's brief narrative focuses largely on the night of the insurrection, in brutal detail, with a small portion at the beginning devoted to Turner's upbringing. Significantly, Equiano's narrative is not framed by white authors, a rarity in the slave narrative genre. Turner's is framed elaborately by Thomas Gray, the white lawyer who heard and transposed his confession. Gray in fact leads the reader to foregone conclusions about Turner in his preface, though he insists that "this is a faithful record of [Turner's] confessions" (245). It may well be a faithful transposition of Turner's voice, but Gray's introduction describes Turner and his followers as a "fiendish band" of "remorseless murderers" whose "flinty bosoms" could not be penetrated by human decency, so intent were they to enact their "hellish purposes" (246). Such editorializing in the introduction is reinforced in the concluding paragraphs, also in Gray's voice, in which he twice uses the phrase "fiend-like" to describe Turner (262). The main text of Turner's confessions is sprinkled with Gray's questions and parenthetical asides.

That said, Turner comes across in his *Confessions* not only as a force to be reckoned with, but a voice to be heard. He and Equiano have in common the conviction that they were singled out by God; Equiano writes, "I was named *Olaudah*, which, in our language, signifies vicissitude or fortune also, one favoured, and having a loud voice and well spoken" (59). Equiano has a belief in divine providence, that he will be protected on earth (if God is willing) and/or provided for in heaven. Turner has an "impression that I was ordained for some great purpose in the hands of the Almighty" (251). He has visions and revelations; the Spirit of God speaks to him like it "spoke to the prophets in former days," and this divine selection makes him a natural leader, for his fellow slaves "believed and said my wisdom came from God" (251). Such a conviction demonstrates the different ways in which religion can be interpreted under a system like slavery: religion can be used to reinforce social hierarchies, to provide comfort for the oppressed, or to present opportunities for empowerment. Equiano does everything in his power to be baptized so he can be accepted into the Christian community. Turner and his followers, denied baptism, take it upon themselves to enact a baptism with the approval of the same Spirit who spoke to Turner. He uses the language of the Bible, as do all authors of slave narratives, but here it is used to justify revolution: "Christ had laid down the yoke he had borne for the sins of men, [so] that I should take it on and fight against the Serpent, for the time was fast approaching when the first should be last and the last should be first" (253). When Gray asks him if he now sees the error of such thinking, he replies, "Was not Christ crucified?" (253). More than a prophet, Turner sees himself as a martyr: righteous, divinely chosen, not susceptible to human sin.

As a literary work, *Confessions* labors to persuade the reader that Turner's own interpretation of his insurrection and of his role in it is valid, despite Gray's damning language. So convinced is Turner that the bloody events of his insurrection were not only justified, but prescribed by God, that the reader must at the very least take notice, if not fully agree. Gray's introduction insists that this insurrection was "entirely local," the unfortunate product of a criminal mastermind who managed to influence those around him to enact bloody deeds (247). In the conclusion, Gray believes that Turner's deeds were not linked to other insurrections happening about the same time; yet Turner replies, ominously, "can you not think the same ideas, and strange appearances about this time in the heaven's [sic] might prompt others, as well as myself, to this undertaking" (261). These are Turner's final words, and they echo as strongly as the judge's final words in the document proper, which pronounce that he will "be hung by the neck until you are dead! dead! dead! and may the Lord have mercy upon your soul" (264–265). The tension between these two voices – the slave rebellion leader and the white judge who sentences him – is significant in that it destabilizes any notion that a single story will lead to a uniform interpretation, especially a story that is so imbued with passion, violence, and indignation. Although Gray's framing of the tale is a prominent feature of the text, Turner's voice comes through loud and clear. *The Confessions of Nat Turner* was an instant bestseller and has provided much fodder for reinterpretations and retellings in the nearly two centuries since it was published.

Without question, the most famous slave narrative is Frederick Douglass's *Narrative of the Life of Frederick Douglass, An American Slave. Written by Himself* (1845). With over a hundred published slave narratives extant including three written by Douglass, the reasons for this narrative's rise to the top of the genre have to do with critical reception, Douglass's own reputation, and the consistency and strength of his voice and vision. The "American" in Douglass's title signals the evolution of the genre into a uniquely American form. The subtitles of Gronniosaw's and Equiano's narratives associate them with Africa, and Nat Turner's subtitle marks him as the leader of an insurrection. None of them mentions America in the title nor uses the word "slave."

The rhetorical purpose of Douglass's narrative is clear from the outset: its aim is to further the cause of the abolitionist movement, which was gaining considerable steam when his *Narrative* was published in 1845. The familiar testimonies by white authors that frame the beginning of Douglass's *Narrative* were penned by the prominent abolitionists William Lloyd Garrison and Wendell Phillips. Garrison's letter takes it as a given that Douglass, whose oratorical skills were well known, has written the work without editorial interference, "in his own style, and according to the best of his ability" (273). The emphasis here is subtle, but important: Douglass is an individual, a man with his own voice, his own motivations, and his own story to tell, emerging from a backdrop of countless other such stories; as Garrison writes, "The experience of FREDERICK DOUGLASS, as a slave, was not a peculiar one; his lot was not especially a hard one; his case may be regarded as a very fair specimen of the treatment of slaves in Maryland" (273). Garrison conditions the reader to respond to the work emotionally and as a precisely described literary work, selecting scenes from the text and praising them for their economy and ability to affect anyone reading them who does not "have a flinty heart" (273). Readers are poised to receive the work not as a propaganda piece, but as what it claims to be: the narrative of a life, described in terms of the way one man rose above his enslavement through a combination of strength of body, mind, and spirit. In this way, his narrative meshes with the other great thinkers of his time, the American transcendentalists.

The structure of Douglass's narrative is worth noting. It is divided into eleven chapters, plus an appendix. The first nine chapters combined are shorter than the last two, particularly chapter ten, which contains the significant development that truly enables Douglass's transformation. In this emphasis, it is a model of the dramatic structure that governs great stories, in which complications result in rising action that lead to a climax. The first two chapters illustrate the masterful way Douglass repeats motifs and foreshadows later events, all while simply telling the story of his life. Both chapters begin gently and factually, with simple statements about the author's youth, then lead on to a deep understanding of the nature of slavery from his perspective. In the first chapter, having established how little he knows of his own origins (including his age), he brings the reader abruptly into one of the scenes of cruelty. His master strips his aunt to the waist, ties her to a hook in the joist on the ceiling "put in for the purpose" of tormenting slaves, and commences to whip her brutally, swearing all the while. Douglass says, "I was so terrified and horror-stricken at the sight, that I hid myself in a closet, and dared not venture out till long after the bloody transaction was over. I expected it would be my turn next. It was all new to me. I had never seen any thing like it before" (285). With its emphasis on the author's vision, this passage ensures not only that Douglass is destined to be a victim of slavery, but is destined also to witness the sufferings of its many other victims, and to testify on their behalf.

The second chapter repeats the factual tone that began the first chapter, but Douglass again pushes the reader to understand the depths of the slave's condition. Instead of seeing violence in this case, the reader is encouraged to hear the songs the slaves sing, and to interpret them. Relating the songs' lyrics and describing the way they sound, Douglass emphasizes the sorrow at their heart and argues, "I have sometimes thought that the mere hearing of those songs would do more to impress some minds with the horrible character of slavery, than the reading of whole volumes of philosophy on the subject could do" (290). In a population denied the right to literacy, music is a vital and even central means of expression. Douglass anticipates the modern reader's need to pay careful attention to vernacular expression in more recent African American music: the underlying meaning of jazz, the blues, soul, R&B, hip-hop, and rap in recent years as they intersect with the study of literature. Douglass admits that even he didn't understand the meaning of these "sorrow songs" while he was close to them, but now that he is no longer a slave, his perspective has deepened: "They told a tale of woe which was then altogether beyond my feeble comprehension; they were tones loud, long, and deep; they breathed the prayer and complaint of souls boiling over with the bitterest anguish. Every tone was a testimony against slavery, and a prayer to God for deliverance from chains" (290). This analysis complements and amplifies his description of his aunt being whipped in the preceding chapter: the reader can now not only see but hear the devastating effects of slavery on body, mind, and spirit.

The narrative progresses to demonstrate Douglass's increasing awareness of his condition. He details many ways in which slave owners exert complete control over their slaves through physical and psychological punishment. In one affecting scene, a notoriously brutal overseer whips a slave named Demby so viciously that he runs into the river for relief. He is ordered to come out on the count of three. When he refuses, he is shot dead. This disregard for the life of a slave is a grotesque extension of Aunt Hester's whipping, and Douglass is doomed to witness it help-lessly. Interwoven with such scenes are descriptions of the ways that slave owners controlled the minds and behavior of slaves, leading them into depths of fear and despair. Hope rises and is dashed in a seemingly endless cycle, as Douglass begins to see his way out of his situation. One significant moment occurs when he meets his new mistress, Sophia Auld, who is described in angelic terms, in stark contrast to the language of hell and damnation that infuses the early chapters: "Her face was made of heavenly smiles, and her voice of tranquil music" (303). Sophia is credited with teaching Douglass the rudiments of reading, which end up being one key to his freedom. As someone associated with the evils of slavery, though, her kindness cannot last: "The fatal poison of irresponsible power was already in her hands, and soon commenced its infernal work. That cheerful eye, under the influence of slavery, soon became red with rage" (303). This fallen angel succumbs to her husband's demands that she no longer allow Douglass to read, because if he were allowed to do so, "he would at once become unmanageable, and of no value to his master. As to himself, it could do him no good, but a great deal of harm. It would make him discontented and unhappy" (303). Overhearing these words leads Douglass to a revelation: "I now understood what had been to me a most perplexing difficulty – to wit, the white man's power to enslave the black man.... From that moment, I understood the pathway from slavery to freedom" (303–304). Master Auld unwittingly gives Douglass what he needs to transcend his condition: the desire for equality, achieved through the acquisition of knowledge.

And yet, literacy alone is not enough. Douglass's mind is freed through this revelation, but his body remains enslaved. Through a series of beatings – suffered rather than witnessed this time – Douglass is made to submit repeatedly. Because Douglass is clearly "unmanageable," as Auld predicted he would be, his new master hires a notorious slave breaker named Covey to discipline him. Clearly still affected by the heartless death of Demby, Douglass is justifiably frightened of Covey, and he initially sinks into despair. Witnessing the symbolic freedom of sailing ships, he bares his soul: "O, why was I born a man, of whom to make a brute!....God, deliver me! Let me be free! Is there any God? Why am I a slave?" (325). His desire for freedom seems desperate here as he cheapens his own life, and still regards himself as a "brute" rather than a man. Covey beats him and starves him, and he struggles on, deliriously, admitting, "I was broken in body, soul, and spirit.... behold a man transformed into a brute" (328). Having reached this low point, he manages to restore belief, and promises, "You have seen how a man was made a slave; you shall see how a slave was made a man" (326).

Douglass's transformation is described in terms that recall Christ's crucifixion and resurrection. His trial begins at three o'clock in the afternoon, the time of Christ's death. He falls three times, as Christ did carrying his cross, and he is bleeding from a head wound, as Christ did due to his crown of thorns. When Covey has him pinned to the ground, Douglass writes, "at this moment – from whence came the spirit I don't know – I resolved to fight; and suiting my action to the resolution, I seized Covey hard by the throat; and as I did so, I rose" (330). This resurrection comes from an unidentified "spirit," and Douglass's Christian readers would thus easily see this as analogous to their savior's story. But Douglass also discusses how an older slave named Sandy had just given him "a certain *root*, which, if I would take some of it with me, carrying it *always on my right side*, would render it impossible for Mr. Covey, or any other white man, to whip me" (329). He initially rejects this talisman as superstition, but ends up carrying it and in fact does not rule out the possibility that his success in beating Covey has something to do with the root. The root symbolizes his connection to a non-Christian belief system, to other slaves, and to his ancestry ("roots"). The whole incident is based on both belief and inner strength, and Western/Christian beliefs alone do not fully explain Douglass's triumph. In fact, Douglass is quite critical of religious hypocrisy throughout the narrative, and defends his position in the Appendix: "those unacquainted with my religious views [might] suppose me an opponent of all religion....What I have said respecting and against religion, I mean strictly to apply to the *slaveholding religion* of this land" (363). Although it is heavily qualified, largely because the abolitionist cause and Christian faith were intertwined, Douglass's critique of religion is bold and opens up the possibility of alternative ways of interpreting human experience at a time when Christianity was largely unquestioned.

Although Sojourner Truth's *Narrative* (1850) does not break from Christian thinking, it is a significant development from Douglass's narrative in other regards: (1) it is the first American slave narrative from a woman's perspective, and (2) Truth uses the convention of the third person in her narrative. Though it is in her voice, she regards her slave self as a character of sorts and refers to herself by her initial name (Isabella) when she was young, and as Sojourner Truth after she changed her name. This third-person mode gives her considerable ironic distance from her subject, and she even employs sarcasm in making the argument, repeatedly, that slaves are human beings regardless of systematic attempts to dehumanize them. Even though the main intent of Truth's narrative is this basic humanist message, her narrative is couched in religious rhetoric that is arguably its dominant feature.

Truth was a prominent speechmaker in her time and is perhaps best remembered for her speech "Ain't I a Woman?" Her rhetorical strength is clear in her *Narrative* as well. Truth's work foreshadows Harriet Jacobs's much longer narrative in its emphasis on family, particularly the traumas that the female slave feels when members of her family are taken from her. In the following passage her sarcasm blends with her feelings of indignation as a mother whose children are taken away: "In process of time, Isabella found herself the mother of five children, and she rejoiced in being permitted to be the instrument of increasing the property of her oppressors! Think, dear reader, without a blush, if you can, for one moment, of a *mother* thus willingly, and with *pride*, laying her own children, the 'flesh of her flesh,' on the altar of slavery….But we must remember that beings capable of such sacrifices are not mothers; they are only 'things,' 'chattels,' 'property'" (593–594). Her message that slaves must be regarded as people before attitudes toward abolition can change is consistent through her narrative, though her sarcasm isn't always this direct.

Truth spares nothing from her narrative: neither emotional, bloody descriptions nor feelings of despair and outrage. Yet her ultimate focus is on her conversion and thoroughgoing dedication to Christianity. Her perspective is that of a missionary as well as an abolitionist. One of the longest and most fascinating incidents in her narrative involves a notorious preacher known as Matthias who enters the house of Isabella and her companion Mr. Pierson, and delivers to them in fire-and-brimstone manner his intractable beliefs, many of which derive from the Old Testament, but some of which are his inventions. At the heart of his harangue is his strong belief that women should be suppressed. Truth resists this fanaticism, shows its dangers, and emphasizes the need to receive the Bible without distortion. She prefers having children read the Bible to her because adults, in doing so, would always add their interpretations, and she wanted "to see what her own mind could make out of the record, and that, she said, was what she wanted, and not what others thought it to mean" (648). Her final chapters show her equally committed to abolition, true Christianity, and the insistence that reform must be based on an adjustment of attitude that would include slaves within the definition of humanity.

The Beginnings of Fiction

The slave narrative genre was not, of course, fiction. At the same time, as Robert Stepto points out, "a slave narrative is *not* necessarily an autobiography….We need to observe the finer shades between the more easily discernible categories of narration" (6). Novels were the dominant literary genre in the mid-nineteenth century, and the best-selling novel of that century was Harriet Beecher Stowe's *Uncle Tom's Cabin* (1852), a novel that derived from slave narratives and that is often credited with catalyzing the Civil War. As the slave narrative genre grew and developed, the line between it and the novel blurred, giving the authors of slave narratives more creative control over their stories.

Especially notable in this regard is Harriet Jacobs's *Incidents in the Life of a Slave Girl* (1861). She begins her preface by insisting on the work's truthfulness: "Reader, be assured this narrative is no fiction" (119). Her editor, the abolitionist Lydia Maria Child, admits, "some incidents in her story are more romantic than fiction" (121). Jacobs immediately moves in the direction of fiction by giving her narrator a pseudonym, Linda Brent. This convention is especially significant because of the established convention in slave narrative prefaces of declaring that the work is written by the author himself or herself, and also because of the importance of naming within them: Douglass, for instance, tells of the origins of his impulse to rename himself after Sir Walter Scott's poem *The Lady of the Lake*, and Sojourner Truth discusses her renaming explicitly. Jacobs says in her introduction that she has given some of her characters fictitious names because she "deemed it kind and considerate towards others to pursue this course" (119). The reason she changed her own name may have been to avoid any identifications between herself and her former fellow slaves, but the artistic effect is to give Jacobs creative distance from the "slave girl" who is the work's heroine.

This is not to suggest that any of the incidents in the work are fictional or even "exaggerated," and indeed she insists that they are not (although it is possible to see some embellishments when one compares, for instance, the actual newspaper notice of her escape with the version she includes in her narrative). It is merely to mark the significance of this departure from the established conventions of the slave narrative. Even the title indicates a movement toward the conventions of fiction: "incidents" are episodic, like novel chapters. Moreover, Jacobs's book relies heavily on dialogue, which does not hold a prominent place in earlier slave narratives if it is included at all, and she titles her chapters in addition to numbering them, following a nineteenth-century novel convention. The intended audience of Jacobs's narrative – northern white women – is explicit in Child's introduction, which speaks of "the hope of arousing conscientious and reflecting women at the North to a sense of their duty in the exertion of moral influence on the question of Slavery" (122). A narrative that borrowed some novelistic conventions would have immediate appeal amongst this readership, who were accustomed to reading novels.

As most current readers tend to read Douglass's and Jacobs's slave narratives first, or maybe exclusively, it is common practice to compare them in terms of gender. As Jacobs writes, "Slavery is terrible for men; but it is far more terrible for women. Superadded to the burden common to all, *they* have wrongs, and sufferings, and mortifications peculiarly their own" (207). Jacobs's slave experience is obviously different from Douglass's in terms of sexual politics: whereas male slaves were used for work, female slaves were also used to breed more slaves, and frequently for the sexual pleasure of their masters. Also, Jacobs's narrative is strongly centered around family, especially when compared with Douglass's. Her desire to escape is compromised by the duty she feels toward her children, and the narrative's most striking feature is her description of the confined space in which she lived for years, tantalizingly close to her children, who did not know she was there. When we look at Douglass's narrative through the lens of gender, it reflects the stereotypical male ability to move through the world, whereas Jacobs's movement is constrained by her domestic duties. Douglass's shorter narrative is characterized by violence, pragmatism, and a sometimes cool distance from the events he narrates, whereas Jacobs's is decidedly more emotional, more leisurely in its narrative pace, and more focused on the verbal sexual harassment of her master, Mr. Flint, than on the brute force of slave breakers we see in Douglass's work.

Yet a comparison based on gender is only one way of approaching Jacobs's text, and it may be limiting in terms of what her narrative offers. One useful way to approach *Incidents in the Life of a Slave Girl* is as a document strongly influenced not only by the Bible, which is evident throughout the book through quotation and paraphrase, but also by the law. Lovalerie King sees the narrative "as a literal and figurative rejection of the laws sanctioning slavery and allowing the expropriation of her basic human rights, as well as an indictment of the related ethical code" (47). Jacobs's book can productively be read in the context of the so-called Compromise of 1850, which was a strengthening of the fugitive slave laws of the late eighteenth century, designed to balance power between the North and the South as a way of averting the Civil War. The Compromise gave financial incentives to slave catchers while denying accused escaped slaves the right to testify at their own trials. Another significant precursor to Jacobs's narrative is the now famous case of *La Amistad*, a slave ship in which the slaves mutinied at sea, raising questions about slaves' rights as citizens. Jacobs's narrative asks one question repeatedly, and from different angles: what rights did slaves have?

The question is not just legal, but moral. Linda Brent believes that she, like all women, has a right to her body, specifically regarding her decisions about sex, and Mr. Flint's attempts to preserve her virginity for himself, even while hiding his intentions from his suspicious wife, are directly at odds with this belief. Flint and Linda frequently square off over legal issues, such as the validity of a will or the fact that Linda technically belongs to Flint's daughter rather than to him. Jacobs writes, "[Flint] told me I was his property; that I must be subject to his will in all things. My soul revolted against the mean tyranny. But where could I turn for protection?... there is no shadow of law to protect [slave girls] from insult, from violence, or even from death" (151). Jacobs steadfastly refuses to think of herself as property. Her soul's rebellion in the above passage is matched by her mind's rebellion throughout, and she eventually arrives at a position of extreme confidence: "I had a woman's pride, and a mother's love for my children; and I resolved that out of the darkness of this hour a brighter dawn should rise for them. My master had power and law on his side; I had a determined will. There is might in each" (216).

Jacobs's determined will is eventually mightier than Flint's legally derived power. He is not able to preserve her virginity, nor to capture her once she escapes, nor to convince her through a forged letter to return, nor finally to extort money from her to buy her own freedom. A friend does buy her freedom, an act that disappoints her because she firmly believes that no one has ever had the right to own her, and the legitimacy of anyone's claim to her should not be validated. There is a sense of weariness at the end of her long narrative when she admits, "The dream of my life is not yet realized. I do not sit with my children in a home of my own" (350). Despite her considerable triumphs, she still does not enjoy the basic privileges that her intended readers do. And yet, she is exuberant that she and her children are no longer slaves. She expresses this sentiment through direct address: "Reader, my story ends with freedom; not in the usual way, with marriage" (350). The "usual" ending she speaks of applies to novels, not to slave narratives, reinforcing the fuzziness of the line between them.

Jacobs may have helped pave the way with her inventive slave narrative that borrowed fictional techniques, but the first African American novel is William Wells

Brown's *Clotel, or The President's Daughter* (1853). It is a novel in the sense that it is a sustained fictional narrative with multiple plots, but *Clotel* is truly a miscellany of genres that borrows directly and liberally from newspaper accounts, poems, short stories, and slave narratives to create an original work. Its tone is also wide-ranging, including scenes of pure sentimentality, passages of fiery polemic, and even humor. Brown has a difficult time training his focus on the title character for long, and her death prior to the novel's conclusion adds to the sense that the novel is only partly interested in her as a character. Its experimental flourishes and self-consciousness make it seem like a novel well ahead of its time rather than one at the origin of the tradition.

Brown plays with the notion of the distinction between fiction and slave narratives throughout the work. One chapter (XXIII) is entitled "Truth Stranger than Fiction." After hearing of ill slaves being purchased for scientific dissection, one white character says to another, "I have often heard what I consider hard stories in abolition meetings in New York about slavery; but now I shall begin to think that many of them are true" (133). On more than one occasion he says of an anecdote he has related, "This, reader, is no fiction" (148, 172), prompting readers to verify the story if they so desire, and even providing the source material should they care to do so. In the conclusion Brown writes, "I may be asked, and no doubt shall, Are the various incidents and scenes related founded in truth? I answer, Yes" (226). It is somewhat ironic that he should feel compelled to defend the truthfulness of a work of fiction, but *Clotel* is so intertwined with the slave narrative genre that such a defense is fitting.

Brown is also the author of an important slave narrative, *Narrative of William W. Brown, A Fugitive Slave* (1847), and he includes a shortened variation on it entitled *Narrative of the Life and Escape of William Wells Brown* as the introduction to *Clotel*. This "sketch of the author's life" is cleverly written in the third person. It begins, "William Wells Brown, the subject of this narrative, was born a slave in Lexington, Kentucky;" in this way, as Robert S. Levine points out, "[Brown] challenged the convention of the time that had white abolitionists writing such prefaces as a way of 'legitimating' the efforts of the black author" (49). This third-person rendering of his own life represents Brown's willingness to take full creative control of his writing as he had participated in the framing convention in his 1847 narrative, with a brief preface by J.C. Hathaway. He also quotes himself in the initial sketch in *Clotel*, adding to the sense of playfulness and reliance on other published material that typify the novel.

The narrative voice of *Clotel* is, like other aspects of it, varied. It occasionally highlights the kind of general pronouncements about the nature of slavery common in slave narratives, made for the benefit of the ignorant outsider, such as the following: "In all the large towns in the Southern States, there is a class of slaves who are permitted to hire their time of their owners, and for which they pay a high price" (84). At other times the narrator indulges in sentimentality, as when Clotel and her lover Horatio are parting: "Her voice was choked for utterance, and the tears flowed freely, as she bent her lips toward him. He folded her convulsively in his arms, and imprinted a long impassioned kiss on that mouth, which had never spoken to him but in love and blessing. With efforts like a death-pang she at length raised her head from his heaving bosom" (121). Frequently, he turns the narrative over directly to his sources, reprinting newspaper stories verbatim, and even quoting from Jefferson's *Notes on the State of Virginia* as well as the *Declaration of Independence*, gaining irony through the assertion that Jefferson is Clotel's father.

By working in a mode that might be described as an expansive definition of fiction, Brown is able to advance a strong critique of slavery by framing it in terms of a dialogue between his fictional characters. The subplot involving Reverend John Peck, his daughter Georgiana, and Peck's friend Carlton is especially fruitful in this regard as it enables Brown to deride religious hypocrisy. Carlton exposes his friend's weak thinking; he tells Peck, "I am no great admirer of either the Bible or slavery. My heart is my guide: my conscience is my Bible" (108). Georgiana, a committed abolitionist, is emboldened by Carlton's words to rebel against her father's authority: "as whatever accords with the will of God, in any manifestation of it should be done and persisted in, so whatever opposes that will should not be done, and if done, should be abandoned....True Christian love is of an enlarged, disinterested nature" (109). Although the lengthy speeches of Brown's characters are not plausible as authentic representations of speech, they serve their purpose of mixing rational abolitionist arguments with stories of the heart-wrenching experiences of slaves.

Each slave narrative emphasizes a different aspect of the slave experience. Brown's novel takes on many aspects, but places special emphasis on the process of valuation, the devastation of families being sundered, creative methods of escape, and the effects of miscegenation. The main plot of Clotel's life involves all of these, and it is difficult to isolate the singular emphasis in Brown's novel. Like many of the first novels in English, it is ambitious in scope, and it revels in its miscellaneous nature. His final address, though, is to "British Christians"– *Clotel* was published in England where Brown was in exile because of the Fugitive Slave Law – and is couched in biblical rhetoric (226). This suggests that the original intent of the novel was to persuade a very specific audience, and the reader is aware of the prevalence of other topics besides abolition within the work, such as the temperance movement. For all of the creative freedom *Clotel* enjoys as the first African American novel, it exhibits the same pressures evident in many slave narratives to advance the cause of abolition first and foremost.

Two rather more conventional novels conclude the era of slavery. Both were recovered in recent years by Henry Louis Gates, Jr. The first, Hannah Crafts's *The Bondwoman's Narrative*, was unpublished until 2002, and its date of composition and the identity of the author are still a matter of some debate. Gates believes that the manuscript was written in 1855 (286); an authentication report included in the 2002 published version concludes that it had to have been written between 1853 and 1861 (310), affirming that it is indeed one of the earliest African American novels, but not necessarily the first by an African American woman. So little is known about Hannah Crafts that her racial identity is a matter of speculation, even as she identifies herself as "A Fugitive Slave Recently Escaped from North Carolina" in the novel's subtitle (1).

Scholars have demonstrated how Crafts was influenced by white novelists of the time such as Dickens and Charlotte Brontë, but one can also see traces of Brown's *Clotel*, such as her reference to "truth stranger than fiction" (3) in her preface, or the chapter title "A Mystery Unraveled" which echoes Brown's "A Mystery." Such echoes may be coincidental, but the similarities between *The Bondwoman's Narrative* and other novels that derive from the slave experience, as well as the connection between these novels and slave narratives, suggests a potent urgency at the origin of the African American literary tradition to treat the theme of slavery and its variations as often as possible. In short, in the years leading up to the Civil War there was no topic for black writers other than slavery and the need for its abolition, and yet the range of possibilities afforded by this topic broadened as the tradition developed and the genre expanded.

Crafts's contribution is to infuse her narrative with the gothic and sentimental conventions of the time, even while maintaining a compelling first-person voice throughout in order to convince the reader of the authenticity of her own experience. A ghost story told by the character Lizzy is embedded within the larger narrative, just as humorous and morbid anecdotes are embedded in *Clotel*, demonstrating that authors were keen to expand the horizon of the slave narrative as it merges with fiction. The plot of *The Bondwoman's Narrative* contains some implausible incidents that clearly mark it as fiction, and its diction is artificial in marked contrast to slave narratives, but its coherence and earnestness, as much as its potential significance as an historical document, account for the tremendous amount of attention it received when Gates published it in 2002.

Harriet E. Wilson's *Our Nig* is another significant early African American novel. Published in 1859, *Our Nig* spent many years in obscurity until Gates republished and called attention to it in 1983, nearly two decades before he discovered *The Bondwoman's Narrative*. Unlike Hannah Crafts, the identity of the author of *Our Nig* is well documented. She was famous not only as an author, but as a "spiritualist" and as the inventor and distributor of a popular hair care product. The poor reception of *Our Nig* may have ended Wilson's writing career, although it may simply be possible that she said all she wanted to say in this work of clearly autobiographical fiction. *Our Nig* is an important link between the conventions of the slave narrative and the themes that dominate the half-century of African American prose in the aftermath of slavery. Chiefly, the novel demonstrates how the legacy of racial discrimination, forged in the crucible of slavery, was not limited to the practice of slavery, and was destined to remain in place in American society for a long time.

The frontispiece of *Our Nig* describes it as "Sketches from the life of a free black, in a two-story white house, north, showing that slavery's shadows fall even there." Those "shadows" are made manifest in the treatment of the protagonist, Frado (known also as "Nig"), by the family who indentures her. The child of a white mother and black father in New Hampshire, Frado is described as "a beautiful mulatto, with long, curly black hair, and handsome, roguish eyes, sparkling with an exuberance of spirit almost beyond restraint" (11). This "exuberance of spirit" gets her in trouble; even her mother, deciding where to send her after realizing she cannot take care of her children, describes her as a "wild, frolicky thing, [who] means to do jest as she's a mind to" (12). Such spirit could be a positive survival tool for a character in the situation that Frado finds herself in, but a strong sense of racial self-loathing cancels it out.

Abused by the Bellmonts, the family that takes her in when her mother abandons her, Frado is also mistreated by the children in her school, who immediately cry, "See that nigger....I won't play with her" (19). Her teacher tries to correct the children, but Frado's perception of her own difference and the fact that she is treated as inferior because of it has affected her. The lesson is reinforced, to put it mildly, in the Bellmonts' home, particularly by the matriarch and by her daughter Mary. Mrs. Bellmont frequently says things like, "Take that nigger out of my sight" (28). At one point, Frado discusses such treatment with the sympathetic Aunt Abby, asking, "Did the same God that made [Mrs. Bellmont] make me?" and concluding, "Well, then, I don't like him....Because he made her white, and me black. Why didn't he make us *both* white?" (28–29). James Bellmont, Frado's favorite member of the family, later overhears her lamenting, "why was I made? why can't I die? Oh, what have I to live for....all because I am black!" (42).

Nearly all of her damaged psychological state is caused by Mary and Mrs. Bellmont, and the reader shares Frado's elation when they die. And yet, death is even more complex and freighted with meaning than usual in this novel because of its ubiquity and because of the Christian promise of heaven, which Frado does not feel is available to her because of her race. When James Bellmont takes ill, Frado enters a prolonged crisis, partly because she now aspires to enter heaven only so she can be with the saintly James. She attends a religious meeting because, "Her doubt was, *is* there a heaven for the black?" The minister urges, "Come to Christ...all, young or old, white or black, bond or free, come all to Christ for pardon; repent, believe" (47). This message does not take right away because Mrs. Bellmont, the most powerful person in her life, "hardly believed [Frado] had a soul" (48). Moreover, she teaches Frado that "prayer was for whites, not for blacks" (52). Frado concludes, "She did not love God; she did not serve him or know how to" (55).

The remainder of the narrative moves quickly, making the resolution to Frado's psychological and social problems seem incomplete. She leaves the Bellmont family, marries, is left alone by her husband, bears a child, and leaves him in the care of another. In her travels throughout New England, she learns lessons that are more practical than spiritual. Even though she is "black, feeble, and poor," she manages to learn how to make straw bonnets to sell, and also learns from the woman who teaches her that skill "the value of useful books," presumably beyond the Bible (69). The epigraph to each chapter flaunts Wilson's wide and varied literary knowledge, including poetry in addition to Bible verses. Because of the secular instruction she receives, "Frado experienced a new impulse. She felt herself capable of elevation; she felt that this book information supplied an undefined dissatisfaction she had long felt, but could not express. Every leisure moment was carefully applied to self-improvement" (69). She has not left God or religion behind by any means in the book's hasty final pages, but she says that we are likely to see her "busily employed in preparing her merchandise....Nothing turns her from her steadfast purpose of elevating herself" (72). Certainly, this elevation brings her closer to the kingdom of God, but there is a strong sense that she is motivated just as much by the desire to succeed materially in the world that has beaten her down so systematically.

Conclusion

The early years of published African American literature, from its origins in the eighteenth century through the end of the Civil War, treated slavery almost exclusively, but not uniformly. Slavery is based on systematic dehumanization, but the proliferation of black writing during this period is evidence of slaves' resistance to such treatment. Despite the extraordinary measures slave owners took to prevent black writing – from psychological and physical torment to anti-literacy laws – the writing that survives developed into the foundation for some of the most profound and valuable works in the American literary canon. The story of slavery and all of its horrors – the subtle as well as the evident – is one that must be heard repeatedly, and, as recent writers such as Toni Morrison and Thylias Moss have demonstrated, one that must be revisited continuously as Americans come to terms with the most shameful episode in their history.

Suggestions for Further Reading

Bruce, Dickson D., Jr. *The Origins of African American Literature*. Charlottesville, VA and London: University Press of Virginia, 2001. Print.

Carretta, Vincent. *Phillis Wheatley: Biography of a Genius in Bondage*. Athens, GA: University of Georgia Press, 2011. Print.

Davis, Charles T. and Henry Louis Gates, Jr., eds. *The Slave's Narrative*. Oxford and New York, NY: Oxford University Press, 1985. Print.

Fisch, Audrey, ed. *The Cambridge Companion to the African American Slave Narrative*. Cambridge: Cambridge University Press, 2007. Print.

Shields, John C. and Eric D. Lamore. *New Essays on Phillis Wheatley*. Knoxville, TN: University of Tennessee Press, 2011. Print.

3

RECONSTRUCTION THROUGH THE 1910S

The Emancipation Proclamation marked the end of slavery in the United States, but also signaled the beginning of a long period of social debate about how to heal the wounds left by the Civil War. The debate is not over: there are still legal arguments being made about possible governmental reparations to the descendants of slaves, and the facts of racism and hate crimes still produce daily headlines, to say nothing of the more subtle forms of discrimination that persist. There is a developing body of neo-slave narratives (also called new narratives of slavery) in the twenty-first century, and rhetoric about exploitation is often couched in antebellum terms, such as when the singer Prince, protesting his contract with Warner Brothers Records, tattooed the word "slave" on his face, or when the filmmaker Spike Lee, during the making of his film *Malcolm X*, referred to Warner Brothers Studio as a "plantation." The wounds of slavery have healed slowly, if at all.

And yet there was a rush in the immediate aftermath of the Civil War to move quickly past the pain and to address the problems of inequality. The social/political project known as Reconstruction (originally Radical Reconstruction) was a deliberate attempt to enfranchise blacks, especially in the realm of government. Reconstruction lasted just over a decade (1865–1877), and at its end American society was in disarray with regard to race relations. Although the project initially succeeded in placing a number of southern blacks in political offices, it looks like a failure from our current historical vantage point, partly because it caused a backlash that included a horrifying number of lynchings, as hate groups like the Ku Klux Klan arose. Also, the appointment of blacks to political positions was undercut by southern states passing nefarious laws that restricted many blacks' right to vote, including poll taxes, residency requirements, and literacy tests. The post-Reconstruction period from 1877 through to roughly 1900 was a despairing, dark period in African American history.

A leader had to emerge who would articulate the issues and propose a viable way forward, especially after the death of the venerable Frederick Douglass in 1895. In the wake of the Civil War, the focus was on social programs and public policy more than on literature, and most scholars and general readers agree that the half-century following the Emancipation Proclamation did not produce the greatest works in African American literary history in terms of artistic accomplishment and creativity. At the same time, literature in the years following slavery lay some important groundwork for future works in the way it caused Americans to confront the thorny social problems they were facing. An era of tremendous change, growth, and prosperity, the end of the nineteenth century and beginning of the twentieth marked a fresh start in African American letters. It was characterized by the main question about whether African American thought was best served by training one's focus on the past, the present, or the future.

Non-fiction Prose During and After Reconstruction: Differences of Opinion

Non-fiction prose continued to hold a prominent place in African American letters after the Civil War just as it had done before in the form of the slave narrative. Some writers (notably Douglass) from the era of slavery continued to publish in this genre. One of the most notable prose writers of this era who has gained renewed attention in recent years is the fiery Ida B. Wells-Barnett. She is known primarily as a journalist, yet that term does not deter scholars from including her in the literary tradition. It is significant that African American writers were contributing to journalism as paid professionals: Anna Julia Cooper, William Monroe Trotter, Charlotte Forten Grimke, Pauline E. Hopkins, and W.E.B. DuBois (discussed below) were among the other black writers allowing their voices to be heard in journalistic venues during the late nineteenth century, and black writers of later eras (such as Langston Hughes and James Baldwin) did not limit themselves exclusively to "literary" genres. The essay was, in fact, the natural heir to the slave narrative as a literary tool of social reform, and its popularity and power in the late nineteenth century command attention.

Wells-Barnett's main crusade was against lynching, and her two publications *Southern Horrors* (1892) and *A Red Record* (1895) are powerful testimonies to the racial terror of that time. She was also fearless in her willingness to accuse southern white men of crimes, and one of her essays nearly cost her her life, as a white mob demolished the office of *Memphis Free Speech*, the journal in which she had published an uncompromising accusatory essay about the lynching of three black women. Her facts are incontrovertible, and her voice is consistently strong, so the moral outrage behind it cannot be ignored, as in this passage from *A Red Record:*

> If the Southern people in defense of their lawlessness, would tell the truth and admit that colored men and women are lynched for almost any offense, from murder to a misdemeanor, there would not now be the necessity for this

defense. But when they intentionally, maliciously and constantly belie the record and bolster up these falsehoods by the words of legislators, preachers, governors and bishops, then the Negro must give to the world his side of the awful story.

(679)

Wells-Barnett helped to give that side of the story, with no less urgency or passion than the authors of slave narratives argued for the abolition of slavery.

It is not surprising that one of the best-selling works written in the half-century after the Emancipation Proclamation derived directly from the slave narrative, since that genre had become firmly established as the heart of black American writing. Booker T. Washington – a spokesman, presidential advisor, and one of the founders of the Tuskegee Institute – was the most prominent African American leader at the end of the nineteenth century and beginning of the twentieth. His autobiography *Up From Slavery* (1901) might be described as an ex-slave narrative, for although it begins as many slave narratives do ("I was born a slave"), the focus is very much on the "Up" in the title, not the "Slavery" (1). It is a work that showcases individual progress as a way of inspiring a race. It also generated controversy as some critics saw Washington's unflappable optimism as both naïve and the wrong approach to healing the wounds of a nation more plagued by racism than Washington acknowledged. Still, his upbeat, pragmatic formula was highly persuasive, and his influence cannot be overstated.

Washington's introduction to his work is more reminiscent of Benjamin Franklin's formative *Autobiography* than it is of a slave narrative. In his preface he states, "I have tried to tell a simple, straightforward story, with no attempt at embellishment. My regret is that what I have attempted to do has been done so imperfectly" (Preface). This humility, coupled with a preference for the "simple," sets the tone for Washington's work, as it had for Franklin's. The reader, it is expected, would have known the reputation of both men by the time they put pen to paper, so they do not need to establish their authority. In Washington's case, the supposed imperfection of his writing, he claims, is due to the fact that he has been extra-ordinarily busy advancing opportunities for his race, notably the establishment and maintenance of his crowning achievement: the Tuskegee Institute, a teachers' college that set the precedent for historically black colleges and universities. In short, he claims that if his work is flawed, it is because he has been so industrious, and hard work and perseverance are in fact the greatest virtues an individual can have, according to his book.

When Washington describes his years as a slave, he emphasizes not abuse, as slave narratives tend to do, but rather extreme poverty, which carries over into his early years as a free man. The worst experience he suffered as a slave was that he had to wear an uncomfortable flax shirt. He takes pains to point out that, from his perspective, the members of his race "entertain no feelings of bitterness against the whites before and during the war," and even that the nature of relations between former slaves and former slave owners after the war was amicable (10). While making it clear that slavery was a horrible institution, he chooses to see the possible good that came out of it: "the ten million Negroes inhabiting this country, who themselves or whose ancestors went through the school of American slavery, are in a stronger and more hopeful condition, materially, intellectually, morally, and religiously, than is true of an equal number of black people in any other portion of the globe" (11–12). He goes even further: "the black man got nearly as much out of slavery as the white man did" (12). This statement is shocking when taken out of context. Ever practical and positive-thinking, Washington suggests that white people became so dependent on blacks during slavery that they are unable to function independently in slavery's aftermath. This suggestion is consistent with his descriptions of the dismal conditions faced by students in the early years of the Tuskegee Institute over which he presided: rising up out of adversity is better than beginning in comfortable surroundings from one's birth, since it necessitates a drive to succeed.

Washington's story repeats a few core themes and concentrates on a single message: hard work, patience, and *practical* education are the keys to moving forward in post-slavery America. His chapter "Boyhood Days" shows both how he makes the best of the limited opportunities available to him and how he creates opportunities, especially through learning to read. He hears of the Hampton Institute, a school for African Americans in Virginia, and is bent on attending it, but he also teaches himself to read in a way similar to Douglass, by persuading local literate boys to teach him. While not losing sight of formal education, he places great emphasis on the practical lessons he picks up. Under the stern eye of Mrs. Ruffner, who hires him as a servant, he learns the value of cleanliness and order, two virtues that he heralds throughout the book: "the lessons that I learned in the home of Mrs. Ruffner were as valuable to me as any education I have ever gotten anywhere since" (31). When he finally gets to Hampton, his "college examination" is to clean a room thoroughly, which he does, claiming, "never did any youth pass an examination for entrance into Harvard or Yale that gave him more genuine satisfaction" (38).

Although Washington's pride and sense of dignity are clear and undeniable, contemporary readers are likely to see this task, and many like it described in *Up From Slavery*, as menial and subservient rather than truly empowering. His fixation on personal hygiene as a high form of salvation occasionally becomes almost absurd: "In all my teaching I have watched carefully the influence of the toothbrush, and I am convinced that there are few single agencies of civilization that are more far-reaching" (54). He is dismissive of the efforts of certain black people in the Reconstruction era to learn Latin and Greek, claiming that those who pursued such study "seemed to know less about life and its conditions as they would meet it at their homes" (63). In all cases, a pursuit of the practical trumps any aspiration to the higher echelons of culture. His credo is this: "Nothing ever comes to one, that is worth having, except as a result of hard work" (136).

While his single-minded optimism and belief in meritocracy – that hard work leads to success – are more beneficial than paralysis or despair, there are certain naïve strains here. For instance, he looks back on the Ku Klux Klan as a phenomenon of the past, claiming, "To-day there are no such organizations in the South, and the fact that such ever existed is almost forgotten by both races" (56). The Ku Klux Klan and other racist organizations were in fact to resurge throughout the twentieth century, demonstrating the dangers of believing that racial discrimination ever really ends, even if it dissipates or takes different forms. And yet, there is something awe-inspiring in the way that Washington presses forward into a future in which he strongly believes that no one will harbor any race prejudice, and that the spirit of self-improvement will lead not only to the uplift of his race, but to a peaceful and prosperous nation free of poverty and other forms of misery.

Washington had numerous followers, but also a significant number of detractors. The most prominent of the detractors was without question W.E.B. DuBois, who would go on to become one of the most influential black thinkers of the twentieth century. DuBois, the first African American to earn a Ph.D. from Harvard, may have bristled at Washington's dismissal of New England education as a solution for southern blacks, but his opposition to Washington's ideas was not personal. The two diverged starkly on the question of how African Americans should proceed after the failures of Reconstruction in the post-Civil War years. DuBois made his opinions clear in his 1903 book *The Souls of Black Folk*, especially in the chapter "Of Mr. Booker T. Washington and Others." DuBois's opposition was inspired mostly by Washington's 1895 speech that came to be known as "The Atlanta Compromise," later parodied in Ralph Ellison's magisterial novel *Invisible Man* (1952) (see Chapter Five). Washington's speech to southern businessmen definitely sent the message that "separate but equal" – the principle behind a number of segregation laws, upheld in the Supreme Court decision Plessy v. Ferguson (1896) – was an acceptable social solution, and it assured white entrepreneurs that they could count on blacks to continue to work without complaint, and without demands for full equality.

DuBois acknowledges Washington's tireless spirit and concedes the point that his rise to power from humble beginnings is impressive; and yet he speaks of "a feeling of deep regret, sorrow, and apprehension" among black people in response to the ideas Washington has set forth which were taken as the only solutions to the racial problems plaguing the United States (394). DuBois turns to history to assert that, although the ultimate goal of blacks might be assimilation, the means of achieving it is through "self-assertion and self-development" (397) as opposed to accommodation. He says that Washington "represents in Negro thought the old attitude of adjustment and submission" at a peculiar time in history, given the opportunities that blacks should seize: "Mr. Washington's programme naturally takes an economic cast, becoming a gospel of Work and Money to such an extent as apparently almost completely to overshadow the higher aims of life" (398). Washington's dismissal of book learning in particular must have disturbed the highly educated DuBois. He points to three ideals that Washington's ideas sacrifice: "First, political power, Second, insistence on civil rights, Third, higher education of Negro youth" (398). According to DuBois, these sacrifices in the name of industrial education, wealth, and knuckling under to the demands of the new South led to widespread disenfranchisement and disappointment. Moreover, even true economic progress is unlikely, according to DuBois, if a people "are deprived of political rights, made a servile caste, and allowed only the most meagre chance for developing their exceptional men" (399). DuBois uses his critique of Washington to advance his own belief that African Americans at the turn of the twentieth century should not shrink from any "lofty" goals of equal treatment in social or political realms.

The split between Washington's and DuBois's ways of thinking is frequently held up as a rift in black society, but their influence is much broader than the debate they spawned. These men were both race leaders with very different backgrounds and different intents, but in terms of literature, they appeal to two very different types of readers. DuBois's indignation and intellectual analysis reaches back to Douglass and forward to James Baldwin, Ralph Ellison, bell hooks, and Cornel West later in the twentieth century. Washington's legacy is in a populist literature, the potentially inspirational pragmatism found in self-help books and popular autobiographies. In terms of literary influence, DuBois has made a much greater impact, largely due to another concept he advances in *The Souls of Black Folk*. At the beginning of this extraordinary work, he writes, "Herein lie buried many things which if read with patience may show the strange meaning of being black here in the dawning of the Twentieth Century. This meaning is not without interest to you, Gentle Reader; for the problem of the Twentieth Century is the problem of the color-line" (359). DuBois calls for a certain type of reader, a "patient" one who is keen to understand a "strange meaning" rather than a simple one. He does not identify his addressed "Gentle Reader" by race: the problem he speaks of affects all Americans.

The idea he articulates in the first chapter of *The Souls of Black Folk* is that of double-consciousness. Many of the greatest African American literary works of the twentieth century can be productively analyzed through this concept, and some are directly indebted to it. He begins his first chapter by identifying a psychological separation between himself and "the other world," the one that considers him "a problem" (363). He relates an anecdote from his youth when a young, presumably white girl refuses a card from him as he and his schoolmates exchange them in a frivolous ritual: "Then it dawned upon me with a certain suddenness that I was different from the others; or like, mayhap, in heart and life and longing, but shut out from their world by a vast veil" (364). A veil distorts vision from both sides, and DuBois is uncertain whether to tear down the veil, to hide behind it, or to imagine himself above it, in a world where neither he nor other members of his race matter. But the ultimate effect of the veil is to alienate him, and to cause him to change the way he sees himself:

> the Negro is a sort of seventh son, born with a veil, and gifted with second-sight in this American world, – a world which yields him no true self-consciousness, but only lets him see himself through the revelation of the other world. It is a peculiar sensation, this double-consciousness, this sense of always looking at one's self through the eyes of others, of measuring one's soul by the tape of

a world that looks on in amused contempt and pity. One ever feels his two-ness, – an American, a Negro; two souls, two thoughts, two unreconciled strivings; two warring ideals in one dark body, whose dogged strength alone keeps it from being torn asunder.

(364–365)

The significance of this concept of double-consciousness is immense, and students of African American literature should invariably read this entire chapter of DuBois's work (or better, the entire book) to fully understand it. The main points discernible from these passages at least indicate that DuBois is aware of the way "the eyes of others" distort his own identity, how the problem is psychological as well as social, and how "two warring ideals" in one body create a problem for anyone attempting to achieve anything like true fulfillment.

DuBois contributed consistently and prolifically to African American letters throughout the twentieth century until his death in 1963. Much of his writing might be characterized as history or sociology instead of literature, but he did not shy away from any literary genre, including fiction, and his style is in marked contrast to the straightforward, unadorned style of Washington. A work like *The Souls of Black Folk* is not easy to classify, and it stands along with *Walden* (1854) or *The Education of Henry Adams* (1918) as a brilliant, original American work.

Poets Emerge

The slave narrative genre so dominated the antebellum era that African American poetry was not common or widely distributed during this time, with a few exceptions. Phillis Wheatley was, of course, the most prominent exception, and other less prominent poets (such as Lucy Terry and George Moses Horton) did produce some work worthy of our attention, but aside from the oral tradition of song lyrics, which was quite fertile, poetry does not hold a prominent place in the African American literary tradition until the late nineteenth century. During the era of abolition, one of the most prominent anti-slave poets was white (John Greenleaf Whittier), but Frances E.W. Harper grew to prominence during the 1850s and remained a major voice in African American poetry (as well as other genres) until her death in 1911. Her imperative was to use literature in all its forms for social reform and protest. Her accomplishments were made possible by tireless energy and encompassed accomplishments not only in literature but in education and her involvement in socially progressive organizations.

Her earliest poems, especially those published in the landmark 1853 collection *Poems on Miscellaneous Subjects*, are direct protests against slavery, often with an emphasis on its impact on families. Written mostly in four-line stanzas with end rhymes, these poems are designed for maximum emotional impact. A poem like "The Slave Mother" directly involves both the speaker and the reader from the beginning: "Heard you that shriek? It rose / So wildly on the air, / It seemed as if a burden'd heart / Was breaking in despair" (1–4). The reader must confront the terrible contradiction of the subject's life: she is a mother, and yet the child she is trying to protect is "not hers" because of the laws of slavery (17). The reader witnesses the archetypal scene of a slave child and mother being sundered, but is not able to help, or to speak out in protest. The shrieks return at the end of the poem and resound, causing us to hear and to try to process the madness we are witnessing.

Harper's poetry after the Civil War – and there is a great deal of it – frames some of the important postwar social issues that plagued black Americans and the nation as a whole. In "Aunt Chloe's Politics" (1872) Harper creates a humble, unpretentious speaker who claims, "Of course, I don't know very much / About these politics," yet goes on to advance a critique of the hypocrisy of the political scene in the Reconstruction era (1–2). She concludes with an affirmation of the voting process as well as wariness about its corruption: "Though I thinks a heap of voting, / I go for voting clean" (19–20), that is, voting without the taint of corruption. Harper's poems rarely stray from this common sense voice while unflinchingly addressing the crucial topics of the time, such as the inequality of education in the South and the perseverance of discrimination. Although few would say that her poetry stands alongside the greatest in the tradition in terms of originality of form, striking imagery, or inventive use of figurative language, it is clearly and consistently a poetry of protest designed to stir emotion, and it is relentless even after the end of the Civil War in its focus on the social issues that affect African Americans.

The equally prolific poet Paul Laurence Dunbar (1872–1906) also wrote in multiple genres, and also generally wrote in a folk idiom. His legacy has not been uniformly appreciated, though, even though he, like Harper, was tremendously popular in his time. Dunbar's life was cut short by tuberculosis, but in a little more than a decade, beginning with his first poetry collection *Oak and Ivy* (1893), he produced an astonishing body of work. Much of his poetry is written in dialect verse, the ostensible aim of which is to preserve in print the authentic speech of black speakers. The actual effect of dialect, in the racially tense years of the late nineteenth century, was to make black speakers vulnerable to ridicule. Writing of Dunbar's public readings to white audiences in both the South and North, Keith Leonard argues that both audiences "were comforted by charming tales of a largely contented and inferior people" (207). Dialect was employed not only in verse, but also in fiction and the theater. The rise of the minstrel show – an offshoot of vaudeville theater that lampooned stock black characters who were superstitious, uneducated, and foolish – made the association between dialect and racial subjugation clear.

This is not to say that Dunbar was in any way responsible for inventing the use of dialect, either in verse or in any literary form. Many black writers used it consistently in every literary genre, from the slave narrative through some of the great works of fiction and poetry in the early twentieth century, and white writers such as Mark Twain used it not only for humor, but as a way of giving black characters a distinctive and often powerful voice. One of the most popular series of books in the late nineteenth century was comprised of the so-called Uncle Remus stories. Collected by white southern folklorist Joel Chandler Harris, these stories derived from tales passed down through the oral tradition. Harris's rendition of them in written dialect did not prepare them well to withstand the test of time, and the benevolent uncle character who tells them aligns the stories with many other stock African American stereotypes that proliferated in the late nineteenth and early twentieth centuries.

Not all of Dunbar's verse is characterized by dialect, but that which is has generated controversy. If poetry has an obligation to raise consciousness about social ills, much of Dunbar's dialect poetry did not fulfill that obligation. Yet the function of poetry is an open question, and certainly varies over time and between practitioners. Dunbar's gift was to paint characters through their voices, whether writing in verse or in other forms. There is a lyricism and humor in Dunbar's dialect verse as well as a celebration of life that could be considered freeing, and yet his tendency to look back on the past or to look out on the present with an uncritical eye is part of what rankled for his detractors. In his somewhat lengthy poem "The Party," for instance, he depicts the following scene: "All de folks f'om fou' plantations was invited, an' dey come, / Dey come troopin' thick ez chillun when dey hyeahs a fife an' drum" (3–4). This perspective is somewhat patronizing, and although the poem celebrates the party-goers, the modern reader is likely to cringe at its stereotyping; likewise when a preacher is called on to bless the feast, and he says, "Lawd, look down in tendah mussy on sich generous hea'ts ez dese; / Make us truly thankful, amen. Pass dat possum, ef you please!" (79–80).

But Dunbar was a more complex writer than such examples might indicate. His own pronouncements about his dialect poems suggest that he wasn't comfortable with them, and the range of his poetic styles as well as his versatility in other genres reveals a writer of broad gifts who was, in fact, well aware of the racial crisis of his lifetime. In his poem "Douglass," for instance, he speaks of the need for guidance from the strongest voice from the slave era: "Ah, Douglass, we have fall'n on evil days, / Such days as thou, not even thou didst know....Oh, for thy voice high-sounding o'er the storm, / For thy strong arm to guide the shivering bark, / The blast-defying power of thy form, / To give us comfort through the lonely dark" (1–2, 11–14). It is not explicit what the "evil days" or "lonely dark" refer to, but it is clear that the poet senses a crisis that is not apparent in his lighter verse.

As the author of a deep body of writing that is not always consistent or that does not always please readers looking for righteous indignation among the black writers of the past, Dunbar provides an interesting case study for students attempting to understand post-bellum African American writing. As one of the first writers to attempt to make a living at the craft, Dunbar certainly had to make accommodations to the white literary establishment if he was to be published and recognized. At the same time, his work occasionally reveals flashes of resistance and ambiguity, if not direct protest. His most enduring poem, "We Wear the Mask," is one of the earliest expressions of this crucial concept in African American letters: "We smile, but, O great Christ, our cries / To thee from tortured souls arise. / We sing, but oh the clay is vile / Beneath our feet, and long the mile; / But let the world dream otherwise, / We wear the mask!" (10–15). This conclusion demonstrates that the accommodation so often associated with Dunbar's poetry has an underside, a sorrow beneath the singing, cries beneath the smiles. The practice of creating a persona that will not threaten or offend those in power is described here as inevitable: Dunbar does not say, "we choose to wear the mask," but implies that it's something he and other black people do as a matter of necessity. It is a richly ambiguous poem, and, if nothing else, it crystallizes the concerns of many late-nineteenth-century black writers and black Americans more generally, as they struggled between overcoming the damage of a racist past and embracing the flimsy promise of a better future.

The rise of Dunbar as the central African American poetic figure of the last decade of the nineteenth century and first decade of the twentieth was remarkable, and although his long-term influence has not been as profound as the great poet of the next generation, Langston Hughes, he left a strong impression on his contemporaries. In his elegiac poem "Paul Laurence Dunbar," James D. Corrothers writes, "Dunbar, no poet wears your laurels now; / None rises, singing, from your race like you. / Dark melodist, immortal….A wide world heard you, and it loved you so / It stilled its heart to list the strains you sang, / And o'er your happy songs its plaudits rang" (15–17, 26–28). Though Corrothers was clearly someone who had aspired to wear the laurels of the foremost black poet, here he acknowledges the superiority of Dunbar's achievement. Like Dunbar, he wrote in both dialect and Standard English, reinforcing a vexing artistic dilemma of the period.

Other black poets who emerged at the end of the nineteenth century were occasionally marked by their reluctance to treat race as the subject of their verse. Alice Moore Dunbar Nelson, wife of Paul Laurence Dunbar, was one of these poets; in general, her subjects were domesticity or nature rather than race, and she did not employ dialect in her poems. William Stanley Braithwaite is another, dealing with themes common to the English Romantic poets who influenced him. Mark Sanders notes that this critically neglected era of poetry can be divided into two camps: the dialect poetry that was limited in terms of creative freedom and political progress and the Romantic-influenced poetry that was "a reaction to dialect, or perhaps its correction" (223). Still, he argues that this generation of poets is noteworthy for a number of reasons, including their voicing of African Americans' claim to inclusion and the representation of black female voices within the tradition.

The beginning of the twentieth century brought more poetic voices that anticipated the next generation of poets who would be central to the Harlem Renaissance. James Weldon Johnson and Fenton Johnson were hybrids of the vernacular and intellectual traditions that are also evident in the non-fiction and fiction of the time. Fenton Johnson's poem "Tired" indicates some of the despair of the black working class. The speaker begins, "I am tired of work; I am tired of building up somebody else's civilization" (1). He suggests that he and his wife stop working and let that civilization go to ruin, and also that they indulge in excessive liquor and "Throw the children into the river; civilization has given us too many. It is better to die than to grow up and find that you are colored" (6). The despondency of this poem is not characteristic of all of Fenton Johnson's work, but it indicates that not everyone could endure the "mask" that Dunbar identified.

James Weldon Johnson, whose novel *The Autobiography of an Ex-Colored Man* (1912) is discussed later in this chapter, was an accomplished writer and social activist whose works span the earliest decade of the twentieth century and the Harlem Renaissance of the 1920s. His early poetic works are more characteristic of the dialect verse of Dunbar, but he gradually came to reject this mode, a principle he underscores in his preface to *The Book of American Negro Poetry* (1922), an early and influential anthology (see Chapter Four). He wrote the inspirational lyrics to the song, "Lift Ev'ry Voice and Sing," considered by many to be the black national anthem, including these lyrics: "Sing a song full of the faith that the dark past has taught us / Sing a song full of the hope that the present has brought us; / Facing the rising sun / Of our new day begun, / Let us march on till victory is won" (5–9). These lyrics represent a hopeful strain within a larger body of work that did not shy away from anger at the crimes of both history and the present.

Fiction for a New Century: Double-consciousness and Passing Narratives

Although African American fiction began to develop toward the end of the slave narrative era before the Civil War, it would not achieve its fullest expressions until the middle of the twentieth century. The reasons behind this relatively slow development are varied. It may have been that the social problems created by the aftermath of the Civil War and Reconstruction were so pressing that the best black prose writers gravitated toward non-fictional forms, following the lead of the slave narratives, in order to express the quandary of black experience in the late nineteenth century directly, without the veil of fiction. Also, it is possible that writers and readers alike had a difficult time identifying the central thematic concerns of the African American experience post-slavery that might have been framed best in fiction. This is not to say that no black fiction writers existed during this period, but rather that a full, unrestrained expression of black experience in fiction would take a little longer to emerge. Dunbar wrote some noteworthy fiction, but poetry remained his primary genre.

Frances E.W. Harper, whose poetry is discussed earlier in this chapter, published a significant and enduring novel, her second, in 1892: *Iola Leroy, or Shadows Uplifted*. As the subtitle makes clear, the emphasis of the novel is on racial "uplift," the common term in the late nineteenth century for initiatives that would promote black social advancement in the aftermath of slavery. As in Washington's work, there is in Harper's novel a tremendous amount of optimism about the future of race relations. Unlike Washington's work, though, there is also a significant emphasis on the sins of the past. *Iola Leroy* is a historical novel that turns a critical eye on both the past and present while holding out hope for a better future.

Harper's perspective is that of a social activist as much as a novelist. The artistry of the novel suffers as a result, but *Iola Leroy* does help to articulate a number of issues that lingered for black Americans following the Civil War. It is heavy on dialogue, a tactic that enables Harper to put the voices of black, white, and mixed-race characters in conversation about social issues. The mixed-race characters, including the title character, are the most fully realized characters in the book, as they embody for Harper one of the most salient issues of the time: the ethics of light-skinned black people "passing" for white, or aspiring to join the majority race while denying their African/slave ancestry in order to advance socially. The passing narrative would come to dominate black fiction for the next quarter-century.

In many cases, the passing narrative is about the hazards of attempting to wear this particular mask, and *Iola Leroy* is no exception. What is interesting about the novel is the consistency with which characters who can pass refuse to do so. There is an emerging race pride evident in Harper's novel along with a host of other issues related to the late-nineteenth-century black experience, including the link between the temperance movement and racial social reform, the necessity of preserving family connections, the pros and (mostly) cons of entertaining the possibility of sending ex-slaves to Africa, the importance of formal education for blacks, the rise of hate groups and their relationship to segregation laws, and many more besides.

The intent of the novel is clearly social reform. As the author says in her after-word, "From threads of fact and fiction I have woven a story whose mission will not be in vain if it awaken in the hearts of our countrymen a stronger sense of justice and a more Christlike humanity in behalf of those whom the fortunes of war threw, homeless, ignorant and poor, upon the threshold of a new era" (215). In some ways, it continues the tradition of late antebellum fiction like Wilson's *Our Nig* (1859) in this regard. Yet Walker has the advantage of a historical perspective that bridges the gap between slavery-era and post-slavery narratives. Beginning as it does during the Civil War, the novel shows a direct line between the perspectives that made slavery possible and the enduring prejudices that perpetuated racism after slavery's abolition.

The title character is a light-skinned black woman raised in slavery despite her master's/father's wishes to free her and her mother. Her father married and manu-mitted her and her mother, but after his death the law was manipulated by one of his friends, and Iola returned to slavery until the war. This unfortunate incident is in some ways necessary for her development because she is destined to address the social problems of all suffering people, not just herself.

One of the interesting dimensions of *Iola Leroy* is the way it both uses and resists the conventional marriage plot. From the moment she is introduced, Iola is clearly a catch, and the book progresses toward a traditional comic resolution. But she is not the typical nineteenth-century heroine in this regard because she has little interest in romance or marriage, and in fact she rejects her first suitor, a white doctor she meets during her years as a nurse. Even while rejecting Dr. Gresham she engages him in a debate about race relations while acknowledging their different races: "I believe the time will come when the civilization of the negro will assume a better phase than you Anglo-Saxons possess" (89). He later renews his proposal, and she again rebuffs him, claiming, "When mistaken for a white woman, I should hear things alleged against the [black] race at which my blood would boil" (177). He is flabbergasted that she would not claim the social advantages he offers her, and others are similarly shocked at her brother Harry's decision to join the black regiment during the Civil War when he could have easily passed for white.

Iola and Harry are bent on reuniting their scattered family more than they are motivated by marriage and economic success, respectively. The importance of family relates to the vital need to privilege race pride over individual gain; as Harry says, after reuniting with his mother and sister, "Now that I have linked my fortunes to the race I intend to do all I can for its elevation" (155). Iola is similarly motivated by the desire to discover her proper role for helping her people move into a future that fosters racial equality. Her eventual husband, Dr. Latimer, suggests writing, and she responds, "I would do it if I could, not for the money it might bring, but for the good it might do" (199). He argues that her writing is a moral imperative: "out of the race must come its own thinkers and writers. Authors belonging to the white race have written good racial books, for which I am deeply grateful, but it seems to be almost impossible for a white man to put himself completely in our place" (199). Literature is part of a larger project, from Harper's point of view, by which African Americans must forge their destiny while making important contributions to American culture more generally.

In terms of African American fiction, Harper and her antebellum predecessors do not hold as solid a position as Charles Waddell Chesnutt, often regarded as the first professional black American fiction writer whose achievements in that genre were parallel to Dunbar's in poetry. Chesnutt eventually gave up writing altogether, due largely to his frustration with critics and his difficulty in earning a living, but his body of work, including a half-dozen posthumously published novels, represents a significant watershed in the development of African American fiction. He is con-sidered the most important writer in that genre before the Harlem Renaissance. Chesnutt is remembered primarily as a short story writer and especially for his celebrated tales in the collection *The Conjure Woman* (1899). Of Chesnutt's short fiction, William Dean Howells, one of the most influential critics and publishing leaders of the era, wrote, "We had known the nethermost world of the grotesque and comical negro and the terrible and tragic negro through the white observer on the outside, and black character in its lyrical moods we had known from such an inside witness as Mr. Paul Dunbar; but it had remained for Mr. Chesnutt to acquaint us with those regions where the paler shades dwell as hopelessly, with relation to ourselves, as the blackest negro" (161). Howells' perspective says something about Chesnutt's intended audience: white people (the "we" he posits). This may be true, for there is a contrast between Harper's emphasis on race pride and Chesnutt's rendering of a much more troubled psychology that implies the need for deep self-reflection on the part of ex-slaves and the descendants of slaves, especially those mixed-race individuals light-skinned enough to pass for white ("the paler shades").

Chesnutt's artistic gifts allowed him to render post-bellum black life with considerable ambiguity and subtlety.

Although his short stories remain his best-known works, Chesnutt published three novels in quick succession in the first five years of the twentieth century. He was so discouraged by the mediocre-to-poor reception of the third, *The Colonel's Dream* (1905), that he essentially gave up on publishing afterwards. A number of his unpublished novels have appeared in print for the first time in recent years, and Chesnutt's legacy is still very much in flux. During his lifetime, though, he enjoyed meteoric success followed by relative obscurity, a fate that was repeated by a number of writers in the next generation, such as Jean Toomer, Nella Larsen, and Zora Neale Hurston.

Chesnutt's first novel, *The House Behind the Cedars* (1900), is a passing novel that provides a valuable contrast to Harper's *Iola Leroy*, and that sets up a number of themes that were taken up in the Harlem Renaissance. Passing is only one of Harper's concerns, and her novel leads to the easy conclusion that its practice is traitorous to the black race and should never be undertaken under any circumstances. Chesnutt explores the psychology of passing and does not lead his readers to any easy conclusions about it, but encourages them to understand it as a potential metaphor for the dangers of forgetting or denying the past.

The original title of *The House Behind the Cedars* was *Rena* after its heroine, Rowena Walden. Rena is, like Iola Leroy, of mixed race and light-skinned enough to pass for white. She is also caught up in a marriage plot with two suitors, and she also devotes herself to teaching. But she has far less agency than Iola does, and far less strength or support. She is an archetype for a figure that became known as "the tragic mulatto," a fictional character (often a woman) whose mixed-race heritage limits her choices and her control over her fate to such a degree that she ends up unfulfilled, insane, or dead by the end of the narrative.

Rena and her brother John rename themselves Warwick and move to South Carolina, where the laws governing their racial identity are less restrictive, to pass for white as a way of rising out of their lowly station. John is a lawyer and Rena is a notable beauty. During a scene that explicitly links the South to feudalism, Rena draws the attention of George Tryon during a jousting tournament. They fall in love and become engaged. Rena has to return home to care for her mother, and George happens to be in town at the same time. He discovers her racial identity and promptly flees. The narrator declares, "One curse of negro slavery was, and one part of its baleful heritage is, that it poisoned the fountains of human sympathy" (118). The novel is a test case for this principle, and because of the endurance of this poison, Chesnutt questions the harmonious racial future projected in novels like *Iola Leroy*.

The tragic circumstances that surround Rena are deeply ingrained in the culture of her time, and reach back to slavery itself. Blackness is considered shameful in white society, a secret to be concealed by Rena and her family: "The taint of black blood was the unpardonable sin, from the unmerited penalty of which there was no escape except by concealment" (127–128). Since blackness is cast in this way in the regional culture of the time, a character like Rena feels as though she has only one choice with regard to her racial identity: to deny it. Tryon, her suitor, also feels bound to the racial essentialism of his culture. When a racist doctor toasts "the Anglo-Saxon race: may it remain forever, as now, the head and front of creation, never yielding its rights, and ready always to die, if need be, in defense of its liberties!" Tryon raises his glass enthusiastically (136). He soon thereafter discovers that Rena is of mixed race and he becomes profoundly confused: "At first he could see nothing but the fraud of which he had been made the victim. A negro girl had been foisted upon him for a white woman, and he had almost committed the unpardonable sin against his race of marrying her" (143). These terms are bombastic, and they become grotesque in his dreams: "In all her fair young beauty [Rena] stood before him, and then by some hellish magic she was slowly transformed into a hideous black hag" (147).

George Tryon's perspective reveals the sickness that stalks the South in the years after slavery. Chesnutt, like Walker, reveals where it comes from by reaching into the past to connect the racism of the immediate post-Civil War period with the crisis of the present. It is not just sympathy that has been jeopardized by the fact of slavery, but love. Rena cries to her brother: "[George] looked at me as though I were not even a human being. I do not love him any longer, John; I would not marry him if I were white, or he were as I am" (180). Yet her love persists despite this declaration, and George discovers that he also loves her in defiance of his culture's demands: "Reason, common-sense, the instinctive ready-made judgments of his training and environment – the deep-seated prejudices of race and caste – commanded him to dismiss Rena from his thoughts. His stubborn heart simply would not let go" (192). Although this sentiment and George's determination make it seem possible that he will simply move beyond his racism and atone for his behavior, Chesnutt does not allow for such a facile conclusion. George attempts to apologize and to renew their engagement, but Rena has been too damaged by the look she registered when George, at least for an instant, regarded her as though she were not human. She says to him in a letter replying to his renewed courtship: "You are white, and you have given me to understand that I am black. I accept the classification, however unfair, and the consequences, however unjust" (258). She is neither in control of her ability to determine her racial identity through "passing," nor is she able to change the entrenched perceptions of black inferiority that pervade her culture. DuBois's double-consciousness and the psychological complications of "wearing the mask" that Dunbar speaks of are both evident in Rena, and she is broken by the undercurrent of racism that flows beneath American culture around the turn of the twentieth century. The promises of love and reconciliation between two individuals are not strong enough to withstand it.

The other two novels Chesnutt published in his lifetime were focused on racial violence. *The Marrow of Tradition* (1901) took on the subject of an actual historical event: race riots (or, more accurately, a massacre carried out by a racist organization) that occurred in Wilmington, North Carolina in 1898. Through this passionate novel, Chesnutt established himself as a bold writer who did not shy away from the tense atmosphere of his lifetime. His celebrated stories in *The Conjure Woman* were much more subtle and muted by comparison. *The Colonel's Dream* (1905) told the story of the difficulty of redeveloping the South economically given the persistence of racist codes. In all of the novels there is a sacrificial victim whose death does not necessarily bring about the positive change it was meant to. There is a palpable pessimism in them that may have put off readers eager for some cheery news about race relations.

Chesnutt's short fiction included early stories that are thought-compelling variations on the familiar Uncle Remus tales. In *The Conjure Woman*, Uncle Julius, whose folkways are evident in his dialect, narrates tales of post-plantation life to a northern couple. The first of these, and one of the best known of Chesnutt's stories, is "The Goopher'd Grapevine." The story Uncle Julius tells is fantastical and entertaining, but it masks the teller's ulterior motives: to continue to have a place to live and prosper despite the northern couple's plan to buy the plantation for their own benefit. The tension of northern investment in the dilapidated southern economy is also the ethical issue at the heart of *The Colonel's Dream*.

The issue of passing is also one that recurs in Chesnutt's short fiction, notably in the title story of his second collection *The Wife of His Youth* (1899). The protagonist of this story, Mr. Ryder, is a leader in a social group known as "the Blue Vein Society." Its members are named as such because, though of mixed race, they are light-skinned enough to reveal blue veins. They deny that color prejudice is a prerequisite for membership, but it is clear to the reader that they are snobs who aspire to the trappings of white upper-middle-class culture. Ryder says, "I have no race prejudice…but we people of mixed blood are ground between the upper and the nether millstone. Our fate lies between absorption by the white race and extinction in the black" (105). His desire is to be absorbed as much as possible into the white world. He is challenged, though, when an ex-slave comes to his house looking for her husband, from whom she was separated many years before. The title makes clear that she is Ryder's wife, though he is not legally bound to her because slave marriages were not valid after the war. He must face the ethical dilemma of clinging to his newly invented identity or acknowledging the woman who represents the shame and ignominy of his past. His dilemma is one shared by all of the members of the Blue Vein Society, and his narrating the story of the wife of his youth calls them back to their core selves: "There were some present who had seen, and others who had heard their fathers and grandfathers tell, the wrongs and sufferings of this past generation, and all of them still felt, in their darker moments, the shadow hanging over them" (111). The shadow of slavery is not one that can be denied or transcended without social and psychological consequences. That fact is the driving force behind much of Chesnutt's work.

One of the most significant works of fiction published in the early twentieth century prior to the Harlem Renaissance is James Weldon Johnson's short novel *The Autobiography of an Ex-Colored Man*. Johnson renders many of DuBois's concerns in fiction, and he also anticipates the racial anxiety of Harlem Renaissance writers like Countee Cullen and Nella Larsen. His novel, though uneven in terms of narrative pacing, certainly influenced one of the central works in the African American tradition, Ellison's *Invisible Man*.

The preface to *The Autobiography of an Ex-Colored Man* opens with a metaphor that derives explicitly from DuBois; the book's publishers write, "In these pages it is as though a veil had been drawn aside: the reader is given a view of the inner life of the Negro in America" (3). The novel's memorable opening chapter shows the narrator innocently living through school rituals, such as a spelling bee in which he excels. He witnesses a group of white students tormenting black students and, after a black student retaliates, he tells his mother "how one of the 'niggers' had struck a boy with a slate. I shall never forget how she turned on me. 'Don't you ever use that word again....You ought to be ashamed of yourself'" (12). He soon discovers that his teacher groups him with the black students and forgets his mother's directive as he rushes home and asks her, "mother, tell me, am I a nigger?" (13). He also asks her flatly if she is white, and she tells him she is not, but that his long absent father is.

His consciousness shifts immediately. He regards others but especially himself differently as a result of this half-understood knowledge. Again echoing DuBois, he writes,

> From that time I looked out through other eyes, my thoughts were colored, my words dictated, my actions limited by one dominating, all-pervading idea which constantly increased in force and weight until I finally realized in it a great, tangible fact. And this is the dwarfing, warping, distorting influence which operates upon each colored man in the United States. He is forced to take his outlook on all things, not from the viewpoint of a citizen, or a man, or even a human being, but from the viewpoint of a *colored* man.
>
> *(15)*

Race, in short, becomes the primary defining factor in the narrator's life, and his growth as a citizen and as a man more generally is inhibited by it.

The narrator gradually learns more about his identity as a mixed-race child from the South. He turns to *Uncle Tom's Cabin* (1852) as a guidebook to his ancestry and finds it a valuable representation of the past. But balancing the influence of that novel is a speech by a young black classmate at their graduation from grammar school. The enthusiasm of this young boy on the subject of the Haitian revolutionary Toussaint L'Ouverture is transferred to the narrator: "I felt leap within me pride that I was colored; and I began to form wild dreams of bringing glory and honor to the Negro race" (29–30). This nascent pride is at war with simmering racial shame throughout, and it is the narrator's lifelong challenge to work through these warring elements.

After his school days and the premature death of his mother, the narrator embarks on a number of journeys that cast him in the role of an observer of the white world, the black world, and occasionally the demimonde in which the two blend, sometimes violently. His initial attempt at attending college ends quickly when he is robbed of his life savings. He takes up various jobs afterwards, followed by a spate of gambling and studying music. All the while, his racial identity is in flux as he is capable of passing for white. His passion is for playing piano, and, after witnessing a lurid murder in New York, he agrees to travel to Europe with a wealthy white patron who wants him to perform occasionally. He is especially fond of playing European classical music in a ragtime idiom, but he has an epiphany that this practice squanders his talents, and also that it prevents him from fully expressing his identity. He vows to reclaim his African American ancestry by becoming a composer and acknowledging that he is biracial. His patron tries to dissuade him, claiming, "I can imagine no more dissatisfied human being than an educated, cultured, and refined colored man in the United States" (88). His point is one that troubles the narrator: essentially, the patron's belief is that individuals cannot change society's opinions about race, and that the only duty of the individual is to pursue personal fulfillment. Nevertheless, the narrator returns to America to study black culture in the South as a way of informing his musical aspirations.

The narrator's journey through the South, like his experiences in New York, cast him in the role of an observer, and the novel at times resembles non-fiction. During his travels he witnesses a lynching, listens to extensive conversations about the race question, and attends a religious revival which causes him to become attuned to important oratorical performance skills inherent in black culture, just as he witnessed as a child when he felt a surge of race pride. His experiences on both sides of the color line leave him in a quandary, and he resolves to let society determine his racial identity:

> I finally made up my mind that I would neither disclaim the black race nor claim the white race; but that I would change my name, raise a mustache, and let the world take me for what it would; that it was not necessary for me to go about with a label of inferiority pasted across my forehead. All the while I understood that it was not discouragement or fear or search for a larger field of action and opportunity that was driving me out of the Negro race. I knew that it was shame, unbearable shame. Shame at being identified with a people that could with impunity be treated worse than animals.
>
> *(115)*

This realization in theory does the narrator no good until he puts it into practice. His final trial is to admit his racial identity to a white woman whom he loves. This moment is key in illustrating the crux of double-consciousness: the narrator sees himself through the eyes of his white lover, and yet has the forbearance to reveal himself in her eyes in terms of his complex heritage. The challenge going forward from this moment is not only to understand the social motivations behind "passing" for white, as the narrator has, but to reconcile those motivations with individual psychological needs. *The Autobiography of an Ex-Colored Man* is valuable for the way it expresses and explores the quandary of this issue in early-twentieth-century America.

Conclusion

The half-century following the Civil War was clearly an era fraught with confusion and disagreement. Black writers were beginning to gain a foothold in the white literary establishment, but the demands of a fickle reading public did not safeguard the long-term success of their endeavors. The public disagreement between Washington and DuBois is valuable for highlighting very real concerns about the tension between the desire for social progress and the reality of psychological damage as an invisible aftereffect of the Civil War. DuBois's concept of double-consciousness is the most salient concept from the era, and it resists Washington's program for racial uplift in ways that demarcate the forking path of African American thought.

The evolution of the slave narrative and its development into fictional forms can be illustrated with a fairly straightforward line, but after slavery was abolished, the tradition dispersed in many divergent directions. Poetry, too, began as a form of social protest, but developed into a number of separate schools. Even during the next era, the Harlem Renaissance, which purported to gather and celebrate the artistic accomplishments of African Americans, this divergence lingered and further developed. Overall, the period of Reconstruction through the early decades of the twentieth century saw the emergence of a number of significant writers who advanced some of the themes that served as the foundation for later thought. Their decisions to focus on the past, the present, or the future underscore the fact that they were living in a volatile period of history.

Suggestions for Further Reading

Blum, Edward J. and Jason R. Young. *The Souls of W.E.B. DuBois: New Essays and Reflections*. Macon, GA: Mercer University Press, 2009. Print.

Gardner, Eric. *Unexpected Places: Relocating Nineteenth-Century African American Literature*. Jackson, MS: Mississippi University Press, 2009. Print.

Gilroy, Paul. *The Black Atlantic: Modernity and Double-Consciousness*. London: Verso, 1993. Print.

Harrell, Willie J., Jr., ed. *We Wear the Mask: Paul Laurence Dunbar and the Politics of Representative Reality*. Kent, OH: Kent State University Press, 2010. Print.

McCaskill, Barbara and Caroline Gebhard, eds. *Post-Bellum, Pre-Harlem: African American Literature and Culture, 1877–1919*. New York, NY: New York University Press, 2006. Print.

McElrath, Joseph R., Jr., ed. *Critical Essays on Charles W. Chesnutt*. New York, NY: G.K. Hall, 1999. Print.

Smethurst, James Edward. *The African American Roots of Modernism: From Reconstruction to the Harlem Renaissance*. Chapel Hill, NC: North Carolina University Press, 2011. Print.

Wells-Barnett, Ida B. *Southern Horrors and Other Writings: The Anti-Lynching Campaign of Ida B. Wells, 1892–1900*. Ed. Jacqueline Jones Royster. Boston, MA: Bedford, 1997. Print.

4

THE ERA OF THE HARLEM RENAISSANCE

The period known as the Harlem Renaissance (also called the "New Negro" Renaissance) is mostly associated with the 1920s, though its beginnings can be traced to the years just prior, and some of its spirit continued to exist in the years just after, until the Great Depression brought about a new set of issues that further changed the nature of African American literature. During the 1920s, an unprecedented amount of black writing was published and accepted by the white literary establishment, promising not only a better future for race relations, but, equally importantly, a new sense of black race pride. F. Scott Fitzgerald dubbed the 1920s "The Jazz Age," and the development of that musical form is central to other African American cultural developments at the time. But although some of the architects and builders of the Renaissance wanted it to be seen as a purely artistic movement, it is evident that the literary tug-of-war of the Reconstruction era between sociopolitical thought and art-for-art's-sake continued.

The word "renaissance" connotes a rebirth, but it also refers to a focused period of extraordinary cultural production. The Harlem Renaissance fulfills both connotations; a new optimism replaced the mood of cultural uncertainty that characterized black America in the late nineteenth and early twentieth centuries, and it manifested itself in a spectacular artistic outburst. There is some debate about whether or not the Harlem Renaissance was a spontaneous outpouring of art or a socially and politically manufactured phenomenon: a conscious attempt to atone for the failures of Reconstruction. David Levering Lewis writes, "The Harlem Renaissance was a somewhat forced phenomenon, a cultural nationalism of the parlor, institutionally encouraged and directed by leaders of the national civil rights establishment for the paramount purpose of improving race relations in a time of extreme national backlash, caused in large part by economic gains won by Afro-Americans during the Great War" (xiii). Nathan Irvin Huggins begins his essential study of the movement with the observation, "It is a rare and intriguing moment when a people decide that they are the instruments of history-making and race-building" (3).

Whether or not the Renaissance is regarded as somewhat "forced" or self-conscious, the fact remains that the period represents a significant breakthrough for black artists in general and black writers in particular. For the first time in the African American literary tradition, there was a wide range of subject matter, a willingness to experiment with form, and the emergence of a vast array of diverse voices that did not always sing in harmony. Moreover, the publishing industry had changed dramatically to accommodate this surge of new authors. There were more opportunities, beginning with a host of high quality literary magazines, dedicated to disseminating the work of black writers. Though short-lived, it was a heady period that marks a significant turn in the trajectory of the African American literary tradition. At the very least, as Huggins argues, it succeeded in infusing black life with a newfound sense of dignity and accomplishment that had largely been absent, underdeveloped, or patchy in earlier periods.

Three related historical catalysts caused the Renaissance to happen when and where it did. The first catalyst, modern industrialization, created jobs in northern cities, especially the burgeoning automobile industry, but also shipbuilding and weapons manufacturing. The second catalyst was World War I (1914–1918), which not only necessitated the manufacture of ships and weapons, but also drew many men into military service, thus changing the dynamic of the workplace dramatically. The third catalyst was the so-called Great Migration, which involved the relocation of an estimated 1.5 million African Americans from the agricultural South to the industrial North in the early years of the twentieth century. Compounding the effects of a period of heavy migration from Europe to the United States beginning in the late nineteenth century, this movement caused northern cities – not only New York, but also Chicago and Detroit, the new capital of the automobile industry – to swell and sprawl with dizzying speed. In terms of African Americans, the culture of the rural South had to adapt to dynamic urban settings in the North. The proliferation of jazz, blues, dance, and theater so often associated with the Harlem Renaissance is a tangible representation of this adaptation, and the establishment of new publishing venues and political organizations, as well as the creation of substantial, enduring literary texts, marks the period indelibly as a highly significant moment.

Literary historians and anthology editors have presented works of the Harlem Renaissance in various ways: by genre, chronologically, and thematically. This chapter concentrates, given the limited space, on the issues and controversies of the period, focusing on the central authors of the Renaissance, in hopes that the reader will find ample cause to pursue some of the less prominent voices, of whom there are many. As the first discernibly coherent period in African American literary history, the Harlem Renaissance is profoundly important, and it would seem that it presents a stable story for students of the black literary tradition: that black artists shook off the devastation of the past in order to produce a body of literature that was free, celebratory, and forward-thinking. As time has gone on, though, critics have begun to see the complexities of the period. As Emily Bernard summarizes, "More than progress, the theme of the New Negro Movement is contradiction" (268).

A Period Defined, Redefined, and Debated

The Harlem Renaissance is the first period of African American literary history that fostered widespread disagreement about what black American literature should be. Although Washington and DuBois had engaged in a thoroughgoing social debate in the years prior to the Renaissance, the primary focus of their dispute was not literature. DuBois went on to be a leading critical voice within the Renaissance as well as a practitioner: in addition to essays, he contributed a novel, and was also an editor and general tastemaker while the Renaissance flourished. Washington's death (1915) predated the Renaissance, but there is little indication that he would have been an active participant in it had he lived longer: his pragmatic view of social progress would not have mixed comfortably with the cerebral and artistic achievements of the 1920s.

Part of the divergence in perspective seen during the Renaissance that endures even today has to do with social class. DuBois helped to frame that debate with his identification of a group he called "the talented tenth" – the ten percent of blacks who would be responsible for leading the race into the future; as he put it, the race's "exceptional men" ("Talented," 842). Consistent with his opposition to Washington, he believed that these race leaders would be developed through traditional higher education rather than through labor training. He was cautious, though, to draw a distinction between the character and intelligence of these leaders and the elitism of wealth; he writes, "If we make money the object of man-training, we shall develop money-makers but not necessarily men" ("Talented," 842). Later a dedicated communist, DuBois certainly was not responsible for fostering class-based elitism during the Renaissance, but such a divide was evident, and the phrase "talented tenth" connotes a cultural split that might easily be mistranslated from DuBois's intentions to highlight social class divisions. One of the central points of debate amongst the practitioners and critics of the period was the question of whether African American literature was meant to speak for the experiences of the whole race, the "talented tenth" who were interested in art and education, the common folk, or individuals.

Another debate about the so-called "New Negro" literature was whether it was either "new" or "Negro." In other words, was this literature a modern breakthrough or just a continuation of the existing African American tradition into the modern era? Was it specifically an African American outpouring of expression or were black artists just adding their perspective to white literary forms, that is, ones that whites would not only recognize and appreciate (and buy), but that would also not significantly challenge their preconceived notions of black life? (Later in the century, the more radical black writers of the Black Arts Movement would denigrate the period as being too tame). Related to this last question is the crucial rhetorical question of audience: was the literature of the Harlem Renaissance meant, like slave narratives, to educate and persuade white readers about black social realities, or was it an unbridled outpouring of artistic expression without a specific intended audience?

Five foundational works of non-fiction help to frame these debates. The first is James Weldon Johnson's preface to *The Book of American Negro Poetry* (1922). Huggins identifies Johnson, along with DuBois, as the "old guard" of the Renaissance; both men's influence was established before the period got into full swing. As a leading critic, Johnson had the obligation not only to assemble the first African American poetry anthology, but also to establish the standards that would argue for its inherent merit. He begins his introduction by discussing black contributions to American popular music and dance, which he calls "lower forms of art" than poetry and literature more generally even while arguing "that they are evidence of a power that will some day be applied to the higher forms" (17). He identifies the race struggle as the single force that was inhibiting white southerners as well as talented blacks from producing great literature. At the same time, he points to the African American poetic tradition that had been established long before the 1920s, reaching back to Phillis Wheatley and running through Paul Laurence Dunbar (discussed in Chapters Two and Three, respectively). He contrasts their styles to the new poets, who, for instance, largely reject the dialect verse that Dunbar often employed. Johnson believed that such dialect could only lead in two directions, "humor and pathos," and thus was not useful for the new, vibrant landscape of the Harlem Renaissance (41). Drawing a parallel with the achievements of the recent literary revival in Ireland, Johnson argues that black poets need to

> find a form that will express the racial spirit by symbols from within rather than by symbols from without, such as the mere mutilation of English spelling and pronunciation…but which will still hold the racial flavor; a form expressing the imagery, the idioms, the peculiar turns of thought, and the distinctive humor and pathos, too, of the Negro, but which will also be capable of voicing the deepest and highest emotions and aspirations, and allow of the widest range of subjects and the widest scope of treatment.
>
> *(41–42)*

This emphasis on broadness is the final note of Johnson's preface, in which he introduces some of the brightest new lights on the black literary scene, the ones whom he felt would lead other black poets into a new world in which, eventually, a poet's "own individual artistic gifts" become more important than his or her treatment of "racial themes" (42). Twenty-first-century readers will likely find the anthology less inspiring than the great poetic works that came out of the Renaissance, and will look in vain for the names of the two most prominent poets of the era (Langston Hughes and Countee Cullen), who had not yet become established. Still, as the opening salvo in a debate about literary taste, Johnson's preface is instructive, and it sets forth terms that could be disputed or reinforced as black writers took to their typewriters.

A second crucial work of non-fiction is Alain Locke's "The New Negro" (1925), an essay in which the author not only defines this emerging type, but embeds in his definition a progressive, optimistic tone for the future. He speaks of a definite change from the Old Negro to the New Negro, but says that the change did not happen as dramatically as it might have appeared to because "the Old Negro had long become more of a myth than a man" (3). This myth involved, partly, the notion of the "Negro problem" from the preceding era, a patronizing attitude that rendered a black person "more of a formula than a human being," one who depended upon help from social reformers and politicians. Shaking off this legacy, Locke points to the "new psychology" and "new spirit" of the "New Negro," the definite, optimistic change that has come from within despite continued trying circumstances (3). Locke believed that his people had overcome the urge to become cynical, or to fight prejudice with more prejudice, and were poised to shift "from the arid fields of controversy and debate to the productive fields of creative expression" (15). Art, in other words, marks the arrival of the New Negro, who is no longer content to continue to fight battles only through policy debates.

A third essay, George Schuyler's "The Negro-Art Hokum" (1926), has a skeptical, even sardonic tone with regard to art. It challenges the growing establishment of banner-carriers for the Renaissance by saying that there is, essentially, no such thing as black art – at least not yet. The creative expressions that are characteristic of black life in America, according to Schuyler, are actually associated just with a single region or social class, rather than with the race as a whole. He believes that these expressions are found in dance and music. In terms of literature, painting, and sculpture, "it is identical in kind with the literature, painting, and sculpture of white Americans; that is, it shows more or less evidence of European influence" (25). He pushes his critique even deeper when he writes "that the Aframerican is merely a lampblacked Anglo-Saxon" (25). Since his black peers, like whites, are overly simplistic in their thinking and base it on crude, widely circulated stereotypes, Schuyler argues, there's not much possibility for the rise of authentic art. Part of his point is that American culture is bland and not terribly inspirational, but he also rejects the notion that black art must necessarily reflect something "peculiar" about black experience, because that distinction from white experience will invariably reinforce racial hierarchy (26).

A fourth essay that can help to frame the debates is Langston Hughes's famous manifesto "The Negro Artist and the Racial Mountain" (1926). This essay was conceived as a direct response to Schuyler's, and also in direct response to Countee Cullen, who is the unnamed black poet in the opening paragraph, the one who expresses a desire, in Hughes's interpretation, to be relieved from the burdens of writing about his race, and by extension, wishes "to be white" (91). Hughes uses the metaphor of a mountain to describe that psychological barrier which separates individual artists from the art they create. In favor of distinctiveness in black art, Hughes cautions the black artist against submitting to American "standardization" (91). Lurking within this tendency toward the desire for assimilation is a feeling of racial shame that prevents the black artist from "discover[ing] himself and his people," especially "the low-down folks, the so-called common element" who comprise the majority of the race (92). Hughes celebrates these common people, both in this essay and throughout his career, because of their self-confidence, their authentic claim to individuality. Hughes's essay is a clarion call to fellow black artists not to be afraid of expressing the truths of their own people, and of themselves as individuals. Accusing white art of dullness, he implores black artists not to imitate it out of a sense of fear, timidity, and the need for acceptance. He points to jazz as a model for his literary art because jazz is "one of the inherent expressions of Negro life in America; the eternal tom-tom beating in the Negro soul – the tom-tom of revolt against weariness in a white world, a world of subway trains, and work, work, work; the tom-tom of joy and laughter, and pain swallowed in a smile" (94–95). Accepting such expressions as truth, even if they don't conform to preconceived "white" notions of what art should be, is essential, and the artist must embrace his freedom. He ends the essay memorably by stating that the artist should not care whether either white or black audiences accept his work: "We build our temples for tomorrow, strong as we know how, and we stand on top of the mountain, free within ourselves" (95). Freedom – always a complicated word within African American literature – here refers to *individual* freedom: of spirit, of thought, of expression, all within a racial context.

The final essay to be considered, actually a 1926 speech W.E.B. DuBois gave to introduce the recipient of the prestigious Spingarn Medal, was entitled "Criteria of Negro Art." It is much less prescriptive than the title implies, but it underscores both Johnson's and Locke's views on the relationship of the "New Negro" to the past and affirms Hughes's belief that the artist must be absolutely free: "In all sorts of ways we are hemmed in and our new young artists have got to fight their way to freedom" (758). He describes these limitations as customs inherited from whites, sexual guilt, religion, and shame over the past. He insists that black art must be devoted to Truth and Justice, both capitalized along with Beauty. Art has an obligation to uphold Justice and to depict Truth, and he claims that black people have to uphold Truth and Justice when whites do not: "Thus all art is propaganda and ever must be, despite the wailing of the purists. I stand in utter shamelessness and say that whatever art I have for writing has been used always for propaganda for gaining the right of black folk to love and enjoy" (757). DuBois is using "propaganda" here as a way of linking black experience with dignity, which can only be achieved through that ideal combination of Truth and Justice. This combination is not only endemic to black art in the 1920s, but, as DuBois sees it, to all great art throughout history. (Locke, in a 1928 essay entitled "Art or Propaganda?", has a different viewpoint: he claims that Renaissance artists "must choose art and put aside propaganda" [Ervin, 49]).

These essays together provide an outline of the main currents of thought in the Renaissance, and demonstrate the varied directions these currents took at the points where these writers disagreed with one another. Renaissance artists would have had a difficult time pleasing all of these writers simultaneously. Hughes's idea that black artists should express themselves according to their own intuition was a noble (if utopian) ideal, but clearly critics existed who would complicate that ideal. They actively altered the tastes of readers as well as the output of writers.

New Wine in Old Bottles, Old Wine in New Bottles

The *form* this art would take would engender as much debate and variety as we see in these varied conceptions of the nature of New Negro Art. The Harlem Renaissance took place during a time of cultural and artistic upheaval – a.k.a. Modernism – in which social structures and literary expressions were undergoing radical change and revision. In Europe, James Joyce, Virginia Woolf, and American expatriate Gertrude Stein were producing stream-of-consciousness novels that violated every convention associated with fiction, and similar experimental works, notably by William Faulkner, proliferated domestically. Poets, led by T.S. Eliot and Ezra Pound, were busy discovering ways to "make it new," in Pound's words, and dramatists, led by Eugene O'Neill, were bringing new energies and techniques to the stage. This is not to say that traditional types of literature were not also being produced simultaneously, but there was unusual acceptance of the avant-garde in the 1920s, perhaps even an expectation of it.

It is thus not surprising that the New Negro Renaissance work that recent critics and students study and puzzle over more than any other is *Cane*, Jean Toomer's enigmatic 1923 masterpiece. Critics have wondered whether to consider it a collection of stories and poems or a novel. Its three sections begin with cryptic drawings that resemble the phases of a moon, or parentheses. Clearly, Toomer was willing to embrace the avant-garde spirit of the 1920s by resorting to ambiguous symbols. *Cane* is slippery, full of symbols and moods. Since it was Toomer's only major work, we don't have many clues to draw from to contextualize his developing genius. It stands in its own corner, both part of and apart from the more accessible works of the Renaissance. Its importance was noted right away, and other writers at the time were conscious of the long shadow it threw; the novelist Wallace Thurman, in his satirical 1932 novel *Infants of the Spring*, writes, "I know of only one Negro [author] who has the elements of greatness, and that's Jean Toomer. The rest of us are merely journeymen, planting seed for someone else to harvest" (221).

Darwin Turner, in his introduction to the 1975 edition of *Cane*, traces Toomer's intense intellectual journey in the years prior to writing it. Believing at first in an almost mystical merging of the races, Toomer continually revised his intellectual position on racial identity, and this fluidity of thought is evident in *Cane*. In a letter to *The Liberator* he wrote, "I am naturally and inevitably an American. I have strived for a spiritual fusion analogous to the fact of racial intermingling....Within the last two or three years, however, my growing need for artistic expression has pulled me deeper and deeper into the Negro group....It has stimulated and fertilized whatever creative talent I may contain within me" (Toomer, 128). The stories and poetic sketches in the first section of *Cane* reflect the inspiration he derived from listening to songs and speeches in the South. These dense, imagistic pieces have intrigued readers since their publication. Their subjects include race relations, sexual desire, and violence, all against the backdrop of a landscape described with atmospheric precision. The landscape and characters seem inextricable, as in these sentences from "Fern:" "Face flowed into her eyes. Flowed in soft cream foam and plaintive ripples, in such a way that wherever your glance may momentarily have rested, it immediately thereafter wavered in the direction of her eyes" (16). Many of the early stories are just a page or two long, but the second section closes with a more substantial story, "Bona and Paul," about unfulfilled sexual longing and biracial anxiety. It culminates in Paul's vision of a beautiful racial intermingling, as he expresses it to a worker at a café: "I came back to tell you, brother, that white faces are petals of roses. That dark faces are petals of dusk. That I am going out and gather petals. That I am going out and know her whom I brought here with me to these Gardens which are purple like a bed of roses would be at dusk" (80). The final section is completely comprised of "Kabnis," a long story reminiscent of Joyce or Faulkner involving a redefinition of religion, based on the idea, haltingly expressed by an old man, that the nation must atone for the sins of its past, especially "th sin th white folks 'mitted when they made th Bible lie" (117). Such moments sparkle forth in *Cane*, yet the reader who attempts to summarize the book's importance in a simplistic way will invariably fail.

Other than *Cane*, much of the Renaissance fiction that has withstood the test of time is realism, and its experimentation or stylistic flourishes have to do with voice. One exception is the work of Richard Bruce Nugent, whose 1926 short story "Smoke, Lilies and Jade" is noteworthy not only because of its stream-of-consciousness motif (sentence fragments linked with ellipses, forsaking conventional capitalization), but also because of its frank treatment of same-sex desire, perhaps the first overt instance of this subject in African American literature. The story names some of the great figures of the Renaissance (Langston, Zora) as the narrator copes with the feelings associated with kissing another man: "Alex closed his eyes...how did one act...his pulse was hammering..." (579). It ends as many modern works do, by refusing to end: "*To Be Continued...*" (583). The story cannot be said to be race-conscious in the way most Renaissance works are and in fact it has little to do with racial identity. The absence of that subject demonstrates the freedom that Hughes describes in "The Negro Artist and the Racial Mountain," but Hughes's assumption is that black artists will continue to treat the subject of black identity with that freedom.

Many of the great poets associated with the Harlem Renaissance are a bit tamer than their white modernist counterparts in terms of experimentation with form. Jamaican-born Claude McKay, for instance, wrote a great number of poems, including the famous declaration of defiance, "If We Must Die." In this strong-voiced poem, McKay rallies his readers to "[fight] back" against the "cowardly pack" who have cornered them (14, 13). Like virtually all of McKay's poems, this one is a textbook Shakespearean sonnet, a 14-line poem in iambic pentameter with a specific rhyme scheme and structure. Although there is nothing wrong with poetic expression in sonnet form or any traditional form, the fact that Harlem Renaissance authors such as McKay employed it indicates a certain tentativeness on the part of black poets of the 1920s to create new forms to match their new mindset.

Countee Cullen, perhaps the most prominent poet of the Harlem Renaissance besides Hughes, was also a traditionalist with regard to form, though not to the same degree as McKay. One of Cullen's most famous poems, "Yet Do I Marvel," is also a straight Shakespearean sonnet. This poem uses its three quatrains to build an argument that questions God's tendency to torment his creatures. Why, for instance, does "the little buried mole [continue] blind" (3)? Why, in mythology, are figures like Tantalus and Sisyphus doomed for eternity? The poet acknowledges that God must have a reason, and that He does not have any obligation to explain himself to individual mortals. The couplet at the end of the argument, though, suggests that God would not be able to explain this circumstance: "Yet do I marvel at this curious thing: / To make a poet black, and bid him sing!" (13–14). The context for the poem is of supreme importance as the reader attempts to understand the poet's conundrum: why is it especially puzzling that God would make a black poet? Following the examples from earlier in the poem, is this another example of divine unfairness, or even cruelty? What are the specific impediments to being a black poet? The poem asks the reader to rely on his or her knowledge of the history of the times. A few possibilities exist: black poets faced publishing obstacles, or they were not as easily accepted by critics, or, perhaps, they were obligated to write about racial themes exclusively. This final explanation is one that troubles Cullen as the unnamed poet in Hughes's essay "The Negro Artist and the Racial Mountain." No matter how we interpret the sonnet's final couplet, it is clear that the condition of the black poet is a trying one, from Cullen's point of view. By expressing this conflict in a sonnet, Cullen was insisting on his mastery of poetic diction while communicating anxiety over his racial identity.

The use of the sonnet form in particular might have been a self-conscious way to link the Harlem Renaissance to the English Renaissance, during which Shakespeare penned his sonnets. There is within this impulse the desire to be taken seriously and to add to the annals of what is considered high art. Still, detractors could identify the employment of traditional poetic forms as imitative of white European culture, or, worse, retrograde, as the sonnet form was hundreds of years old at this point, and this was supposed to be the expression of the "New Negro." Moreover, with experimental white poets like Pound and Eliot gaining a great deal of attention, poems that employed strict meter and end rhyme sounded somewhat naïve, regardless of their content.

Langston Hughes exhibited a willingness to invent new conventions, and his were not the same inventions as those of Pound or Eliot, who increasingly tended toward abstraction and obscure allusions in the 1920s. Hughes deliberately employed the rhythms and sounds of jazz in his early works. Often deceptively simple, Hughes's poems are truly liberated from the modernist-era burdens of trying to impress audiences with abstruseness and erudition. He commands the reader's attention not with a whisper or a shout, but rather with the clarity and precision of a self-confident voice speaking the common man's language with grace.

The strength of Hughes's early poems derives from his subjective point of view, his use of an expressive "I" who exists both as an individual and as a racial everyman. Take, for example, two of his frequently anthologized early poems, "I, Too," and "The Negro Speaks of Rivers." In "I, Too," he responds to Walt Whitman's 1860 poem, "I Hear America Singing." Hughes points to the fact that Whitman's celebratory poem does not include the voices of black people (despite its publication on the eve of the Civil War), and insists on adding his voice to the "varied carols" that Whitman heard. Hughes's speaker is "the darker brother" who is sent to eat in the kitchen when company comes. He resents this discrimination, but does not allow it to define him, or to keep him down. Rather, he focuses on the future, and on the resources he can marshal in the present to ensure his survival: "I laugh, / And eat well, / And grow strong" (5–7). By defining himself, he ends up focusing on his own self-worth and beauty rather than allowing bitterness or self-doubt to weigh him down. In terms of presentation, he picks up from Whitman's idea, but does not imitate his form. Compared to Whitman's characteristic litanies and lengthy lines, Hughes's poem is spare and stripped down. In "The Negro Speaks of Rivers," the speaker relies on his experience and wisdom: "I've known rivers....My soul has grown deep like the rivers" (11, 13). The "I" of this poem is again both individual and collective, and is able to range over time and space to communicate with body and soul. The poem is like a river, rhythmic and eternal. Moreover, it links Africa and America by pointing specifically to both the exploitation of black labor and a sense of survival and endurance that prevent the speaker from wallowing in despair. It is a poem of growth rather than erosion. Hughes's focus on common speech, familiar images, and especially the idiom of jazz and blues in verse became extremely influential not only during the Renaissance, but as a model for later black writers who were eager to develop an original voice to communicate the African American experience.

Racial Self-doubt

If part of the ostensible intent of the Renaissance was to provide black people with positive images of racial pride, as is evident in many of Hughes's early poems, one can also see in many works of this time a nagging counterweight to those images. For every speaker like the one who not only "sings America" but triumphantly *is* America in Hughes's "I, Too," there is the voice of an individual who is paralyzed or alienated by society's attempts to oppress him. Huggins describes this phenomenon as "a strong odor of...pathos and self-doubt" (69). One prominent example can be seen in Cullen's devastating short poem, "Incident":

> Once riding in old Baltimore
> Heart-filled, head-filled with glee,
> I saw a Baltimorean
> Keep looking straight at me.

Now I was eight and very small,
And he was no whit bigger,
And so I smiled, but he poked out
His tongue, and called me "Nigger."

I saw the whole of Baltimore
From May until December;
Of all the things that happened there
That's all that I remember.

The sense of deflation brought about by the racial epithet at the center of the poem is palpable, and has a profound, lasting effect on the speaker. We know that he was eight when the "incident" took place, but the sense is that he is much older now. Profound psychological trauma lingers in the speaker's head, and causes him to fixate on what happened to him rather than on how he reacted. He retreats into his own damaged mind, unable to move past the incident, and unable to salvage anything positive from his travels. The poem's simple, child-like rhythm and rhyme scheme contribute to its horrifying effect: the loss of innocence and the stagnation of individual growth in a racial context would unsettle even the most optimistic "New Negro."

Hughes's poetry, for all of its ebullience and self-assuredness, also reveals some of the "pathos and self-doubt" Huggins identifies, especially when discussing biracial characters. Such anger grinds against the pride and racial self-acceptance that dominate Hughes's early poems. In his poem "Cross," the title of which connotes not only a crossroads but a "cross to bear," the biracial speaker states: "If ever I cursed my white old man / I take my curses back. / If ever I cursed my black old mother / And wished she were in hell, / I'm sorry for that evil wish / And now I wish her well" (2–7). This may sound like an attempt to come to terms with the racial mixing of one's ancestry in a less violent way than in "Mulatto," where his speaker is fixated on patricidal fantasies, but this speaker is left without a racial identity: "My old man died in a fine big house. / My ma died in a shack. / I wonder where I'm gonna die, / Being neither white nor black?" (9–12). It is noteworthy that the speaker doesn't imagine himself as *both* white and black in this final line, but rather neither one. There is a flavor of fatalism in the last few lines: the speaker's black mother is doomed to poverty and the speaker is unable to control or even identify his own racial identity.

Fittingly, this poem is the epigraph to one of the most troubling extended meditations on the quandary between progressive self-assuredness and racial self-doubt of the period, Nella Larsen's novella *Passing* (1929). Like Jean Toomer, Larsen is a highly important but enigmatic literary figure who published two celebrated novellas in quick succession before fading into obscurity. The first of these novels, *Quicksand* (1928), which DuBois praised as "the best piece of fiction that Negro America has produced since the heyday of Chesnutt," tells the story of a conflicted young woman named Helga Crane (ix). Initially a teacher in the South, Helga is disgusted by the teachings of a preacher who extols the virtues of her school because it teaches African Americans "to stay in their places" (3). The school, modeled on Tuskegee, trains blacks to be "hewers of wood and drawers of water," and she regards the school as "a big knife with cruelly sharp edges ruthlessly cutting all to a pattern, the white man's pattern" (3, 4). She clearly has to flee from this oppressive atmosphere, and she does, but she seems destined from the start to fail to find happiness elsewhere: "She could neither conform, nor be happy in her unconformity" (7). Like the speaker of Hughes's "Cross," her identity is defined in terms of neither/nor rather than both/and.

Helga's conflicts are not limited to race, but include a number of social issues: the pressures of social decorum, sexual longing in conflict with repression, and the rigidity of gender roles, to name a few. She often feels confined by social circumstances and, yearning for a better life, moves on. In this regard *Quicksand* is a lucid example of what Farah Jasmine Griffin defines as a migration narrative, "one of the twentieth century's dominant forms of cultural production," which includes as one of its many features an early departure from the South, which "is portrayed as an immediate, identifiable, and oppressive power" (3, 4). Helga cannot stand the South and so moves to Chicago, where she was born. She visits a rich uncle on her mother's side – her white ancestry – but he rejects Helga, and she learns from her uncle's new wife that her parents were not married. This encounter reveals the depth of her troubled mind, her own prejudice against the blackness within her: "Worst of all was the fact that under the stinging hurt she understood and sympathized with Mrs. Nilssen's point of view....She saw herself as an obscene sore...at all costs to be hidden" (29). Realizing that she has no "people" in Chicago, she flees to New York.

Harlem initially seems to be the solution to her conflict. Surrounded by black people, she immediately feels at home: "Harlem, teeming black Harlem, had welcomed her and lulled her into something that was, she was certain, peace and contentment" (43). Helga's trouble, though, is not inherent in any place. Even though she hates the South and feels rejected in Chicago, her problem is firmly lodged in her mind: "Somewhere, within her, in a deep recess, crouched discontent" (47). The novel showcases her alienation and suggests that it is related to the race prejudice that surrounds her. Yet it does not do so in a simple way. Her great friend in New York, Anne Grey, is obsessed with the race problem and dedicates her life to racial uplift, which frustrates Helga: "Why, Helga wondered, with unreasoning exasperation, didn't they find something else to talk of? Why must the race problem always creep in?" (52). This sentiment is born of a desire to do away with the concept of race altogether because of the anxiety it has caused her, and it fuels her own conflicted feelings about her identity: "It was as if she were shut up, boxed up, with hundreds of her race, closed up with that something in the racial character which had always been to her, inexplicable, alien. Why, she demanded in fierce rebellion, should she be yoked to these despised black folk?" (54–55). This startling statement of racial self-loathing contrasts starkly with the feelings of happiness she experienced when she first came to Harlem.

Her move to Denmark, the country of her mother's ancestry, is both surprising, since it will call attention to her racial identity, and predictable, since it allows her to remove herself from the Harlem she both loathes and loves. She longs for "that blessed sense of belonging to herself alone and not to a race," and she initially feels that Denmark is her true home, but she begins to become self-conscious after receiving copious attention as an "exotic" (64). She refuses an offer of marriage to a Danish man, claiming: "if we were married, you might come to be ashamed of me, to hate me, to hate all dark people. My mother did that" (88). She projects this hatred onto the man who loves her and thus reveals her own inherent conflict in no uncertain terms. She returns to New York, trying one last time to embrace her black heritage, but she is too damaged, too confused. The novel ends with her submitting to a life that she had never wanted, marrying a black man and bearing five children, and returning to the South that she had once despised. A bleak book with a frustrating protagonist, *Quicksand* exemplifies the tension between optimism and pessimism during the Renaissance. Helga, a victim of DuBoisian double-consciousness, reflects the psychological damage caused by the racial politics of the time.

Larsen's other celebrated novella, *Passing*, is no less tragic or conflicted. It also features a troubled female protagonist, Irene Redfield, who is drawn out of her conventional middle-class life by a friend, Clare Kendry, who has been passing for white. Clare has married a vociferous white racist who refers to her jokingly as "Nig" because of her dark skin (170). Her marriage highlights not only the danger of her situation, as Irene regards it, but also the psychological perversity of it. Irene is stunned by Clare's willingness to put up with her husband's abusive language, but she, too, is guilty of remaining quiet while "in reality seething with anger, mortification, shame" (174). Irene tries to distance herself from Clare, but finds herself drawn into her friend's orbit. Irene realizes that she "cared nothing for the race. She only belonged to it" (182). Her own conflicted feelings surface and contain some of the same elements of racial self-doubt evident in *Quicksand*. *Passing* also shares with the earlier novella an inquiry into Freud's theories, specifically of the consequences of burying violence and sexual desire in the unconscious; Irene wonders, "Was she never to be free of it, that fear which crouched, always, deep down within her, stealing away the sense of security, the feeling of permanence, from the life which she had so admirably arranged for them all, and desired so ardently to have remain as it was?" (187). All facets of her identity are on shaky ground partly because of her own ambiguous racial identity and consequent ability to "pass." Her response is to turn against her friend, to regard Clare as a kind of enemy to herself and to her stable existence. She realizes her dilemma: "She was caught between two allegiances, different, yet the same. Herself. Her race. Race! The thing that bound and suffocated her....Irene Redfield wished, for the first time in her life, that she had not been born a Negro" (225). The novel's violent and ambiguous conclusion offers no solution either for the desire of light-skinned black people to pass or for the wounded feelings of those who are indirectly affected by others' passing.

Larsen certainly did not invent the passing narrative. It was in fact a somewhat common trope in the Renaissance, and it had been established in earlier periods, such as in the works of Chesnutt (as described in Chapter Three). In Larsen's novel it is charged with a violence and intensity that highlights psychological issues as much as social ones. A somewhat more tempered rendition of the topic can be seen in Jessie Fauset's *Plum Bun* (1929), published the same year. Fauset, the editor of the prominent journal *The Crisis* during the formative years of the Renaissance, struggled to enter the canon of Renaissance works in the mid-twentieth century because her work seemed more conservative in style than the works of some of her cohorts. But *Plum Bun* has experienced a critical revival in recent years, partly because of its artistic maturity, and partly because it has come to be regarded as more than simply another "passing" tale. Deborah McDowell has argued convincingly that the novel demonstrates "a thematic and ironic complexity [and] a stylistic subtlety," as it takes on not only the subject of passing, but also the topic of women's limited roles, all the while critiquing the romance form it employs (x). *Plum Bun* can usefully expand the concerns of the two women novelists from the Renaissance one typically reads as representative (Larsen and Hurston).

Plum Bun takes its title and its chapter epigraphs from a children's rhyme ("To market, to market, to buy a plum bun"). It can be read as a novel about how maturity brings with it a more realistic, if not disillusioned, perspective. Angela Murray, the novel's protagonist, like Larsen's Irene Redfield, is drawn to the social benefits of passing for white, but is mindful of what it means to accept the social prejudice that passing is complicit in. At the same time, she is intent on "marketing" herself as a marriageable young woman. Her involvement with Roger, a wealthy white New Yorker, does not end in marriage, but rather in Angela's realization about the dangers of treating both passing and love as a "game," as she does: "a game against public tradition on the one hand and family instinct on the other" (146). The "game" has consequences, not only for her, but for her beloved sister Virginia, who is darker skinned and who is well aware of the consequences of Angela's behavior. When Virginia meets her in a railway station, Angela denies her sister in front of Roger, and she is immediately filled with regret: "Surely no ambition, no pinnacle of safety was supposed to call for the sacrifice of a sister" (159). The importance of family over the pursuit of individual social climbing is Fauset's main concern. *Plum Bun* is subtitled "A Novel Without a Moral," but it does seem to clearly excoriate Angela's immature behavior, not only for passing, but for treating marriage as a game and herself as a commodity. Fauset's novel ends more comically than either of Larsen's does, but many of the contentious issues and anxieties of the Renaissance – about assimilation, class mobility at the cost of heritage, race pride, and freedom – are also evident here.

Wallace Thurman, in *The Blacker the Berry…* (1929), looks at race prejudice from a slightly different angle, and his satirical novel is cutting in the way it accuses some light-skinned black people of perpetuating racism. Its protagonist, Emma Lou Watson, realizes early on that her very dark skin color prevents any sort of social mobility (in contrast with Larsen's characters who are plagued by the choices they make based on the mobility afforded by their light skin color). The narrator of Thurman's novel observes, "The tragedy of her life was that she was too black" (5). Thurman, one of the founders of *Fire!*, the short-lived but very significant Renaissance literary journal that celebrated the exuberance of young black artists, tests the consciences of readers who would compromise black pride. The novel is a useful companion piece to Larsen's *Passing* in that the main character also moves from place to place in the hopes of finding a community where she will fit in. The message in Thurman's novel (admittedly not as eloquent as Larsen's) may be more hopeful; as Martha Cook argues, Emma Lou is eventually able "to move beyond a destructive life of self-hatred through articulating a philosophy that enables her to reject self-sacrifice and continue her search for self-reliance" (141). As a satire, though, Thurman's novel points to some weaknesses within the notion of a black community that the Renaissance largely aspired to.

Common Folks, Folklore, Primitivism

The Renaissance displayed what could be seen as a class divide that fueled a robust debate about the definition of African American culture. Hughes in "The Negro Artist and the Racial Mountain" suggested that black middle-class artists who aspired to the condition of whiteness were self-consciously avoiding black culture (associated with the lower class), opting for the dullness of "Nordics" as opposed to their race's vibrant social life. Larsen's *Quicksand* begins with a similar idea, as Helga, working at a school called Naxos (an anagram of "Saxon"), feels bored by the lack of vitality she experiences in a culture that is too white in its sensibilities. At the same time, there was trepidation over the depiction of black people as "primitives:" sensuous, uninhibited, and passionate, but less cerebral or "cultured" than European Americans.

There is a clear racial essentialism in much of the literature of this period that underscores a racial and cultural divide. From this viewpoint, "Africa" becomes synonymous with a primitive ancestry that has brought underappreciated gifts onto the American scene. Africa is also locked in a battle with the dominant European influences over language, religion, social decorum, and formal education, to name a few. The ever-conflicted Countee Cullen expresses this battle memorably in his lengthy poem "Heritage" in which he repeats, but does not fully answer, the question, "What is Africa to me?" As "One three centuries removed / From the scenes his fathers loved," he does not have a strong connection to Africa, yet its existence torments his body and troubles his mind; he writes, "Ever must I twist and squirm / Writhing like a baited worm / While its primal measures drip / Through my body, crying 'Strip! / Doff this new exuberance. / Come and dance the lover's dance!'" (4.14–19). Even while embracing Christianity and scoffing at the "Quaint, out-landish heathen gods" of his forbears, he feels an unmistakable pull toward the continent he considers primitive (5.1). Hughes expresses a similar sentiment in "Afro American Fragment," in which he repeats the phrase "So long, / So far away / Is Africa," and yet feels attracted to a "song of atavistic land" (1–3, 18).

Not all artists resisted this pull, and many who indulged in the wild abandon of Harlem and similar black neighborhoods associated it with a particular kind of hedonism involving music, dancing, sex, and alcohol (the last of which was outlawed during the 1920s under Prohibition). Deriving from the increasingly influential writings of psychologist Sigmund Freud, one emerging school of thought held that white culture involved a large measure of repression, and that black culture had the opportunity or even the obligation to unleash free expression. Of course, such an idea was rife with stereotyping, and yet it is evident in much of the literature of the time.

Claude McKay's short novel *Home to Harlem* (1928) is a valuable examination of this tension. Considered one of the more important works of fiction of the Renaissance, McKay's novel is heavy on what might be considered the cruder expressions of black culture at the time: drinking, sex, and violence. (DuBois wrote, in a withering review, that McKay's novel "nauseates me, and after the dirtier parts of its filth I feel distinctly like taking a bath" [Gates and McKay, 784]). Its protagonist, Jake Brown, returns from the war in Europe to Harlem with a seemingly insatiable appetite for women and drinking. He witnesses and participates in a number of bar fights, most of which involve territory battles over members of the opposite sex. One memorable fight involves two women who agree to battle naked, in public: "An old custom, perhaps a survival of African tribalism, had been imported from some remote West Indian hillside into a New York back yard" (308–309). The violence of the novel is striking, though much of it seems nearly comical and is connected to the drinking, swearing, and sexual abandon that also permeate the book. At one point, following a different fight between two women, one character says, "It's a shame. Can't you act like decent English people?" (97). The two fighters respond in a Caribbean dialect: "She come boxing me up ovah a dutty-black 'Merican coon" and "Mek a quick move or I'll box you bumbole ovah de moon" (97).

Jake delights in the supercharged emotional atmosphere of Harlem, and makes his way through its speakeasies with pleasure in mind. He is laid low by hangovers and, at one point, a sexually transmitted disease, but is generally undeterred and exuberant. To some extent, *Home to Harlem* echoes Hemingway's *The Sun Also Rises* (1926), that chronicle of Lost Generation angst that traces the experiences of another ex-soldier named Jake who is caught up in a milieu of alcoholic, sexual, and violent abandon (in Spain rather than Harlem). McKay's Jake is not plagued by the same existential angst that unnerves Hemingway's Jake. Initially, a comparison of the novels might lead to the facile conclusion that black hedonists in the 1920s could capitalize on their lack of inhibition to fully plunge into sensual pleasure. But McKay's novel changes and deepens when Jake befriends a Haitian waiter named Ray, an intellectual who teaches him about history and who introduces him to cultural pursuits more substantial than the ones he favors. In a highly atmospheric novel which operates as a portrait of Harlem nightlife as much as a study in character or narrative, the contrast between Ray's intellect and Jake's bodily appetites generates a fruitful inquiry into the so-called primitive and so-called refined forces in dialogue at the time. Ray senses that his cerebral gifts may be a curse: "Thought was not a beautiful and reassuring angel, a thing of soothing music and light laughter and winged images glowing with the rare colors of life. No. It was suffering, horribly real" (156). He is an aspiring artist, and yet is plagued by his relationship to the world he witnesses: "Could he ever create Art? Art, around which vague, incomprehensible words and phrases stormed? What was art, anyway? Was it more than a clear-cut presentation of a vivid impression of life?" (228).

Whether or not McKay expresses his own artistic dilemma through his presentation of Jake and Ray is less important than the fact that he reinforces a common Renaissance dilemma: "Ray felt more and his range was wider and he could not be satisfied with the easy, simple things that sufficed for Jake" (265). The "easy, simple things" strike the dominant note in *Home to Harlem*, and yet they are clearly ripe for misunderstanding. Hedonism may be a reaction to oppression or an attempt to experience life on a deeper level. It may not be simply indulgence in one's bodily appetites, in other words. Toward the novel's conclusion is a lyrical paragraph that expresses both primitivism and its complications: "Haunting rhythm, mingling of naïve wistfulness and charming gayety, now sheering over into mad riotous joy, now, like a jungle mask strange, unfamiliar, disturbing now plunging headlong into the far, dim depths of profundity and rising out as suddenly with a simple childish grin. And the white visitors laugh. They see the grin only. Here are none of the well-patterned, well-made emotions of the respectable world. A laugh might finish in a sob" (337). McKay unearths a complex knot of emotions here to destabilize the opposition between the "respectable world" and the underworld he describes. This complication makes the opposition between the primitive and modern, between common folks and so-called sophisticates, less facile.

Zora Neale Hurston was trained as a folklorist and traveled extensively through the Caribbean and the American South (where she was born) gathering materials for her books *Mules and Men* (1935) and *Tell My Horse* (1938). Her reputation in the 1930s rested as much on these works as on her first two novels, *Jonah's Gourd Vine* (1934) and *Their Eyes Were Watching God* (1937), the latter of which has become her best-known work. Raised in Eatonville, Florida, a town incorporated and run exclusively by black citizens, Hurston was educated first at Howard University and then at Columbia University, where she was the only black student. She remained in Harlem at the height of the Renaissance where she produced early short stories and a play, and co-founded the journal *FIRE!* which was dedicated to allowing black writers to explore any subjects and treatments they wished, not just those that would advance a racially progressive social agenda. She returned to the South to conduct more folkloric research in the 1930s and to work on her novels. Her story from that point on is one of the more compelling ones in American literary history. *Their Eyes Were Watching God*, now an indispensable work, was not well received in its time. Richard Wright, who became the major figure in African American literature in the 1940s, was one of a number of critics who denigrated the book for its supposedly retrograde use of dialect and the author for creating a novel that did no political work, instead opting for what could be regarded as crude entertainment for whites at the expense of black people. Hurston faded into obscurity, but her reputation experienced a dramatic revival in the 1970s and 1980s, led by the efforts of novelist Alice Walker, whose influential essay "In Search of Zora Neale Hurston" led not only to the republication of her books, but to an extraordinary amount of attention paid to them in college classrooms and literary journals.

Some late-twentieth-century critics who championed Hurston – including Walker – argued convincingly that the reason she fell out of favor had much to do with gender bias, and there is merit to that argument. As in many literary traditions, the supposed "great works" tend to showcase male adventure over female domesticity. But another reason for her obscurity was the very strength of her folkloric acuity, which was what caused her to write her works in the dialect that James Weldon Johnson had proclaimed regressive at the beginning of the Renaissance in 1922. Many writers in Hurston's lifetime were clearly keen to move away from certain folk traditions that had devolved, in their worst manifestations, into minstrelsy and racist humor. The revival of Hurston's works in the late twentieth century involved a much more nuanced reading of her work and sought to elevate the voices of common folks, women, and Southern blacks rather than to ignore them.

Hurston may have also suffered for being precisely the kind of artist Hughes describes at the end of "The Negro Artist and the Racial Mountain:" free, comfortable, uninhibited, and, to some extent, willing to move through life untroubled by the racism of the past or even the present. The paralysis evident in the poetry of Cullen or the novels of Larsen does not plague Hurston's work. In her brief essay "How It Feels to Be Colored Me" (1928), she proclaims: "I am not tragically colored. There is no great sorrow dammed up in my soul, nor lurking behind my eyes. I do not mind at all. I do not belong to the sobbing school of Negrohood who hold that nature somehow has given them a lowdown dirty deal and whose feelings are all hurt about it" (Gates and McKay, 1009). The history of slavery, she claims, "fails to register depression with me. Slavery is sixty years in the past" (1009). She goes on to view her race as having an advantage over white people who are and should be troubled by the ghosts of their racist history. Listening to jazz music transports her to Africa; the music "attacks the tonal veil with primitive fury, rending it, clawing it until it breaks through to the jungle beyond. I follow those heathen – follow them exultingly. I dance wildly inside myself; I yell within, I whoop....My face is painted red and yellow and my body is painted blue. My pulse is throbbing like a war drum" (1010). A white companion listening to the same music dryly proclaims the music "good." In this short piece, Hurston dives into the concept of black primitivism head first, with no apologies, while also celebrating blackness and proclaiming that, at times, race is a meaningless concept, and that there is no contradiction in her mind between being black and being American. This seeming triumph over DuBois's double-consciousness sets Hurston apart from many of her contemporaries. Her writings do reflect a certain consciousness of the way white society has constrained black life, especially economically, but in describing "the sobbing school of Negrohood" as she does, Hurston also separates herself from the traditions of literary protest, rage, or depression. The Renaissance, comprised of equal measures of optimism and pessimism about the present and future, was the natural period when such divergent opinions would emerge.

Their Eyes Were Watching God, like much of Hurston's work, demonstrates a deep desire for independence and self-fashioning without sacrificing good-natured humor. It is the story of Janie Crawford, told to her friend Pheoby, who in turn the tom-toms, / Low…slow / Slow…low – / Stirs your blood. / Dance!" (1–6). In addition to atmospheric poems such as these that describe Harlem nightlife, some of Hughes's poems are actual blues lyrics in form and theme, such as this first stanza from "Homesick Blues:" "De railroad bridge's / A sad song in de air. / De railroad bridge's / A sad song in de air. / Ever time de trains pass / I wants to go somewhere" (1–6). By taking the lyrics of a familiar musical form and calling it poetry, Hughes not only draws attention to the value of the blues, but erases the line between high and low art (the high culture of poetry and the vernacular blues). This move represents a significant unburdening for any would-be artist wondering about the place of folk culture in a supposedly refined art form like poetry.

The other Harlem Renaissance poet renowned for his use of the blues is Sterling Brown. He is yet another figure from this era whose success was short-lived. His major work is the poetry collection *Southern Road* (1932), and although he published other poetry, his career afterward was more as a critic and professor at Howard University. He shares with Hurston and Hughes a deep interest in folk culture, particularly that of the South, and the raw force of his poetic voice provides a bridge between Jean Toomer and Richard Wright. He also celebrates black folk heroes, such as the blues singer Ma Rainey:

> O Ma Rainey,
> Sing yo' song;
> Now you's back
> Whah you belong,
> Git way inside us,
> Keep us strong.
>   *(3.1–6)*

The blues, here and throughout Brown's poetry, have the capacity to bond black communities and to restore a sense of pride in a past that is in danger of being forgotten, as in his affecting poem "Remembering Nat Turner" in which the legacy of the slave rebellion leader is misinterpreted and misremembered.

The title poem from Langston Hughes's first collection, "The Weary Blues" (1925), brings many of his concerns together. It actually contains two blues lyrics: the first a refusal to let life's problems depress the singer and the second a worn-down moan of weariness, ending in "I wish that I had died" (29). The piano player who sings these lyrics is the subject of the poem, but there is a curious relationship between him and the speaker, who sits in the café audience exulting at the man's playing: "Sweet Blues! / Coming from a black man's soul. / O Blues!" (14–16). The two seem to move as one at the beginning of the poem, swaying back and forth in time, but the speaker disappears as the poem goes on and the player becomes an ambiguous figure. He has poured his life into his blues for the entertainment of others, and he is left weary. Hughes's concern for workers is evident here, for the blues are a product of labor just as any art form is. The exuberance of the music leads eventually to the poem's tired conclusion, with the weary blues rattling around in the player's mind.

communicates it to the busybody community, who stare at Janie from a porch after she returns from a burial. Janie's story is largely about her growth during her marriages to three husbands. The first is a kind of arranged marriage, set up by her grandmother, who worries that she will disgrace herself by becoming pregnant out of wedlock. The marriage is clearly dull and devoid of passion, and she leaves her first husband to find love with a second, Joe Starks. Joe is a better match for Janie, but he has ambitions to become a "big" man, and his eventual appointment as mayor of the town of Eatonville changes their relationship, causing him to limit Janie's social life and to control her in other ways. Joe's death enables her the freedom to choose another lover. Given her wealth and status she has many suitors, but surprises everyone she knows by selecting a somewhat unlikely candidate named Tea Cake, a man much younger than her and with few prospects. Janie's victory is that she has found love on her own terms, and even though Tea Cake dies tragically and prematurely, the story is a triumph of individual will and self-determination.

The plot takes a back seat to the novel's delight in language, both spoken and written. Hurston not only weaves a tapestry of idioms and phrases peculiar to her subjects, but also paints the setting generously. When Janie waits a year for a suitor, it is described as "a bloom time, and a green time and an orange time" (25). When she experiences love for Tea Cake, "her soul crawled out from its hiding place" (128). Resistance to the novel in its time may be partially attributable to the fact that Janie sums up her own moral at its end, about love and individual experience: "love ain't somthin' lak uh grindstone dat's de same thing everywhere and do de same thing tuh everything it touch....you got tuh *go* there tuh *know* there. Yo' papa and yo' mama and nobody else can't tell yuh and show yuh" (191–192). Since great literature was synonymous with ambiguity in the modern era, such common wisdom, expressed in a folksy voice, did not live up to many critics' expectations. But on the other hand, Langston Hughes, the poster boy of the Renaissance, advanced many of the same ideas as Hurston, and in a similar voice. His essay persona Jesse B. Semple ("Simple") and his poetic persona "Madam" were essentially similar to Hurston's characters. The fact that his reputation did not suffer as Hurston's did may have been because of his overtly political writings during his period of sympathy for communism in the 1930s, or because of his extraordinary, varied, sustained output. Hurston's champions of the late twentieth century, though, would insist that gender bias better explained this discrepancy.

Hughes is primarily known as a poet, yet he wrote in virtually every genre. His play *Mulatto* (1935) enjoyed the longest run on Broadway of any play by an African American playwright and held that record for a quarter century. Hughes also wrote novels and short fiction to great acclaim, and his 1940 autobiography *The Big Sea* is one of the most illuminating extended accounts of the Renaissance from one who was at the center of it. Yet his early poems, strongly influenced by jazz and the blues, helped to expand the horizons of other writers during the Renaissance by celebrating black music, and they remain essential foundational works of that period. In "Danse Africaine" he expresses a similar sentiment to that which Hurston expressed about jazz: "The low beating of the tom-toms, / The slow beating of

Hughes's poem can be read as a fitting conclusion to a study of the Renaissance: it is somewhat inconclusive, conscious of racial identity, celebratory of black life, yet also not immune to the forces that weigh against this celebration. The blues player is both a towering figure of inspiration and a tired worker in need of renewal. The blues come from his soul, as the speaker observes, but also from his body. The flash of unfettered optimism in the poem's first blues lyric – "I's gwine to quit ma frownin' / And put ma troubles on the shelf" (20–21) – proved to be akin to the Renaissance itself, which can now be regarded as a concentrated flurry of artistic production that would never be duplicated, and that led to the many different paths down which African American literature traveled in the ensuing years.

Conclusion

The 1920s and 1930s saw African American literature accessing the freedom that had been difficult to attain in earlier periods. The political imperative to abolish slavery in the pre-Civil War era and the tentativeness of the periods of Reconstruction and its aftermath placed earlier literature into certain pre-fabricated molds. Langston Hughes, among others, challenged himself and his contemporary black writers to embrace their race in all of its expressions and to capture its spirit in writing. Not all writers were as exuberant or as uninhibited as Hughes, and not all of them shared his willingness to employ an accessible, everyman voice. Still, in terms of energy, enthusiasm, and the willingness to take risks, the Harlem Renaissance marked a true liberation for black writers and paved the road for later artists, even those who found other models in African American literary history that they were more eager to emulate.

Suggestions for Further Reading

Huggins, Nathan Irvin. *Harlem Renaissance*. London: Oxford University Press, 1976. Print.

Lewis, David Levering. *When Harlem Was in Vogue*. New York, NY: Knopf, 1981. Print.

Ogbar, Jeffrey. *The Harlem Renaissance Revisited: Politics, Arts, and Letters*. Baltimore, MD: Johns Hopkins University Press, 2010. Print.

Pochmara, Anna. *The Making of the New Negro: Black Authorship, Masculinity, and Sexuality in the Harlem Renaissance*. Amsterdam: Amsterdam University Press, 2011. Print.

Rodgers, Marie E. *The Harlem Renaissance: An Annotated Reference Guide for Student Research*. Englewood, IL: Libraries Unlimited, 1998. Print.

Wall, Cheryl A. *Women of the Harlem Renaissance*. Bloomington, IN: Indiana University Press, 1995. Print.

Wintz, Cary D. and Paul Finkelman, eds. *Encyclopedia of the Harlem Renaissance*. New York, NY: Routledge, 2004. Print.

5

MID-TWENTIETH-CENTURY LITERATURE

Although many Harlem Renaissance writers brought widespread attention to black achievements in literature, most were tied to that very specific period of artistic outpouring in the 1920s, even the ones like Langston Hughes who continued to write prolifically afterward. The Great Depression in the 1930s marked a decisive break: after the end of the Renaissance black writers had to remap the future, and although some writers like Hurston produced their finest work during that decade, it is widely considered a building period for the two decades that followed. Beginning in 1940 a new phenomenon altered the trajectory of African American literature in the mid-twentieth century: literary fame. Although Harlem Renaissance writers had gained a good deal of notoriety, their recognition was more collective than individual, with the possible exception of Hughes and DuBois. Many of Hughes's contemporaries faded when the Renaissance ended, some (such as Toomer and Larsen) having produced very little, and others (notably Hurston) disappearing from public view in the 1930s and 1940s. The writers who followed them were regarded in a much more intense spotlight. In 1950 Gwendolyn Brooks became the first black writer to win the Pulitzer Prize. In 1952 Ralph Ellison's weighty novel *Invisible Man* won the National Book Award. In 1959 Lorraine Hansberry's play *A Raisin in the Sun* debuted on Broadway and was the first play by a black author to win the New York Drama Critics' Best Play of the Year award. With this fame came an unprecedented artistic blossoming. More than ever before, the writers in this tradition were willing to flout convention and to write works that followed Hughes's prescription in "The Negro Artist and the Racial Mountain:" they could only become free when they felt confident enough to write out of intuition and artistic conviction rather than in response to the constraining demands of their audiences. In short, more than ever before, individual African American writers dictated their own terms.

The emergence of three major experimental and iconoclastic black authors in the mid-twentieth century brought African American fiction to new heights.

Richard Wright, Ralph Ellison, and James Baldwin were all public figures who frequently retreated from their fame into exile in order to get their writing done. Wright and Baldwin were expatriates who converged (and clashed) in Paris in the 1940s. Wright remained there until his early death in 1960, while Baldwin shuttled back and forth from France and Turkey to the United States as what he called a "transatlantic commuter" throughout the turbulent period of the Civil Rights Movement and its aftermath. Ellison, after publishing *Invisible Man* in 1952, undisputedly one of the most important and influential novels in the African American tradition, was so overwhelmed by the attention his book received that he struggled, and failed, to follow it up with the novel his public demanded before his death in 1994. Although certainly not the only black writers at the time, Wright, Ellison, and Baldwin collectively demonstrate both the growing attention given to black writers in the mid-twentieth century and the personal costs such notoriety brought.

These three writers were both heirs to the Harlem Renaissance and critics of it. They might productively be regarded as three very different writers who had one thing in common: a willingness to regard the past critically and skeptically, or to recognize the achievements of their predecessors while refusing to worship them. All three wrote non-fiction as well as fiction (and Baldwin also wrote plays, poetry, and a number of works that are difficult to classify). Their non-fiction is marked by sharp analysis of history, culture, and literature. Baldwin was particularly willing to do battle with the literary establishment. His infamous critiques of Wright and of Langston Hughes (as well as white authors including Harriet Beecher Stowe, William Faulkner, and Norman Mailer) demonstrated his brashness and fearlessness. Ellison, in his essay "The World and the Jug" (1963), spoke back harshly to the prominent critic Irving Howe, who had criticized him and Baldwin while praising Wright. Wright himself, a dedicated Marxist, found fault with writers who supported bourgeois values, including many Harlem Renaissance authors who had preceded him. This combativeness may seem distracting from the actual literature these authors produced, but they drew strength from it and, despite Ellison's extreme case of writer's block, they managed to produce a substantial body of highly original work unprecedented in the African American tradition.

Wright, Baldwin, and Ellison in the area of prose, and Gwendolyn Brooks, Robert Hayden, and Margaret Walker in poetry, were only the brightest stars in a new constellation of black writers who commanded attention. This mid-century fame may be attributable to a number of factors: a changing literary scene, the maturing of the tradition, the efforts and ambition of a talented group of writers, or the radical changes taking place in black America that culminated in the Civil Rights Movement. The 1950s in particular was a decade of public demonstration and legal wrangling over the rights of African Americans. Although this political action had been ongoing since the Reconstruction, there was a new urgency to it in the 1950s. The landmark desegregation case of Brown v. the Topeka Board of Education in 1954 marked the end of legal segregation and of Jim Crow laws that had become firmly entrenched in southern society. Despite this important legal victory, the struggle for civil rights and the harmonious society that should have accompanied this change was far from over in the mid-1950s. The year after Brown v. Topeka, a fourteen-year-old black boy named Emmett Till was brutally murdered in Mississippi for allegedly flirting with a white woman. This tragic event was both a catalyst and a caution: the movement toward racial equality was from that point unstoppable, but the fear of fierce violence weighed it down. Through all of the turbulence, the voices of black writers became crucial, especially prior to the national emergence of prominent black political leaders (Malcolm X and Martin Luther King, Jr.) in the 1950s and 1960s.

In general, the enduring African American literature of the 1940s and 1950s was urban, with much of it set in either Chicago or New York. Unlike Harlem Renaissance works, this body of literature tended to focus almost exclusively on urban blight rather than on the opportunities cities might afford. The most prominent feature of black life in the mid-twentieth century as reflected in this literature is poverty, and the limitations to opportunity that coincide with such poverty. There is a deep, tragic strain here: characters, speakers, and narrators in these works struggle to survive in a stingy, hostile world, and they must cope with the knowledge that their lofty dreams only serve to make that struggle more painful.

Richard Wright: *Native Son* and Beyond

A blueprint is generally a document that precedes a project, a design for an imagined future. Wright's "Blueprint for American Negro Writing," published in 1937, after the African American literary tradition had been developing for nearly 200 years, acted somewhat differently: as both a recollection and a prescription. It is his manifesto, just as emphatic as Hughes's "The Negro Artist and the Racial Mountain" published a decade earlier, yet stronger in its ideological conviction. As a blueprint, it does map a way for the future, but it also calls into question the achievements of the past. Wright, raised impoverished in the South and on the hardscrabble streets of Chicago, was drawn to Marxist communism, which had triumphed in Soviet Russia virtually at the beginning of the Harlem Renaissance. Marxist thought was influential throughout urban black communities in the early twentieth century: DuBois and Hughes also moved toward it in the 1930s, and *Invisible Man*, which takes place in the 1930s, includes a lengthy section about a Marxist organization known as The Brotherhood (although Ellison and his narrator ultimately reject it). Marxist influence is evident in Wright's foundational "Blueprint".

"Blueprint for American Negro Writing" begins with a critique of black literary history on three grounds: (1) it has generally been tame and polite, (2) it is too often directed toward white readers, and (3) it has not been understood as contributing meaningfully to American culture. He faults black writers for being less aggressive than blacks in other fields in terms of self-assertion. He is suspicious of overeducated upper-middle class black culture, since it is a hollow imitation of the worst aspects of white culture, and he feels that black writing has ignored a potent source of its own cultural expression: oral folk culture. He writes,

Blues, spirituals, and folk tales recounted from mouth to mouth; the whispered words of a black mother to her black daughter on the ways of men; the confidential wisdom of a black father to his black son; the swapping of sex experiences on street corners from boy to boy in the deepest vernacular; work songs sung under blazing suns – all these formed the channels through which racial wisdom flowed.

(40)

In this regard, Wright falls along a continuum of black writers that connects Frederick Douglass and Langston Hughes before him to Ralph Ellison, Amiri Baraka, Alice Walker, and Toni Morrison after him, to name just a few. All of them recognize the vitality of black folk wisdom, the expressions of the group Baraka called "blues people." This folklore embodies a kind of nationalism that Wright recognizes and does not shy away from. That nationalism is a by-product of the segregation that had been forced upon black Americans.

Wright calls on his contemporary black writers and future ones to accept the profound responsibility of their position, given the waning influence of the black church and the "irresolution" of bourgeois black leaders; the black writer "is being called upon to do no less than create values by which his race is to struggle, live and die" (43). Despite his own political convictions, he insists that he is not asking black writers to align themselves to any "ism," but rather to be aware of their perspective, "that fixed point in intellectual space where a writer stands to view the struggles, hopes, and sufferings of his people" (45). Nonetheless, he acknowledges that his perspective involves a deep sympathy with the working class and with "the hopes and struggles of minority peoples everywhere" (46). He would clearly not consider a black writer's perspective legitimate if it did not ally with the underclass. Also important is "the meaning of the history of their race as though they in one life time had lived it themselves throughout all the long centuries" (47).

That point provides a useful inroad into Wright's masterpiece, the novel *Native Son* (1940). Prior to its publication, he had achieved notoriety from his collection of four novellas *Uncle Tom's Children* (1938), but he regarded his own early work as too sentimental and claimed, extending the logic of the "Blueprint" essay, that he wanted to write something "so hard and deep that [readers] would have to face it without the consolation of tears" (*Native Son*, 454). *Native Son* is as likely today to provoke a complex set of responses as it did in 1940, when it was a Book of the Month selection. (The editors of the first edition considered some of its content too raw and abrasive. They persuaded Wright to expurgate this material, but it has been restored in recent editions). Irving Howe might have been overstating his point when he claimed, "The day *Native Son* appeared, American culture was changed forever," but it is inarguably the case that the trajectory of African American literature was changed forever (152). The novel's sustained cry of pain and confusion continues to resonate. It is possible to name other works by black writers that are more profound, more carefully constructed, more cerebral, or more aesthetically appealing, but it would be much harder to name works that are more passionate, angry, or hard-hitting. *Native Son* was Wright's attempt to express the suffering of black Americans throughout history in one life.

What makes *Native Son* so hard for some readers to cope with is precisely what Wright was aiming for: a protagonist who is not noble or heroic, who invites little sympathy, and whose alienation is exacerbated by his lack of self-knowledge and desire to intimidate others. In addition to communism, Wright was also heavily influenced by literary naturalism, which showcases the stories of doomed men of the American underclass, men whose decisions are tragic because their options are severely limited by the miserable circumstances in which they live. *Native Son* begins in the squalor of a Chicago tenement. Its protagonist, Bigger Thomas, awakens into his impoverished world and his first act is to beat to death a rat in his apartment. Though it might seem like he is acting heroically or chivalrously as the women in his house are terrified, he immediately torments his sister and mother with the corpse of the dead vermin. The narrator explains Bigger's obnoxious behavior: "He hated his family because he knew that they were suffering and that he was powerless to help them....He knew that the moment he allowed what his life meant to enter fully into his consciousness, he would either kill himself or someone else. So he denied himself and acted tough" (10). This toughness is meant to mask his most persistent emotion: fear, the title of the first section of the book. He notes this fear in the rat as he corners it. He sees his only choice as revealing his fear or covering it up by instilling it in others. His dream is to pilot an airplane, but he and his friends determine that they would never be allowed to. This denial of a dream is a subtle way that white power makes itself felt; Bigger says, "Every time I think about it I feel like somebody's poking a red-hot iron down my throat. Goddammit, look! We live here and they live there. We black and they white. They got things and we ain't. They do things and we can't. It's just like living in jail" (20). His visceral reaction to the racial segregation and impoverishment of his life is pure anger, which he suppresses whenever he is in close proximity to white people.

He is as brutal with his friends as he is with his family. He feels the need to assert his dominance and speaks of the need for some sort of violent release from the tautness of his life. Picking fights with friends and strangers doesn't serve to relieve it, though. It is clear that the deeper source of his fear is the world of white, wealthy people that has shut him out and defined him. He derives this feeling from the segregated world in which he lives, but also through portrayals of white and black lives in Hollywood movies and newspapers, both of which figure prominently in the narrative. He glimpses the socialite Mary Dalton in a newsreel at the beginning of a movie and experiences feelings of shame mixed with desire. He coincidentally meets Mary when he goes to work for the Daltons as a chauffeur. Mary rebels against her capitalist father by dating a young communist named Jan. The two of them demand that Bigger drive them to a black part of town, and they encourage him to drink excessively while they try to explain Marxist principles to him. The evening ends in murderous tragedy. As Bigger brings the unconscious Mary home and puts her to bed, he becomes afraid that Mrs. Dalton will catch him in her room, and inadvertently strangles Mary. He then gruesomely decapitates her and incinerates her body in the furnace that he is supposed to tend.

This event precipitates a desperate chain of events that further links Bigger to the cornered rat that he killed at the beginning of the novel. The intensity and pace of the second section, "Flight," matches the first, including a second murder, of Bigger's girlfriend Bessie. Bigger regards his actions as meaningful, if not heroic: "He was living, truly and deeply, no matter what others might think, looking at him with their blind eyes" (239). Blindness is a recurrent touchstone throughout the book, and here it links DuBois's crucial concept of double-consciousness (discussed in Chapter Three) to Ellison's motif of invisibility (discussed later in this chapter). Bigger, though in hiding, is emerging from his static life that represents the antithesis of the American Dream. He feels a twisted sense of accomplishment in the destruction of two young women, both of whom had been kind to him. His feelings about himself gyrate between huge pride in having overcome his paralysis and self-disgust that borders on suicidal feelings. After he is apprehended, he tries to come to terms with his place in the universe: "Maybe he was just unlucky, a man born for dark doom, an obscene joke happening amid a colossal din of siren screams and white faces and circling lances of light under a cold and silken sky" (275). The depth of his despair is at war with his instinctive desire to survive. His feelings struggle against his intellect, and he makes little progress toward self-realization despite the attempts of others – his lawyer, his mother, a preacher, the Daltons, and especially Jan – to forgive him and to explain his behavior. The third section is dominated by his trial, especially by the lengthy speeches of his lawyer, Max Boris, who is a Marxist ideologue. At the novel's conclusion even the sympathetic Max is horrified when Bigger proclaims, "What I killed for must've been good!....When a man kills, it's for something....I didn't know I was really alive in this world until I felt things hard enough to kill for 'em" (429). This conclusion, lacking empathy and remorse, reveals how damaged Bigger is. He doesn't seem redeemable in this world or the next. The question for the reader is not only how society might change to prevent more young men from acting as Bigger did, but what to do with the Biggers who are already here. Wright offers no easy solutions.

Native Son, far removed from the glimmers of optimism for a racially harmonious future projected in some Harlem Renaissance texts, depicts a depraved society that has created its own horror. In his essay "How Bigger was Born" Wright says that "the civilization which had given birth to Bigger contained no spiritual sustenance, had created no culture which could hold and claim his allegiance and faith, had sensitized him and had left him stranded, a free agent to roam the streets of our cities, a hot and whirling vortex of undisciplined and unchannelized impulses" (445). What is striking about this assessment and the book in general is Bigger's alienation and estrangement. He does not have the potential to participate positively in his black community, and his fearful response to the white world is reactionary destruction.

Readers of Wright's celebrated autobiography *Black Boy* (1945) will see that many of the motifs in *Native Son* originated in Wright's own experience. This is not to suggest that Bigger is a variation on his author – Wright in his essay "How Bigger Was Born" points to five models for Bigger who are not him – but rather to understand the circumstances that led the author to write such an impassioned book. In the rich tradition of African American autobiography, *Black Boy* echoes Douglass and anticipates later authors like Baldwin, Malcolm X, and Maya Angelou who confess in detail the trying circumstances of their youth. Wright, whose father abandoned the family, was made to drink in saloons when he was six. He lived all over the South with relatives who would threaten him and beat him in failed attempts to get him to behave. There are scenes of Wright fighting schoolmates and pulling knives and razors on older relatives. He seems like a budding sociopath: when he was very young he set his house on fire and killed a kitten. Like Bigger, he must defend himself, and his response to the world is belligerence born of fear.

And yet, it is also productive to read *Black Boy* on its own terms, separate from *Native Son*. Like all of Wright's work, it engages the reader immediately and sustains forward motion throughout. There is a tremendous feeling of injustice in his personal life that gradually gives way to his critique of injustice in American society more generally, divided as it is along racial and economic lines. As a child, he is ignorant of the white world, which exists at a great distance. As he ages, he faces cruel racism and becomes increasingly alienated. Reading and writing offer salvation. He is ashamed to learn that he has been selling white supremacist newspapers without realizing it, prompting him to become a more critical reader. He faces more injustice when a black newspaper publishes his first story, but refuses to pay him for it. Nonetheless, he remains convinced that his calling is to write: "I dreamed of going north and writing books, novels....I knew that I lived in a country in which the aspirations of black people were limited, marked-off. Yet I felt that I had to go somewhere and do something to redeem my being alive" (168–169). This need to believe in an improved future and to contribute something meaningful to society despite adverse circumstances links Wright's narrative to the slave narratives of the past, where personal freedom is merely a stepping stone to the higher goal of the abolition of slavery. Wright's personal triumphs, in other words, are meant to lead to a place where he can work to improve the lives of other African Americans. Hence, the title of the work reflects the union of the racial with the individual.

As Wright works a number of menial jobs, his fear of and anger toward the white world intensifies. In one scene he earns five dollars fighting another young black man for the entertainment of whites. The experience sickens him and makes him ashamed both of himself and of his adversary. He has to refocus his quest from the mere earning of money to something nobler, and he vows to read all he can, especially the great European and American male writers from the naturalist and modernist traditions: "the impulse to dream had been slowly beaten out of me by experience. Now it surged up again and I hungered for books, new ways of looking and seeing" (249). This crucial development reignites in him the desire to add his own contributions to the literary canon, and it is linked directly to his racial identity: "I now knew what being a Negro meant. I could endure the hunger. I had learned to live with hate. But to feel that there were feelings denied me, that the very breath of life itself was beyond my reach, that more than anything else hurt, wounded me. I had a new hunger" (250). Hunger and pain – physical sensations that plague him his entire life – become the psychological condition that drives him to produce art, and they are evident throughout all of his writing.

The 1940s: New Directions in Women's Writing

Wright clearly established himself as a major force in African American writing with the publication of *Native Son* and *Black Boy*. His sensibility was shared by some of his contemporaries such as Chester Himes, whose 1945 novel *If He Hollers, Let Him Go* is a useful companion piece to *Native Son*. Its protagonist, Bob Jones, has to negotiate racism in the workplace, class warfare, the sometimes confusing effects of communist agitation, and the taboo of interracial sexual desire. Himes served a lengthy prison sentence before beginning his literary career, and many of his works deal with crime and punishment. He wrote a series of detective novels, and a number of his works were made into films, even late in his life when they enjoyed a revival during the era of "Blaxploitation" films in the early 1970s. There is a flavor of the hard-boiled pulp or popular crime novel genre in *Native Son*. Himes was even more strongly influenced by it, and his work makes it clear that the urban underworld that inspired the film noir genre in the 1940s could easily accommodate the black literary imagination.

Yet it is worth noting that this genre is masculine in its sensibilities. Even the titles of Wright's most famous works denote male experience, and women in his and Himes' works are often objectified, and certainly not as fully realized as the male characters. Two prominent black female writers in the 1940s – Gwendolyn Brooks and Margaret Walker – published works that counterbalance the indelicate sensibility of Wright and Himes. A third – Ann Petry – shares some of the gritty naturalism of Wright and Himes, but applies it to female experience.

Brooks, like Wright, was born in the South but raised in Chicago. Her precise, accessible, lush poetry celebrates the lives of common folk using a wide variety of voices. Her career flourished for decades until her death in 2000 at the age of 83, but her earliest works earned her high accolades, especially the Pulitzer Prize-winning *Annie Allen* (1949). The collection coheres around the life of its eponymous subject in three parts; the structure follows her from girlhood to adulthood, framing a mock-heroic middle section titled "The Anniad." This section, in a dizzying flow of words characteristic of Brooks's poetry, is a study in the disillusionment of the romantic young Annie: she begins her romantic journey with "All her harvest buttoned in, / All her ornaments untried" (38) and ends it spent: "Fuchsias gone or gripped or gray, / All hay-colored that was green. / Soft aesthetic looted, lean" (49). Motherhood – specifically the trials of raising children in impoverished circumstances – is a recurrent touchstone in Brooks's work. It is evident in her poems about the death of Emmett Till, published in 1960, which refocus the tragedy on Till's mother (see Chapter Six). In the sonnet sequence "The Children of the Poor," her speaker meditates on her condition, wondering what to give her children, who seem incomplete, "adjudged the leastwise of the land" (52). She refers to them as her "little halves" (53). In the final sonnet she focuses on one: "Life for my child is simple, and is good. / He knows his wish. Yes, but that is not all. / Because I know mine too. / And we both want joy of undeep and unabiding things" (55). She admires her son's indomitable will, his desire that persists despite a lack of success: "But never has he been afraid to reach. / His lesions are legion. / But reaching is his rule" (55). The spirit that moves both mother and child is meant to be inspirational to any who struggle against oppression. Brooks's poetry in general strives to inspire without stooping to sentimentality or false romanticism. The "reaching" that the young child does is an important defiance of the circumstances that could make him miserable.

Margaret Walker is another poet who rose to prominence in the 1940s, though her output thereafter was much less consistent and prolific than that of Gwendolyn Brooks. Like Brooks, she was influenced by Langston Hughes, and she also spent time in Chicago where she met Richard Wright and helped him with research as he composed *Native Son*. Her 1942 collection *For My People* received the prestigious Yale University Younger Poet's award. Her later novel, *Jubilee* (1966), has received increased attention in recent years, but her early poems have garnered the most recognition. The title poem of *For My People* is the most frequently anthologized, and it has the feel of a kind of poetic anthem for African Americans; it begins, "For my people everywhere singing their slave songs repeatedly: their dirges and their ditties and their blues and jubilees, praying their prayers nightly to an unknown god, bending their knees humbly to an unseen power" (1.1–4). In ten oversized lines that swell into stanzas, Walker paints a rich portrait of "her people," who are identified not only by race, but by social class and region. Her subjects are complex: "lost disinherited dispossessed and happy people" as well as "walking blindly spreading joy, losing time being lazy, sleeping when hungry, shouting when burdened, drinking when hopeless" (6.3–4, 7.1–3). The concluding stanza has the qualities of great oratory or a sermon, but it is also complex and ambiguous:

> Let a new earth rise. Let another world be born. Let a bloody peace be written in the sky. Let a second generation full of courage issue forth; let a people loving freedom come to growth. Let a beauty full of healing and a strength of final clenching be the pulsing in our spirits and our blood. Let the martial songs be written, let the dirges disappear. Let a race of men now rise and take control.
>
> *(10.1–8)*

The sensibility here is positioned halfway between the optimistic race pride of the Harlem Renaissance and the militant pushback of the mid-1960s, calling for what might seem a contradiction: a "bloody peace."

Ann Petry's novel *The Street* (1946) complements *Native Son*, redirecting its angry intensity to frame female experiences. Petry published a handful of novels and children's books over the following two decades, but *The Street* is by far her most recognized work. It was the first novel by an African American woman to sell more than a million copies. *The Street* primarily tells the story of Lutie Johnson, although its point of view rotates between her and a number of other characters who live on her street in Harlem. (Paule Marshall borrowed this method for her 1959 novel *Brown Girl, Brownstones*). *The Street* is a passionate, fiery novel whose bleak, tragic strains are evident from the opening paragraph, in which "a cold November wind" torments "a few hurried pedestrians who bent double in an effort to offer the least possible exposed surface to its violent assault" (7). This naturalistic description foreshadows a number of incidents of human violence throughout the novel.

Lutie is a beautiful, young, single mother struggling to survive in hostile circumstances. Virtually all the men in the book desire her sexually, and act on their desires either by physically assaulting her or by attempting to pay her to sleep with them. Chief among these villains is Jones, the superintendent in the building where she rents an apartment. From their first encounter, his violent, obsessive passion for her is clear. He uses her son Bub to get closer to her through a number of schemes that either drive a wedge between Lutie and Bub or that endanger the boy. Jones helps Bub make a shoeshine kit which enrages Lutie, who feels that her son shouldn't have to resort to the menial jobs that seem to be the only ones available to black boys. She realizes Jones is stalking her when she discovers that he has been handling one of her blouses in her absence. He attempts to drag her into a basement to rape her and is only prevented from doing so because a white man named Junto has marked Lutie for himself, and has arranged for her protection. As revenge, Jones sets up Bub to be arrested in a mail theft scheme.

Lutie is trapped by her need for money, which she believes is the key to a better life, and by her beauty, which causes men to see her as nothing more than a sex object. She is a talented singer and is led to understand that she can earn a living that way, but all of the men who encourage this talent are in reality only interested in her sexually. Race and social class are inextricably intertwined in Lutie's mind and in the novel more generally, as it becomes clear that white people control the flow of money and black people have to choose between poverty and pride. The black men in the novel resent the white world for only allowing them menial jobs. A musician named Boots recalls his years as a porter on a train: "He got a handful of silver at the end of each run, and a mountain of silver couldn't pay a man to stay nameless like that. No Name, black my shoes. No Name, hold my coat....Niggers steal. Lock your bag. Niggers lie. Where's my pocketbook?" (165). He admits that his desire for Lutie is an attempt to balance out "a life of saying 'yes sir' to every white bastard who had the price of a Pullman ticket," but that even a hundred Lutie Johnsons would not be enough (165).

Lutie's own sense of degradation and despair is also tied to the white world's control over the economic system. Her life lessons begin during her job as a maid in suburban Connecticut. The rich white people who employ her are obviously miserable: they drink too much, and one inexplicably commits suicide at Christmas. And yet, Lutie desires their material possessions as a step up from the filth and danger of the ghetto. She is aware of "the barrier between her and these people" which she cannot control because "the instant they saw the color of her skin they knew what she must be like; they were so confident about what she must be like they didn't need to know her personally in order to verify their estimate" (34). This prejudice affects the entire society, including Lutie whose resentment gradually turns to all-out rage. The street becomes a symbol for the racial ills of her society: "Streets like the one she lived on were no accident. They were the North's lynch mobs, she thought bitterly; the method the big cities used to keep Negroes in their place....From the time she was born, she had been hemmed into an ever-narrowing space, until now she was very neatly walled in and the wall had been built up brick by brick by eager white hands" (200–201). This realization is complicated by the fact that two black men – Jones and Boots – are the ones who attempt to rape her. They, like her, have been poisoned by race prejudice and now direct their anger toward less powerful members of their own race. Lutie, finally pushed too far, lashes out at Boots and kills him in a blind rage. As she bludgeons him to death, she feels her anger toward her circumstances: the poverty of her street, the prostitution that girls like her resort to, the abandoned mothers, the seedy motives of interracial desire, the lecherous men who won't leave her alone, and finally "the white world which thrust black people into a walled enclosure from which there was no escape" (266). Her murderous rage is just as desperate and irrational as Bigger's is, but her character is much more sympathetic. She appears to get away with murder in the end, fleeing to Chicago, which was, coincidentally, the trap that Bigger couldn't escape from. In her flight, though, she abandons her son, continuing the cycle of despair and leaving the reader with little hope for social change.

Ellison: A Voice from Underground

Native Son was the first novel by an African American to be selected by the once influential Book of the Month Club. Twelve years after its publication, Ellison's *Invisible Man* earned an even higher accolade when it won the National Book Award. In his acceptance speech (published as "Brave Words for a Startling Occasion") Ellison does not name Wright's novel, but comes close when he says that he was not content to use the form of the "'hard-boiled' novel, with its dedication to physical violence, social cynicism and understatement" (*Shadow*, 103). He was hoping for something much grander, and reaches back to the great (white) American novels of the nineteenth century,

> imaginative projections of the conflicts within the human heart which arose when the sacred principles of the Constitution and the Bill of Rights clashed with the practical exigencies of human greed and fear, hate and love. Naturally I was attracted to these writers as a Negro. Whatever they thought of my people per se, in their imaginative economy the Negro symbolized both the man lowest down and the mysterious, underground aspect of human personality.
>
> *(104)*

These quotations should make it clear that Ellison's novel was ambitious and literary, interested in universal human truths as well as racial experience, and concerned with contributing to an ongoing conversation about the benefits and limitations of American rights.

To read and understand *Invisible Man* in all of its depth and complexity requires a great deal of dedication. Although it is not abstract in the way that the works of some of Ellison's influences are (such as James Joyce and William Faulkner), it is cerebral and alludes liberally both to white American and European literary works and historical events and to a number of works from black vernacular and musical traditions. The novel's unnamed narrator, usually referred to as Invisible Man, speaks in a fluid torrent that pulls the reader in just as compellingly as *Native Son* does, yet Invisible Man is much more sympathetic than Bigger, and his story, despite pessimistic or existential strains, offers more hope than *Native Son* does, partly because it allows its beleaguered subject to speak for himself whereas Bigger is never able to articulate his complex feelings.

Although it is strongly plotted, *Invisible Man* is ultimately a novel of ideas. The narrator frames his story with a philosophical prologue and epilogue. Here he introduces his concept of invisibility, a concept related to DuBois's double-consciousness. He tells of how he gets into a street fight with a white racist who has uttered a racial slur at him. Preparing to slit the man's throat, he stops short when he comes to an abrupt realization: "the man had not *seen* me, actually" (4). Throughout the novel Ellison encourages readers to consider what invisibility means. If black people are not recognized in America for their achievements and in all of the rich complexity of their experience, then it is as though they do not truly exist except as projections, shadows, and stereotypical facsimiles. The narrator's recognition of his invisibility initiates a profound search for his identity, ultimately achieved through telling his story.

In the prologue the narrator reveals that he is living in a bizarre underground hole in New York City where he has surrounded himself with over a thousand light bulbs. His circumstances are a form of exile that only makes sense once he has told his story. He begins with his origins in the South, especially his grandfather's death, including cryptic deathbed advice that haunts him throughout the novel. The dying man says, "I never told you, but our life is a war and I have been a traitor all my born days, a spy in the enemy's country ever since I give up my gun back in the Reconstruction. Live with your head in the lion's mouth. I want you to overcome 'em with yeses, undermine 'em with grins, agree 'em to death and destruction, let 'em swoller you till they vomit or bust wide open" (16). This advice is confusing and seemingly contradictory, but one of the lessons the narrator comes to learn is that his life as a black man is filled with contradictions and with wisdom that doesn't make sense, passed down by elders he doesn't respect. Experience would seem to be the better teacher except for the fact that it leaves him in seclusion in a hole in the ground.

The first and perhaps most dramatic event in the narrator's life occurs when he is invited to give a speech to influential white men after he graduates with distinction from his high school. The men are drunk, and the atmosphere is dizzying as they parade a naked white woman around the narrator and a number of his black classmates. They then blindfold the narrator and his classmates and force them to fight one another brutally in a boxing ring in what they term a Battle Royal. Afterward the boys are all invited back into the ring to pick up money, but some of the "coins" are actually electrified pieces of metal that shock the boys when they are touched. All of this humiliation and degradation does not deter the narrator from doing what he had come to do. The speech he delivers parrots Booker T. Washington's Atlanta Exposition speech almost verbatim, and the narrator blusters through it even as the drunken men jeer at him. At a crucial point he unconsciously changes the phrase "social responsibility" to "social equality," and the men suddenly turn sober (31). They ask him to explain that phrase, and he admits that it was a mistake, caused by the fact that he was swallowing blood. This powerful scene can be read as an allegory of the history of slavery and Reconstruction, with the narrator's action limited by forces beyond his control, the result of which is to destroy his community. White men in power are in complete control of him, including the suffering that he not only embodies, but feels compelled to apologize for.

His reward for delivering the speech is a briefcase with a scholarship to a black college modeled after Tuskegee. He carries this briefcase with him throughout his journey, and fills it with objects that determine his fate. His experience at college, which starts idyllically, ends with his expulsion following another surreal incident that strongly echoes the Battle Royal scene. He is given a job driving a rich white trustee named Mr. Norton around the college and its environs. He gets into trouble when he follows the man's orders and drives him first to the house of a poor sharecropper, where they listen to the story of Jim Trueblood who has impregnated his daughter, and afterward to a bar called The Golden Day, where a collection of drunken, insane black men on leave from the local asylum destroy the bar and wound Mr. Norton. The narrator is jealous of Trueblood, who earns money from Mr. Norton for telling his tale, and the narrator is so consumed by shame toward this discredited member of his race that he fails to recognize that his story is not about guilt and incest so much as it is about the redemptive power of the blues. In The Golden Day, the narrator is exposed by one of the released inmates as a puppet of the white establishment, someone too mechanical either to think for himself or to realize the true achievements of his people while he is busy chasing a materialistic American dream.

Invisible Man must learn many lessons throughout his life, but his chief problem is that he doesn't know who to trust, or how to interpret what he sees and hears. The blindness that prevents others from seeing him prevents him from seeing as well. He believes that the college's president, Bledsoe, is not only a good and fair man, but a good role model. Bledsoe expels him and deceives him by giving him envelopes supposedly containing letters of recommendation that he can use to gain employment in New York. The letters actually instruct the powerful white men who read them *not* to hire the narrator, and they essentially echo the words he reads in a dream about his grandfather in the first chapter: "Keep This Nigger-Boy

Running" (33). As long as he is in motion, he can be manipulated. He is a slow learner, though, and he continues to follow the instructions of white men as he finds employment in New York, first as a laborer in a paint factory, and later as a spokesman for The Brotherhood, a socialist organization. Along the way he meets a number of men from the South who speak in a vernacular that he has repressed. These are the people who sing variations on the blues, like Trueblood in his spoken blues story, and the narrator rejects their wisdom because he is so fixated on conventional material success. One of these men, a fast-talking laborer walking around with a cart full of blueprints, says, "Folks is always making plans and changing 'em." When the narrator responds, "that's a mistake. You have to stick to the plan," the laborer looks at him askance and says, "You kinda young, daddy-o" (175). The ability to improvise, to see things for what they are rather than how they appear, is a skill the narrator does not pick up quickly, but it is key to his success throughout life.

While too many ideas swirl around in this enormous, complex novel to detail here, one of the most important ones is the way that history ignores the nameless, powerless black characters who have changed culture in subtle but important ways. One of the narrator's black colleagues in The Brotherhood becomes overwhelmed and leaves what appears to be noble work in order to peddle racist icons on the street. The death of this man at the hands of aggressive police officers provokes a profound change in the narrator. It leads him to an important realization:

> All things, it is said, are duly recorded – all things of importance, that is. But not quite, for actually it is only the known, the seen, the heard and only those events that the recorder regards as important that are put down....What did they ever think of us transitory ones? Ones such as I had been before I found Brotherhood – birds of passage who were too obscure for learned classification, too silent for the most sensitive recorders of sound; of natures too ambiguous for the most ambiguous words, and too distant from the centers of historical decision to sign or even to applaud the signers of historical documents? We who write no novels, histories or other books.
>
> *(439)*

The suffering at the heart of Trueblood's story, the deep wisdom of jazz and the blues, the folk wisdom that the narrator learns in the schoolyard rather than in school have all been lost as official history overlooks them. It is the narrator's role to recover them, which is, without his realizing it, the point of his lengthy story. Even though he remains nameless, he and the other marginal figures he writes about are made visible through his masterful storytelling.

James Baldwin: Exploding Expectations

James Baldwin arrived on the African American literary scene with a bang in the early 1950s, and he was responsible for quite a few other explosions through the turbulent 1960s, the height of his popularity. Baldwin was the *enfant terrible* of the mid-century triumvirate of black novelists who garnered so much attention. One of his first acts was to dismantle *Native Son* in his first book of essays, *Notes of a Native Son* (1955). In one essay he puts Wright's novel in conversation with Harriet Beecher Stowe's novel *Uncle Tom's Cabin* (1852) (which he describes as "a very bad novel"), and calls *Native Son* "a continuation, a complement of that monstrous legend it was written to destroy" (14, 22). According to Baldwin, Wright is only capable of "shouting curses" in his protest novel because he is trapped by the legacy of earlier protest novels, and by the conventions of the protest novel itself (22). Bigger is too much of a myth or symbol, in Baldwin's eyes: not human or nuanced enough. Even as he acknowledges that Bigger's rage lives within himself and within all black people in America, Baldwin is wary of the effect of perpetuating the stereotype that Bigger embodies: "The American image of the Negro lives also in the Negro's heart; and when he has surrendered to this image life has no other possible reality. Then he, like the white enemy with whom he will be locked one day in mortal struggle, has no means save this of asserting his identity" (38). Wright felt betrayed by Baldwin's critique, and shunned the younger writer after having welcomed him in Paris, but Baldwin felt that Wright and others misunderstood him, and he maintained a great deal of respect for his one-time mentor. He had the final word on their fallout in his tribute essay "Alas, Poor Richard" published after Wright's death.

Regardless of Baldwin's intent or the way his early work was received, it was clear upon his publication of *Notes of a Native Son* as well as his novel *Go Tell It on the Mountain* (1953) that he was a fearless young man who was destined to garner a good deal of attention. By the mid-1960s he was inarguably the most prominent black American writer alive. Attorney General Robert Kennedy consulted him about race relations in a famous (and disastrous) 1963 meeting. That same year Baldwin appeared on the cover of *Time* magazine, recognized as much for his speaking engagements in the embattled South as for his literary achievements, which by that point included three novels, a play, and three collections of essays, including his landmark work *The Fire Next Time* (1963). That year marked a turning point in Baldwin's fortunes. His readership declined precipitously by the late 1960s as a host of younger writers emerged. He was deeply affected by the assassinations of Medgar Evers, Malcolm X, and Martin Luther King, Jr., and was afraid for his own safety. Although he continued publishing prolifically until his death in 1987, these later works did not receive anything like the attention his early works garnered. In recent years, scholars have begun to reevaluate these later works, which are gaining as much attention for their path-breaking work on gender and sexuality as for their commentary on race.

Baldwin's rise to prominence doesn't seem likely given his humble beginnings. The oldest child in a family of nine, Baldwin grew up in Harlem in extreme poverty. Bisexuality was not a subject of open discussion in the 1940s when he first discovered his same-sex desire. He was a brilliant student and voracious reader who was denied the opportunities to pursue higher education. His first work was as a boy preacher. Having undergone a violent conversion experience (detailed in his first novel, in the essay "Notes of a Native Son," and again in *The Fire Next Time*), Baldwin developed from a teen proclaiming the word of the Lord to a man who firmly distrusted religion and spoke vociferously against its effects. His first migration out of Harlem brought him to bohemian Greenwich Village in lower Manhattan (where his same-sex desires and interracial mixing were more accepted), to New Jersey (where his first-hand encounters with segregation nearly caused him to commit murder), to Paris, Istanbul, and St.-Paul-de-Vence, France, where he eventually died. The constant motion in his personal life had a parallel in his approach to writing: he was never content to produce the same work twice, and as a result he remains one of the most surprising and broad-reaching figures in the African American literary canon.

His first two novels illustrate this breadth. On its surface, *Go Tell It on the Mountain* looks like a traditional *bildungsroman*: the protagonist, John Grimes, leaves his home in Harlem on his fourteenth birthday to go to the movies. When he returns, his brother has been stabbed in a street fight, and John feels a sense of despair and responsibility. The novel changes considerably from that point, as the long middle section is comprised of three chapters called "The Prayers of the Saints." They are the background stories of three people close to John: his Aunt Florence, his father, and his mother. Since the stories reach back before John's birth, their details are outside of his consciousness, leaving the reader to determine the patterns and relationships that bind these stories of John's elders to his own tale. The novel's resolution does not provide easy answers, but as John is cast to the floor in his violent religious conversion, the themes and plotlines that run throughout the book come together. Baldwin concludes the novel with John calling out to his parents and aunt: "I'm ready....I'm coming. I'm on my way" (221). His progress is really just a prelude to a fuller life.

With such obvious connections to Baldwin's own story – detailed in his essays – readers expected a continuation of a personal story in subsequent works, despite the fact that the novel contains a healthy dose of invention and speculation. His play *The Amen Corner* (1958) provided a little of that expected content as it tells the story of a young man who leaves the church to pursue a career as a musician, reflecting Baldwin's own decision to give up religion for art, but Baldwin's second novel refused vehemently to conform to anyone's expectations. *Giovanni's Room* (1956) caused a sensation, not only being the first novel by an African American writer with a virtually all-white cast, but because its treatment of homosexuality was too frank for many readers in the conservative 1950s. The novel's very existence begs the question as to whether black writers have an obligation to write about race exclusively. Baldwin's pronouncement about America's racial scene in his essays proved that he was a commanding voice to be listened to as the Civil Rights Movement struggled through setbacks and enjoyed victories. Few readers expected that this voice would write about a bisexual white character whose lack of courage to admit his own desires would have disastrous outcomes for himself and others. Baldwin wrote about white characters deliberately in *Giovanni's Room*, thinking that race would cloud the issue of his protagonist's difficulty accepting his sexual identity.

His third novel, the bestselling *Another Country* (1961), combined his concerns about race and bisexuality. A sprawling, challenging novel with multiple storylines and many themes, *Another Country* begins with the suicide of Rufus Scott, an embittered and disenfranchised black musician whose anguish leads to despair. Just before jumping off the George Washington Bridge, Rufus feels sickened by the lack of love he sees in the world around him on the subway: "Many white people and many black people, chained together in time and in space, and by history" (86). He finds no more comfort in the afterlife than he had felt in the underworld: "He stood at the center of the bridge and it was freezing cold. He raised his eyes to heaven. He thought, You bastard, you motherfucking bastard. Ain't I your baby, too?" (87). Rufus's suicide has a massive impact on those he leaves behind, black and white, male and female, lovers, family members, and friends. They all seek, separately and together, to understand the powerful, complex intersection of Rufus's life with their own, and in engaging in this struggle, they are on the path to building a better society, another country where love is possible.

There is no way to simplify Baldwin's message, but it certainly does involve a redefinition of love, a force that can bind society more solidly than the forces that threaten to tear it apart. His most famous short story, "Sonny's Blues," is largely about the difficulties of loving and expressing love for someone who has been a source of disappointment. For Baldwin love is never facile or sentimental; it involves toughness, commitment, and honesty. In *The Fire Next Time* he defines it this way: "I use the word 'love' here not merely in the personal sense but as a state of being, or a state of grace – not in the infantile American sense of being made happy but in the tough and universal sense of quest and daring and growth" (95). This essay, first published in an oversized issue of *The New Yorker* in 1962, crystallizes a number of concerns central to Baldwin's lifelong project. It has a few distinct strains: Baldwin's own story of religious conversion, his first-hand assessment of the rise of the Nation of Islam (whose charismatic spokesman Malcolm X was surging to prominence at the same time), and finally the vexed state of race relations in America. Its dramatic conclusion articulates the crossroads at which America stood at that moment, one that projects both the apocalyptic turbulence and the positive leaps forward of the 1960s:

> Everything now, we must assume, is in our hands; we have no right to assume otherwise. If we – and now I mean the relatively conscious whites and the relatively conscious blacks, who must, like lovers, insist on, or create, the consciousness of the others – do not falter in our duty now, we may be able, handful that we are, to end the racial nightmare, and achieve our country, and change the history of the world. If we do not now dare everything, the fulfillment of that prophecy, re-created from the Bible in song by a slave, is upon us: *God gave Noah the rainbow sign, No more water, the fire next time!*
> *(105–106)*

Baldwin's Jeremiad echoed throughout the 1960s and afterwards as more militant black voices took hold of both art and politics. And yet, Baldwin's bold forays into explorations of same-sex desire significantly complicated his message for some readers whose expectations did not easily accommodate the intersection of racial oppression and homoerotic desire. One such reader was Black Panther Party leader Eldridge Cleaver, whose 1968 memoir *Soul on Ice* contained a vicious, homophobic attack on Baldwin (as discussed in Chapter Six). As Baldwin's work became even more ambitious and more nuanced, his readership declined, but, following Hughes's prescription from "The Negro Artist and the Racial Mountain," he remained unwavering in his convictions, which he stated simply and eloquently in the introduction to his first collection of essays: "I want to be an honest man and a good writer" (*Notes*, 9).

A Raisin in the Sun: Broadway Meets Black America

Lorraine Hansberry's 1959 play *A Raisin in the Sun* was far from being the first play by a black playwright. William Wells Brown, author of a slave narrative and of *Clotel*, the first African American novel, wrote plays in the nineteenth century, and a number of Harlem Renaissance authors including Langston Hughes also wrote plays. Moreover, a rich tradition of musical theater flourished during the Renaissance, as Hughes details in his essay "Harlem: When the Negro Was in Vogue." Nonetheless, African American drama was slower to develop than other genres, and *A Raisin in the Sun* can be seen as the beginning of its modern development. Hansberry's play debuted on Broadway, implying that her dramatic rendering of the lives of struggling black characters was intended for an audience who didn't come from the same circumstances. The stories of characters who felt the same despair as Bigger Thomas and the same aspirations as Invisible Man or Baldwin's John Grimes had to be told wherever possible.

Hansberry was the first prominent black author who was known primarily as a playwright. Had she not succumbed to cancer at a very young age (thirty-five), she would have undoubtedly contributed even more substantially to the black literary canon. *A Raisin in the Sun* has proven to be one of the more enduring plays from the decade that also saw the rise of American theater titans Arthur Miller and Tennessee Williams. Although it is satirized in George C. Wolfe's 1985 parody *The Colored Museum* (see Chapter Seven) as spawning a popular tradition of drama about the frustrations of black, urban, characters against a domestic backdrop, it is without doubt an important work and marks a pivotal moment in black writing.

Hansberry's play takes its title from Langston Hughes's famous poem "Harlem" (1951) which begins with the question, "What happens to a dream deferred?" The play examines the deferred dreams of the Younger family who live in a crowded apartment in Chicago. Their circumstances are not as desperate as those of Bigger Thomas, but they are close, and the play opens in a similar way to Wright's novel, with the sound of an alarm clock, after which the ten-year-old Travis Younger amuses himself by chasing after a rat. The play's psychological heir to Bigger is

Travis's father Walter Lee, an explosive young man who is obsessed with obtaining the material things that seem to be available only to white people. Walter alternates between despair, which leads him to drink, and romanticism, which generally attaches itself to his scheme to invest in a liquor store with some shiftless friends. The Younger family has received an insurance settlement following Walter's father's death, and the play pivots on the ethical question of what to do with the money. Walter and Ruth are expecting their second baby, so Ruth is intent on moving to a larger, nicer home. Walter's sister Beneatha is studying to be a doctor. Walter's mother Lena (known as Mama) would be content to donate the money to her church, but decides to purchase a house with some of it, honoring Ruth's wishes and her grandchildren's needs. She divides the rest between Walter and Beneatha for their separate dreams.

Beneatha's dream is complicated by her relationship with Joseph Asagai, her Nigerian lover. Asagai rattles Beneatha's confidence by accusing her of being an assimilationist because she doesn't style her hair naturally. He teases her for loving him not out of pure affection, but because she is looking for her identity. For part of the play she wears Yoruba robes from Nigeria that Asagai has given her, and there is the sense that her dreams of prestige and success in America are at odds with the values she is drawn to in Africa. Complicating her character further is her budding feminism, which Asagai calls into question: "the world's most liberated women are not liberated at all. You all talk about it too much!" (64). In a comical scene at the opening of the second act, Beneatha, dressed in robes, plays traditional African percussion music while Walter, drunk, play-acts a fantasy that he is an ancient African warrior. Beneatha reveals that she has cut her hair short and is wearing it natural, as Asagai has asked her to do. Her American lover, a college-educated young man named George Murchison, rejects her new look and says of Africa, "Let's face it, baby, your heritage is nothing but a bunch of raggedy-assed spirituals and some grass huts!" (80). She is deeply offended by his remark, but she is also hesitant to accept Asagai's offer to go with him back to Africa.

Beneatha's subplot is significant for a number of reasons, especially as African American literature in the ensuing decades was to come to terms with feminist ideals as well as a renewed interest in traditional African cultural expressions. In *A Raisin in the Sun*, this prototypical character is left overwhelmed and confused. Moreover, her agency is compromised by the actions of her misguided and over-bearing brother, Walter Lee. While Beneatha explores her feminine identity and individual dreams, Mama tells Walter Lee that she trusts him with a share of the insurance money: "It ain't much, but it's all I got in the world and I'm putting it in your hands. I'm telling you to be the head of this family from now on like you supposed to be" (107). Walter swears off drinking at that point and interprets his mother's advice as license to follow his dream to invest in the liquor store. In his exuberance he invests not only his share of the money, but Beneatha's as well. His supposed business partner runs off with it, leaving both himself and his sister without the seed money for their dreams.

The play's ironic reversal comes at the hands of a racist organization that is trying to keep the Youngers out of a white neighborhood in the suburbs. Mama has put one-third of the money down on a house that will provide a cleaner, safer upbringing for Travis and his unborn sibling. When a man named Lindner arrives offering the family a check to bribe them not to move into the neighborhood, the Youngers are still riding high on their dreams, and they send him off curtly. When they learn that Walter has squandered their money, they call Lindner back to recoup their losses. As Lindner is about to present them with the check, Walter changes his mind, claiming, "we are very proud people" and resolves to move into their suburban home regardless of the circumstances (148). The pride that the Youngers claim at the end of the play is an admirable show of strength against a racist society, but *A Raisin in the Sun* raises unresolved questions about the nature of the dreams that have been deferred. Beneatha's individual dreams in particular have been denied through no fault of her own, and she not only has to defer to Walter to make this final decision, but the play ends with both Walter and Mama ridiculing the possibility of her marrying Asagai and moving to Africa. Mama is so proud of the fact that Walter has "come into his manhood" by refusing to be cowed by Lindner's racism that she seems to overlook Beneatha's deferred dreams (151). Moreover, the Youngers may be moving out of an impoverished setting, but they are entering a racially hostile one. The concluding note is of pride and defiance, and yet the question of whether any dreams have truly been fulfilled is left open.

Conclusion

In "The World and the Jug," Ellison resented the implication that Wright's "Blueprint," or the model he had created in *Native Son*, meant that other black writers had to fall into line. Defending himself and Baldwin, he writes, "It is not for me to judge Wright's courage, but I must ask just why it was possible for me to write as I write 'only' because Wright released his anger? Can't I be allowed to release my own?.... Everybody wants to tell us what a Negro is, yet few wish, even in a joke, to be one. But if you would tell me who I am, at least take the trouble to discover what I have been" (*Shadow*, 115). There is still a tension in his words between the obligation for a black writer to write about collective experience and the desire to explore the vast possibilities of individual experience, yet even this debate opened up new avenues of possibility for late-twentieth-century black writers. The unprecedented fame of the writers discussed in this chapter, as well as many more who labored in their considerable shadows, helped to develop the freedom for later writers to experiment and to create works that were both commercially viable and artistically ambitious.

Suggestions for Further Reading

Brown, Stephanie. *The Postwar African American Novel: Protest and Discontent, 1945–1950*. Jackson, MS: Mississippi University Press, 2011. Print.

Jackson, Lawrence Patrick. *The Indignant Generation: A Narrative History of African American Writers and Critics, 1934–1960*. Princeton, NJ: Princeton University Press, 2011. Print.

Kinnamon, Keneth. *Critical Essays on Richard Wright's Native Son*. New York, NY: Twayne, 1997. Print.

Leeming, David. *James Baldwin*. New York, NY: Knopf, 1994. Print.

Posnock, Ross, ed. *The Cambridge Companion to Ralph Ellison*. Cambridge: Cambridge University Press, 2005. Print.

Rampersad, Arnold. *Ralph Ellison: A Biography*. New York, NY: Knopf, 2007. Print.

6

THE 1960S AND THE BLACK ARTS MOVEMENT

1960s America was characterized by turbulent, often violent, changes. It was a decade of assassinations: the black leaders Malcolm X and Martin Luther King, Jr. and the white leaders John and Bobby Kennedy, to name just the most prominent, were all cut down at the height of their influence. Race-based riots in cities like Los Angeles (1965), Detroit (1967), and Newark (1967), as well as widespread protests against American involvement in the Vietnam War, contributed to the unsettled mood. The arts responded with their own revolutionary changes. Mixing black and white forms, popular music evolved quickly and radically, from innocent rock-and-roll paeans to teenage love at the beginning of the decade to the experimental, drug-fueled psychedelia and funk at the end. Visual art embraced popular culture ("pop") in ways that conservative critics found distasteful, while the popular entertainment medium of film urged viewers to consider it as art. Literature brought the once marginal topics, voices, and methods of the Beat Generation and other bohemians into the mainstream, while a brainy, darkly funny new mode called postmodernism evolved.

African American literature in particular underwent some of its more radical changes during the 1960s. The grand achievement of Ralph Ellison, the energetic production of James Baldwin, and the hard look at urban domestic life by women writers like Gwendolyn Brooks, Lorraine Hansberry, and Ann Petry, all discussed in Chapter Five, represented a new rise to prominence of black voices on the literary scene. Although these writers made unique contributions within their respective genres, they weren't especially avant-garde or iconoclastic. This is not to suggest that the great black American works of the 1940s and 1950s were conventional, but they may have looked that way after the 1960s, when black literature strove to identify and rename itself as something unique. Literature became a potent and meaningful tool for the struggling underclass who was the explicit audience for this work, whereas the primary audience of earlier works was, to a large degree, white liberals in need of enlightenment.

One increasing trend among black Americans in the 1960s involved renaming, and this trend can be related to the desire for a black nationalist identity. The very term used to describe the race changed during this decade from "Negro" to "black." ("African American" emerged in the final decade of the twentieth century, where it has remained alongside "black" or "Black" as the acceptable terms of racial identification). *The Autobiography of Malcolm X* (1965) details a series of renamings, as Malcolm Little became known by his street name Detroit Red, then renamed himself Malcolm X, and settled on El-Hajj Malik El-Shabazz just before he was assassinated. The death of Malcolm X prompted a number of young black people to rename themselves, including the leading voices of the most influential black literary trend of the decade, the Black Arts Movement: LeRoi Jones, author of explosive poems, experimental plays, essays, and two books of sophisticated cultural/musical analysis, changed his name in 1967 to Imamu Amiri Baraka. Other writers associated with the movement – Roland Snellings and Don Lee – changed their names to Askia Muhammad Touré and Haki Madhubuti, respectively. With these changes, the Black Arts Movement was solidified. Although its heyday was very short-lived – shorter even than the Harlem Renaissance – it was extraordinarily influential in terms of setting a radical precedent that later black artists could either accept or reject, but one that they definitely couldn't ignore.

The Early 1960s: Moving Toward Radicalism

Richard Wright died in 1960 at the age of 52, but his reign as the most prominent voice in black letters had ended much earlier, as James Baldwin, Ralph Ellison, and Gwendolyn Brooks ascended in the 1950s. Ellison left his readers waiting for the last four decades of his life for the follow-up novel to *Invisible Man* (1952). Baldwin emerged as the most prominent author of African American prose (fiction and non-fiction), while Brooks continued to publish poetry steadily and prolifically. Both Baldwin and Brooks were to change in terms of their aesthetic and their political urgency in the early 1960s, and Ellison's essay collection *Shadow and Act* (1964) is forceful and uncompromising, indicating what the follow-up to *Invisible Man* might have looked like if Ellison had managed to complete it.

Baldwin's landmark essay *The Fire Next Time*, discussed in Chapter Five, marked the high point of his career in 1963. After that point, his readership diminished, beginning with his 1964 play *Blues for Mister Charlie*, his first critical misfire. Robert Bone, whose 1965 study *The Negro Novel in America* was an influential early work of criticism of black prose, called the play "one unspeakably bad propaganda piece" (216). The fact that Baldwin's less subtle and frustrated treatment of race relations could be labeled "bad" and "propaganda" in the mid-1960s indicates that expectations and tastes were changing rapidly. It ran for six months on Broadway, with Baldwin insisting that the ticket prices be kept reasonable to accommodate a black audience that might not otherwise be able to afford it. Biographer David Leeming writes, "*Blues for Mister Charlie* opened on April 23 [1964] to an audience of highly appreciative blacks and sometimes angry and often shocked whites" (238).

Baldwin, who had always moved fluidly between white and black worlds and spoken to both black and white audiences, seemed to have hit a nerve that highlighted the divisions in his country, just as his play illustrated the nation's divisions symbolically, bifurcating the fictional "Plaguetown" into "Blacktown" and "Whitetown" on stage. The howl of anger at racial violence that fuels *Blues for Mister Charlie* is not exactly new in Baldwin: all of his work up to that point certainly contained it, with the exception of *Giovanni's Room* (1956). But the howl is much louder here. Perhaps that is why Baraka, delivering Baldwin's eulogy in 1987, said, "as far as I'm concerned, it was *Blues for Mister Charlie* that announced the Black Arts Movement" (96). Baldwin's play, loosely inspired by the story of Emmett Till, a black boy brutally murdered for whistling at a white woman, is an allegory of the inability of white America and black America to cooperate.

Baldwin's play tells the story of Richard Henry, a young black southerner who had moved north and returned to his hometown only to be murdered by Lyle Britten, a poor white storeowner whose racism is vicious and relentless. Richard dies in the play's opening scene, and yet lives on by inspiring his loved ones and his community to examine the causes and meanings of his senseless, premature death. Richard had been no saint, but his murder had nothing to do with his behavior and everything to do with Lyle's insecurity over the growing power of young black people. Here and elsewhere, Baldwin connects America's racial woes to white sexual insecurity. Richard becomes a vulnerable target when he brags about sleeping with northern white women, and at Lyle's murder trial both Lyle and his wife Jo falsely claim that Richard tried to rape her. The trial that concludes the play indicates the way wealthy whites maintain power and social influence through the institutions they control. Richard's father, Reverend Meridian Henry, had been a steady believer in Christian, non-violent resistance throughout the play, but after Lyle is acquitted, he reveals that he keeps Richard's gun under the Bible in his pulpit; he says, "You know, for us, it all began with the Bible and the gun. Maybe it will end with the Bible and the gun" (120). At a crossroads between prayer and violent resistance, Meridian reveals that he is open to change, and that he is following the lead of the more radical younger generation.

Two of Gwendolyn Brooks's more enduring poems are also based on the murder of Emmett Till. In "A Bronzeville Mother Loiters in Mississippi. Meanwhile, a Mississippi Mother Burns Bacon" (1960), Brooks imagines Till's accuser as someone who has long thought of herself in fairy-tale terms, as a "milk-white maid....Pursued / By the Dark Villain" (6–8). She is troubled by the disruptions in her fairy-tale world, by the fact that "the Dark Villain was a blackish child / Of fourteen," and by the notion that her husband, the "Fine Prince," is capable of cruelty (26–27). She has bloody visions: "She tried, but could not resist the idea / That a red ooze was seeping, spreading darkly, thickly, slowly, / Over her white shoulders, her own shoulders / And all over Earth and Mars" (125–128). The victim's blood permanently stains all the universe, and the accuser cannot shake the memory of seeing Emmett Till's mother in the courtroom and dwelling on the "Decapitated exclamation points in that Other Woman's eyes" (131). In a brief companion poem, "The Last Quatrain of the Ballad of Emmett Till" (1960), Brooks enters the consciousness of Till's mother, who is doomed to an eternity of regret, linked to the bloody red vision of his accuser in the first poem: "She sits in a red room, / drinking black coffee. / She kisses her killed boy. / And she is sorry. / Chaos in windy grays / through a red prairie" (3–8). The flat, short lines of this poem are in stark contrast to the troubled, lengthy, ambiguous ruminations of its companion. The poems together highlight the combination of white confusion and black sorrow and anger that swirl around Till's senseless death.

Till's murder, sadly, was not a unique event during the late 1950s and early 1960s, as the outcry for racial equality spawned racial conflict that revealed a grotesque amount of murderous animosity. Even writers who had plenty of personal/domestic issues to work through could not ignore the need to address this animosity in their imaginative work. By the end of the 1960s both Baldwin and Brooks eventually responded to the tragedy not only of Emmett Till's murder, but to the assassinations of Malcolm X and Martin Luther King, Jr. in 1965 and 1968, respectively. By that point, though, a younger generation of writers had emerged who treated Malcolm X's murder specifically as the enduring subject of their work.

The Death and Afterlife of Malcolm X

The gunshot that felled Malcolm X in Harlem in 1965 might be considered the shot heard round the world for the revolution that was the Black Arts Movement. As the most prominent spokesman for the Nation of Islam, Malcolm X had been a visible figure in the media for nearly a decade before his tragic end. White America became aware of – and scared of – the so-called "Black Muslims" through a 1959 documentary aired on network television entitled *The Hate that Hate Produced*. Prior to 1959 relatively few white Americans were aware of the organization whose influence had spread across large, northern cities. *The Hate that Hate Produced* described the Nation of Islam as a "Black supremacist" group and compared its members to white racist hate groups such as the Ku Klux Klan. Malcolm X, the group's spokesman, was such a charismatic figure that he supplanted the group's leader, the enigmatic Elijah Muhammad, in the public imagination, if not in the organization itself. From the moment the documentary aired, Malcolm X was in front of television cameras and microphones constantly, including in the immediate aftermath of John Kennedy's assassination in 1963, when he egregiously proclaimed that the murder of the beloved president was an example of "the chickens coming home to roost." To paraphrase, white America got what was coming to it for its racist ways. This statement proved ill-advised as well as ill-timed, and Elijah Muhammad had to rein in his firebrand spokesman, deepening a growing rift between them.

The Nation of Islam was a powerful organization spiritually, politically, and socially. Founded in Detroit in 1930 by the mysterious Wallace D. Fard Muhammad, it flourished in the mid-twentieth century in Chicago and other northern urban centers as a magnet for black youths looking for a positive alternative to ghetto life. The organization managed to rescue vast numbers of young black men struggling in the nation's blighted urban neighborhoods by providing them with a structure and a purpose, stressing sobriety, physical health, and spiritual clarity. Throughout the early 1960s and well beyond, the image of well-dressed young black men with short-cropped hair distributing pamphlets and inviting other young men and women to information meetings became a fixture in American cities. Yet the Nation of Islam struggled to transcend its label as a "hate group" based on media representations and on countless pronouncements by Malcolm X and other leaders that were incendiary, provocative, and intimidating. That said, the time was ripe for such an organization to emerge. The Civil Rights Movement achieved a great deal in terms of organization, legislation, and cultural enlightenment, but there was clearly a difference of opinion about the amount of passive non-violence a wounded race would or should endure. As Martin Luther King, Jr. gained influence through his writings and speeches throughout the South, Malcolm X and the Nation of Islam were simultaneously gathering followers in the North with a very different set of goals, a different style of resistance to white oppression, and a different timetable for change.

Ironically, the assassination of Malcolm X is attributed to the Nation of Islam itself. Malcolm X had broken from the group in the years leading up to his death due to a schism between him and Elijah Muhammad. He was threatened and his house was firebombed. He undertook a pilgrimage to Mecca and returned convinced that the Nation of Islam did not truly represent the Islamic faith. As he sought to gain a new group of followers, he was shot in the Audubon Ballroom in Harlem.

Soon after the assassination, *The Autobiography of Malcolm X* was published, and it helped to gain for Malcom X an even larger following than he had during his lifetime. Readers who had no connection to the Nation of Islam were compelled by the story, and he quickly became a cultural hero: a revolutionary martyr who died not because he was a mistrusted leader within his movement, but because he was too powerful to continue to exist in racist America. He functioned symbolically as the prototypical black man who gained influence in America through the strength of his convictions and a cautionary tale about what invariably happens to such men.

The Autobiography of Malcolm X is not technically an autobiography. It was written by Alex Haley and based on hundreds of hours of taped interviews with the subject. Biographer Manning Marable describes it as "more Haley's [autobiography] than its author's" (9). Malcolm X wanted to make sure that the story was his, and dictated a contract that both men signed: "Nothing can be in this book's manuscript that I didn't say, and nothing can be left out that I want in it" (423). The degree to which this wish was fulfilled remains an open question; the book contains a lengthy epilogue, for instance, written by Haley after Malcolm X's death that obviously isn't comprised of Malcolm X's words, and yet it is an essential part of his story. A large part of his historical influence rests on his death, as the assassination of a young leader always fuels speculation about what might have happened if he had lived longer. The *Autobiography* intensifies this trend because its trajectory reveals a man who had suffered through a number of trials and low points, but who had achieved enlightenment and inner peace in his final months. For black readers in the mid-1960s looking for a voice to guide them, the abrupt end of the *Autobiography* denoted a lost leader, a martyr who stood for black empowerment and resistance.

As is true of many inspirational autobiographies, the flaws of the subject's early years are revealed in great detail so that his rise seems especially dramatic. Malcolm Little grew up in impoverishment and transience. His early memories include the premature death of his father, which he believed to be the result of a racially motivated murder, and a hostile attack on his family by the Ku Klux Klan. His mother was unfit to raise her children due to mental illness, and Malcolm had to fend for himself on the streets of various northern cities. He became a hustler as a young man, moving quickly from the menial jobs available to young black men in the mid-century, such as shoe-shiner and railroad car waiter, to a petty criminal involved first in gambling, then in peddling and abusing illegal drugs, then as an underling for a mob boss, and finally as a burglar. The early chapters of the book are thrilling: its subject seems to be getting ahead, approaching every hustle as an opportunity to become a more prosperous and more influential figure. Yet the voice of the mature Malcolm X intrudes consistently to criticize his youthful self. After detailing his years as a delinquent, he writes: "I have never previously told anyone my sordid past in detail. I haven't done it now to sound as though I might be proud of how bad, how evil, I was....I found Allah and the religion of Islam and it completely transformed my life" (163–164).

This transformation occurs in prison after Malcolm is sentenced to ten years for armed robbery. Having fallen to a low point, he initially becomes even more self-reliant, famously teaching himself to read in prison by copying the dictionary word for word; he claims: "I don't think anybody ever got more out of going to prison than I did. In fact, prison enabled me to study far more intensively than I would have if my life had gone differently and I had attended some college" (196). Such messages of empowerment appealed to many poor black readers who had similarly been denied the opportunities enjoyed by their wealthy white counterparts. Malcolm's self-reliance proves the key to true transformation: he uses his newfound literacy to write to Elijah Muhammad, who becomes his spiritual savior by believing in him and thus fostering in him the dignity he had never known.

The remainder of the *Autobiography* documents his compelling life story while spreading a message as strong as slave narratives had more than a century earlier: that black men in America are victims of systematic oppression, and that they have to empower themselves rather than wait for white Americans to accommodate them. The difference is that the *Autobiography* clearly had a black audience in mind. Its goal was not to win over the modern-day equivalents of white abolitionists, though it might have been crafted partially as a warning to white Americans not to underestimate their black brethren. Its clarity and power galvanized a generation and continues to hold sway not only as a fascinating historical document about an important figure, but also as a masterful work of rhetoric.

Malcolm X is a recurrent touchstone and inspirational figure in the work of many Black Arts poets, and he is often described in terms that summon him from the dead or that claim that he lives on. Welton Smith, in his poem "malcolm," creates a speaker who has internalized his hero: "i cannot move / from your voice" (1–2). He later locates this voice: "your voice / is inside me; i loaned / my heart in exchange / for your voice" (25–28). The speaker looks out on the misery of his world and looks back to Malcolm X for guidance about how to cope with it. He eventually reaches deep inside himself and achieves a profound inner connection with the martyred leader who had used the "frenzy" inside himself to combat the injustices of the world:

> now you pace the regions
> of my heart. you know
> my blood and see
> where my tears are made.
> i see the beast
> and hold my frenzy;
> you are not lonely –
> in my heart there are many
> unmarked graves.
>
> *(73–81)*

Malcolm X's murder is nearly an obsession in Smith's poetry, especially in the poems selected for Amiri Baraka and Larry Neal's landmark anthology *Black Fire* (1968). His imagery is filled with violence, pain, and invective. In "The Nigga Section" he addresses Malcolm's murderers directly: "you are the dumbest thing / on the earth the slimiest / most rotten thing in the universe / you motherfuckin germ / you konk-haired blood suckin punks / you serpents of pestilence you / samboes you green witches nawing the heads of infants" (34–40). Smith's landscapes are apocalyptic, haunted by screams, blood, and images of a beast that devours everything in its path. As such, they fit the mood of the times, when artists mixed revolution with surrealism and absurdism to yield a new aesthetic.

Larry Neal in his poem "Malcolm X – An Autobiography" retells Malcolm X's story with a distinct emphasis on his hustling years: "I hustler. I pimp. I unfulfilled black man / bursting with destiny" (25–26). The poem ends with Malcolm in jail experiencing salvation in his vision of Elijah Muhammad: "Allah formed man, I follow / and shake within the very depth of my most imperfect being; / and I bear witness to the Message of Allah / and I bear witness – all praise is due Allah!" (74–77). It is unclear why Neal chooses to end his poetic "autobiography" at this moment: perhaps he wanted to avoid the unpleasant implications of Malcolm's murder at the hands of the Nation of Islam. Regardless of the reason, it is clear that black poets in the late 1960s were reframing the story of Malcolm X to fuel their artistic/political aims.

The Black Arts Movement

To suggest that all Black Arts Movement literature confronted the legacy of Malcolm X would be misleading. He became a recurrent symbol within the movement, but only insofar as he provided a shorthand for its main concerns: promoting solidarity within the black underclass, producing art that was distinctive and unfamiliar, and participating in an overtly political project that fostered or legitimized black nationalism. There were certainly other historical events at play when the movement came into being in the mid-1960s, but this particular murder hit many budding black artists hard. Malcolm X symbolized different things to different people, and yet many associated him with the type of pride that grew out of defiance. In an era when segregation was no longer legal, many black Americans were tired of its longstanding effects: their feelings of inferiority, the blight and poverty of their communities, and their dearth of successful role models outside the church and the sports and entertainment industries. Martin Luther King, Jr. certainly provided for African Americans a strong, steady voice of leadership which organized and defined a movement. His historical importance cannot be overstated. Malcolm X, though, arguably had a more immediate impact on the arts in the 1960s, which responded to the pressure to become politically forceful.

Prior to the inception of the Black Arts Movement, a black artists' collective known as the Umbra Workshop met weekly in the bohemian Lower East Side of Manhattan to practice and discuss a new black aesthetic. This group, which included Black Arts Movement poets Askia Touré and Ishmael Reed, felt excluded by underground collectives of primarily white artists, and wanted to embody cooperation rather than competition among black writers. It was a short-lived project, producing just a handful of journal issues before breaking up, but its spirit carried over into the Black Arts Movement.

Poetry was the dominant genre of the Black Arts Movement, and its features are distinct. Its emphasis on the vernacular puts it in the tradition of Langston Hughes and Sterling Brown from the Harlem Renaissance (see Chapter Four), but it is far more experimental as it seeks to reject all conventions associated with established (white) forms. Black Arts Movement poems tend to use creative spelling, to employ vulgar or offensive language, to forego capitalization and standard punctuation, to break lines unconventionally, and to make use of typographical symbols such as slashes and parentheses to create linguistic ambiguity or disruption. Much of this poetry was intended to be performed: the flouting of conventions used in print forces readers to imagine how the poet's voice might sound in performance.

The Black Arts Movement was defined not only by its aesthetic innovations, which made it distinct from both black writers of previous generations and contemporary white writers, but also by its social aims to promote black solidarity and pride. The two were clearly intertwined, as in this passage by Hoyt Fuller, who helped to define the movement: "the future can be clearly seen in the growing number of black people who are snapping off the shackles of imitation and are wearing their skin, their hair, and their features 'natural' and with pride" (8). After incorporating a poetic illustration of this trend, he writes, "If the poem lacks the resonances of William Shakespeare, that is intentional" (9). In some senses, the movement helps to identify its own aesthetic by rejecting the dominant aesthetic. Its works were not just unconventional, but *anti*-conventional.

Leading proponents of the Black Arts Movement consciously defined it as it was developing. Addison Gayle, Jr.'s introduction to his influential collection of essays, *The Black Aesthetic* (1971), is an excellent overview. He identifies a few characteristics of the new black writing – anger, nationalism, and resistance to white attempts to chronicle the black experience – and also argues that these are not really new. He focuses on the differences between the new black writing and earlier black texts; first, contemporary black writers are at war, and their enemy is no longer the backwards South of the late nineteenth and early twentieth centuries. Racism is everywhere, and it must not only be recognized, but combatted. Second, new black writers must not write with a white audience in mind so they can feel free to express their anger honestly. Third, the best way to achieve an honest perspective is to be willing to "de-Americanize" black thinking and black writing rather than to demonstrate how they fit into an American tradition. The goal was to reject the entrenched standards of white writing and to see black writing as potentially transformative rather than adaptive: "The Black Aesthetic, then, as conceived by this writer, is a corrective – a means of helping black people out of the polluted mainstream of Americanism, and offering logical, reasoned arguments as to why he should not desire to join the ranks of a Norman Mailer or a William Styron" (xxiii). Not coincidentally, these famous white novelists were criticized in the late 1950s and 1960s for their attempts to represent black experience in their work (Mailer in his 1957 essay "The White Negro" and Styron in his 1967 novel *The Confessions of Nat Turner*). Gayle concludes, "To be an American writer is to be an American, and, for black people, there should no longer be honor attached to either position" (xxiii). Such rhetoric was not unusual in an era when many young people, black and white, were vocal opponents to American military involvement in Vietnam. And yet, coming from a black writer, this rhetoric was consistent with the popular idea that black Americans would be better off seceding into their own self-governed units; hence the *Nation* of Islam.

Another influential voice in defining the movement was Larry Neal, who co-edited with Baraka the seminal anthology *Black Fire*. His 1968 essay "The Black Arts Movement" offers one of the most cogent definitions available. He insists (as Baraka consistently does) that black art should never separate the artist from the black masses, taking a firm stand on an issue that had been debated in black writing at least since the Harlem Renaissance: "The Black Arts Movement is radically opposed to any concept of the artist that alienates him from his community" (1960). He links the movement to the 1960s rallying cry for "Black Power" implying that art and politics are so intertwined as to be nearly synonymous. The need for self-determination motivates both art and politics, and Neal embraces the term "nationalism" to describe the aspirations of black artists and black people more generally. He and Gayle agree that the development of a "black aesthetic" involves something stronger than a rejection of the "Western aesthetic." Neal writes, "The cultural values inherent in western history must either be radicalized or destroyed, and we will probably find that even radicalization is impossible" (1960–1961). Neal and other spokesmen for this movement frequently ally the terms "Black" and "Third World," implying solidarity between oppressed people globally. He describes the role of black artists as profoundly "ethical" in that the new black art will fulfill its moral obligation to combat the forces of oppression.

Neal identifies specific aspects of Black Art itself, often relying on Baraka's work for examples. He traces the history of the movement to the Black Arts Repertoire Theatre School, an artist-created space in Harlem that featured plays, concerts, and poetry readings for the masses. The school closed due to what he called "internal problems" (not unlike the Umbra Workshop a few years earlier), but versions of it cropped up in cities and on college campuses nationwide. These spaces were always motivated by grass-roots organizations and anti-establishment attitudes. He sees theater in particular as "potentially the most social of all the arts" in the sense that it can be "an integral part of the socializing process. It exists in direct relationship to the audience it claims to serve" (1965). He and other artists associated with the movement wanted to restore theater to its ancient role in opposition to what they felt was the bland modern version, which he believed was meaningful only as entertainment, and which deliberately excluded the perspectives of black people. He sees the collective goal of black theater, and of all Black Art, as addressing a black audience and as having "as its task a profound reevaluation of the Black man's presence in America" (1972). He claims that the Harlem Renaissance represented a similar flowering, but that it failed because "It did not address itself to the mythology and the life-styles of the Black community. It failed to take roots, to link itself concretely to the struggles of that community, to become its voice and spirit" (1972). Art associated with this new movement, then, had a specific charge. While acknowledging its predecessors generally, it selected a few of them – Frederick Douglass, W.E.B. DuBois, Richard Wright, and the Martiniquan social activist Frantz Fanon – as its true forefathers.

The central figure of the Black Arts Movement is unquestionably Amiri Baraka. Initially associated with the Beat Generation poets and the bohemian Greenwich Village scene of the late 1950s and early 1960s, Baraka published under his birth name LeRoi Jones in the early years of his career. Primarily a poet and playwright, Baraka also published two excellent non-fiction volumes on African American music and culture, including the influential *Blues People* (1963). The assassination of Malcolm X became a central incident in his transformation, but a 1960 trip to Cuba initially caused it. In *The Autobiography of LeRoi Jones* (1984) he speaks of being "shaken" by the trip when Cuban intellectuals "assaulted my pronouncements about not being political." When he claimed that he was a poet, not a politician, they responded: "And so you want to write your poetry and that alone, while most of the world is suffering, your own people included. It is bourgeois individualism" (164). Baraka took this critique to heart: "I was never the same again….It was not enough to write, to feel, to think…one must act!" (166). This commitment to political art is the hallmark of Baraka's long career, one imbued (not surprisingly) with controversy.

Although he labeled himself a poet, Baraka was equally known for his plays and essays. His best-known work is the 1964 play *Dutchman*. This brief but dense play is often read as an allegory of race in America, yet it is abstract and mysterious enough to resist any simple interpretation. There are two main characters in the play: a young black man named Clay and a visibly insane white woman named Lula. The entire play takes place on a subway car, with dramatic effects provided by the lights being turned on and off and the passengers swaying as the train hurtles forward. At the opening of the play, Clay is minding his own business when Lula boards the train and begins to seduce and provoke him. Her seduction makes both Clay and the audience uncomfortable, but her provocation is designed to draw him out of his world just as the Cuban intellectuals drew Baraka out of his complacency; she calls him "a well-known type" and says, "You look like you live in New Jersey with your parents and are trying to grow a beard....You look like you've been reading Chinese poetry and drinking lukewarm sugarless tea" (8). She attacks him for being a fake bohemian intellectual and a boring specimen of the bourgeoisie. She asks him who he thinks he is; when he answers, "Well, in college I thought I was Baudelaire," she responds, "I bet you never once thought you were a black nigger" (19). This is only one of a number of shocking statements that Lula makes, and the effect is to unsettle Clay to the point that he explodes in rage, at which point Lula murders him and dumps his body.

Dutchman does not yield an easy moral or lesson, but it is certainly evident that Baraka is warning young men like Clay to open their eyes and to develop a consciousness that can access rage in a beneficial way. Clay does not see Lula coming because he is too involved in a dull, individual dream that denies his roots. Lula controls him through manipulation and lies, and once he reacts violently, pushing her and screaming at her, she has essentially won. Before she kills him, though, he draws a connection between murderous rage and the arts. In his famous poem "Black Art," Baraka proclaims, "We want poems that kill" (1), and Clay in *Dutchman* says something similar about the jazz and blues musicians from the past: "[Charlie Parker] would've played not a note of music if he just walked up to East Sixty-seventh Street and killed the first ten white people he saw....If Bessie Smith had killed some white people she wouldn't have needed that music" (35). Clay's intent (and Baraka's) is not to incite a race war, but to insist that music, poetry, and drama can become transformative, revolutionary forces for black people if they explore their original voices rather than imitating white ones. Lula considers the message dangerous, and, having awakened an important idea in Clay, she feels she has to dispatch him before he can use it. Her final gesture is to select her next victim, another young black man who boards the subway at the play's conclusion dressed just like Clay.

Baraka's play *The Slave* (1964) is a useful companion piece to *Dutchman*. The two share some features – a small cast, two acts, a single set with flashing lights – but the racial roles are somewhat reversed, as the obviously volatile character (Walker) is black and the white characters are taken off guard by his behavior. The situation and backstory to the play aren't entirely clear, but the audience does know that Walker has entered the living room of the white couple, Grace and Bradford Easley, that he is armed with a gun, and that they have a troubled history. An urban war rages outside, and Walker is directly involved in it. He drinks the Easleys' liquor and holds them at gunpoint, all the while threatening to take away their daughters who are asleep upstairs. The audience gradually learns that the children are his and Grace's. Walker murders Bradford, and both he and Grace are injured by falling debris as the house collapses.

The Slave is often read as an allegory of Baraka's descent into the depths of his mind. The Easleys represent his past appeasement of white bourgeois culture, and they have clearly had a lasting, complex effect on the person he has become. They are at war with his current persona, the black revolutionary Walker, whose rage and passion need some sort of outlet so as not to be trapped in his mind, causing internal anguish and torment. Even deeper in his psyche is the figure of the slave. The same actor who plays Walker opens the play as an old man whose speech devolves into that of a "field hand" as he struggles to communicate an idea to the audience, an idea that negates time and makes history present: "I am much older than I look…or maybe much younger" (45, 44). The figure of the slave is archetypal and troubles Walker's mind just as his past with Grace and the existence of their daughters do. Personal history and communal history thus blend to explain, if not justify, the murderous rage that consumes both Walker and the city that forms the backdrop of the play.

Baraka's poetry develops out of the Beat Generation tradition, emphasizing jazz aesthetics such as improvisation, energetic, free expression, and spontaneous, creative metrical patterns. His work from the beginning tends toward a model like Allen Ginsberg's in that it critiques contemporary culture while validating the perspective of a marginal member of society. The beginning of an early poem, "Look for You Yesterday, Here You Come Today" (1961), gives a sense of his early aesthetic and concerns:

> Part of my charm:
> > envious blues feeling
> > separation of church & state
> > grim calls from drunk debutantes
> Morning never aids me in my quest.
> I have to trim my beard in solitude.
> I try to hum lines from "The Poet In New York."
>
> *(1–7)*

Within a few years, having committed to political art and recognizing the rage within himself, the tone and content of Baraka's poems change dramatically, as in the poem "Black Dada Nihilismus":

> Come up, black dada
>
> nihilismus. Rape the white girls. Rape
> their fathers. Cut the mothers' throats.
> Black dada nihilismus, choke my friends
> in their bedrooms with their drinks spilling
> and restless for tilting hips or dark liver
> lips sucking splinters from the master's thigh.
>
> *(40–46)*

This brief example is just a sampling of the evolution of one of the first black, poetic voices that expressed inner turmoil and anger consistently, without artifice and with great forcefulness. In "A Poem Some People Will Have to Understand" (1969) he expresses firm discontentment with the way things are, including the state of poetry. He has lived too long "Without the preciseness / a violent man could propose" (12–13). He laments the dull stasis of his world, a society that passively awaits "the coming of a natural phenomenon" (19). He ends the poem on a chilling note upon realizing that no "natural phenomenon" has come to save them: "Will the machinegunners please step forward?" (26). Poems must kill, he proclaims, or in this case they must be willing to envision murder: the murder of complacency, of inaction, of spiritual barrenness. The machinegunners at the end of Baraka's poem kill in order to create.

Black Arts Movement writers gravitated primarily toward poetry and drama for their potential to bring audiences together in cultural spaces at the heart of black urban communities. One of the most prolific and influential playwrights to come out of the movement is Ed Bullins. The author of dozens of short plays as well as fiction and essays, Bullins's work is as provocative and controversial as Baraka's. His influences tend more toward mid-twentieth-century existentialist and absurdist authors (especially Albert Camus) than toward the bohemian and Beat poets who influenced Baraka. Bullins has endured well beyond the era of the Black Arts Movement, yet like Baraka he remains associated with it.

Bullins began his career with the essay "The Polished Protest" (1963) by critiquing James Baldwin similarly to the way that Baldwin had criticized Richard Wright. Lamenting the notion that Baldwin's writing had become co-opted by a trend toward "stale, oft-chewed phrases and arguments…restated for a newly curious *white* readership," Bullins complains that "Baldwin's newer fiction and caustic essays" are characterized by "an insidious commonness [that] has replaced the traditional types of Negro writing, and this new 'slick' version is being imbued with gimmicks and cuteness" (280, 281). He attributes the problem not only to artists, but to publishers who are reluctant to take risks when publishing black authors. Black publishers are just as bad as white publishers, in Bullins's estimation; calling them "the 'Uncle Toms' of the literary world," he says, they "fight to bury another [black writer] that smacks of quality beneath the garbage of materialism and pseudo-hipness" (283).

Bullins sets the standard for his own art through this critique: it must be bold, experimental, and indifferent to marketplace success if it is to be art. Publishing and producing plays outside of the mainstream literary industry is one step toward accomplishing this ideal. The nature of Bullins's plays reinforces this spirit of indepen-dence and bravery in the face of both racial discrimination and a bland, bourgeois culture. Though no single play from Bullins's *oeuvre* has emerged as the definitive or representative one, "The Electronic Nigger" (1967) showcases a number of his concerns as they are laid out in "The Polished Protest." Set in a college creative writing classroom on the first day of class, this play stages a direct conflict between the authentic and the inauthentic in literature. Baldwin is even evoked by name when the antagonist, A.T. Carpentier, comments on his own bombastic language: "splendid word, 'conundrum,' heh, what? Jimmie Baldwin uses it brilliantly on occasion" (48). Carpentier arrives in the classroom to challenge and confound the instructor, Mr. Jones. They engage in a verbal battle throughout the drama, fueled by the seeming non-sequiturs of the students in the class who side with either the flustered teacher or the aggressive student. Pushed to the brink of rage, Jones addresses Carpentier directly: "Does not the writer have some type of obligation to remove some of the intellectual as well as political, moral, and social tyranny that infects this culture? What do all the large words in creation serve you, my Black brother, if you are a complete whitewashed man?" (58). Carpentier, described in the stage directions as darker-skinned than Jones, has relinquished his blackness and accuses Jones of "preach[ing] bigotry, black nationalism and fascism" (58). Jones is horrified that anyone takes Carpentier seriously, but since he himself has been co-opted by the white higher education establishment, he does not have the fortitude to resist him. Carpentier robotically destroys any semblance of coherence in the classroom, and Jones weakly instructs his students, if they still have the creative urge within them, to pursue it elsewhere. Though he feels defeated, this conclusion may in fact be a triumph as it puts art in a less artificial realm than the college classroom.

Prison as Platform and Corral

More than college classrooms, prison cells became in the 1960s a space where convicted black men and women spoke out. Prison was the site of one of Malcolm X's transformations as described in his *Autobiography*. It was also the site of Martin Luther King, Jr.'s most enduring work of literature, "Letter from Birmingham Jail" (1963). King was best known for his motivational speeches, and these speeches and his collected essays are works of startling clarity and historical significance. His willingness to be incarcerated for his beliefs and to use his incarceration to speak truth to power struck a nerve not only because of King's rhetorical brilliance, but because prison populations were overrepresented by black people in the 1960s, a trend that has continued unabated into the twenty-first century. Prison literature has become a prominent category within American literature over the past half-century.

The confluence of prison literature and African American authors had begun much earlier. *The Confessions of Nat Turner* is a kind of prison narrative, *Native Son* (1940) ends in prison, and the work of Chester Himes is largely associated with the dramas of incarceration. King and Malcolm X, though, reveal how prison fails as a space of social control. If prison is meant to function as a regulated mirror image of the ghettos of the nation's blighted urban centers, the effect of both was to destroy the souls of those who inhabited them: the ghettos through neglect, the prisons through scrutiny and regulation. These leaders, though, demonstrated how prison could be turned into a platform for reflection, self-education, and righteous proclamation. King writes of his reasons for being in Birmingham in the first place. His method of non-violent resistance brought him and his followers to Birmingham where law enforcement officials violently squelched demonstrations for civil rights, and he insisted that this problem was a national phenomenon rather than a personal vendetta from an "outsider": "Anyone who lives inside the United States can never be considered an outsider anywhere within its bounds" (118). The inside/outside distinction makes his position as a prisoner even more poignant. The literal and figurative divide of the prison wall is meant to separate absolutely "law-abiding" citizens from criminals, but King claims a deep connection between himself and his fellow citizens from behind this wall: "injustice is here....Injustice anywhere is a threat to justice everywhere" (117–118).

Of course, the very fact of his incarceration calls into question the justice system. He has been arrested for unlawful demonstration, but the cause of this demonstration is unquestionably just. He argues, "We have waited for more than 340 years for our constitutional and God-given rights....There comes a time when the cup of endurance runs over, and men are no longer willing to be plunged into the abyss of despair" (120–121). Between these two statements he provides a litany of reasons behind his impatience on behalf of all black Americans who have been beaten down by the forces of discrimination backed by the law itself. He arrives at a persuasive conclusion: "there are two types of laws: just and unjust. I would be the first to advocate obeying just laws. One has not only a legal but a moral responsibility to obey just laws. Conversely, one has a moral responsibility to disobey unjust laws" (121). Malcolm X was jailed for failing to obey a just law, yet he derived power from what he did with his incarceration. King was jailed for disobeying an unjust law, and his power came from articulating the moral imperative that everyone had to follow his lead. Both refused to be controlled and defined by the bars that surrounded them.

The most prominent prison poet to emerge in the 1960s was Etheridge Knight, who moved from poverty to drug addiction to petty theft. He was sentenced in 1960 to a lengthy term for purse-snatching. While in prison he was inspired by *The Autobiography of Malcolm X* and by contemporary poets including Sonia Sanchez (whom he later married). His first collection, *Poems from Prison* (1968), revealed a poet who was aware both of the fatalism of his predicament and committed to working against it through cultivating a poetic voice that was unique, honest, and moving. Prison acted not only as his material reality, but also as a metaphor for any oppressive forces, including drug addiction, racism, and poverty. The goal of his work was not literal revolution, but liberation and enlightenment. In a brief poem, "On the Yard," another prisoner whom he describes as a "fascist" asks him why he isn't doing anything (line 2). He responds that he is writing, which is doing something, but he concludes, the "beautiful fascist / didn't buy / it – nor / did I / completely" (18–22). Elsewhere he wonders, "can there anything / good come out of / prison," also after meditating on himself as a poet ("Cell Song," 14–16).

Although Knight's work is associated with the Black Arts Movement and shares many of its features – poems about Malcolm X, reliance on the vernacular, use of language that might be considered crude or vulgar, and creative typography – it occasionally tends more toward the personal or confessional than the work of other Black Arts Movement poets. In "Feeling Fucked Up," after learning that his lover has left him, he rejects a litany of people and things central to the movement's typical icons: "Fuck Coltrane…and Malcolm fuck the revolution fuck freedom fuck / the whole muthafucking thing / all I want now is my woman back / so my soul can sing" (8, 15–18). Still, in two companion poems – "Evolutionary Poem No. 1," written in 1972, four years after he was released from prison, and "Evolutionary Poem No. 2," written in 1979 – he shows the "evolution" from focusing on the individual to focusing on the collective. The first poem, in its entirety, reads, "I ain't got nobody / that I can depend on / 'cept myself." The second reads, "We ain't got nobody / that we can depend on / 'cept ourselves." Prison, it seems, has served initially to isolate him, but the deeper he thinks about it, the more he begins to regard the experience as the catalyst for solidarity.

The Black Panther Party for Self-Defense was founded in 1966. It grew out of the Black Power movement to which, as Larry Neal described it, the Black Arts Movement was the "aesthetic sister." The Black Panthers were a militant organization whose ostensible aim was to defend black communities against police brutality as well as to foster humane values in those communities, especially through education. The Panthers' identity was, from the beginning, intertwined with incarceration. Co-founder Huey Newton had just been released from prison when he joined Bobby Seale to initiate the organization. He was again jailed in 1967 for involuntary manslaughter following the death of an Oakland police officer and the lengthy campaign for his release became a *cause célèbre*. Others would be added to a growing list of such causes, including Angela Davis, George Jackson, and Assata Shakur, all of whom eventually published influential autobiographies (or, in Jackson's case, a series of letters published posthumously as *Soledad Brother* [1970]). The Panthers were a visible presence by the time of Newton's second arrest, wearing their trademark red berets and sunglasses, occasionally carrying rifles in news photographs that were intentionally menacing, though the original intent of the group was "self-defense." In 1968, immediately after the assassination of King, Eldridge Cleaver (the party's Minister of Information) and Bobby Hutton were involved in another skirmish with the Oakland police. Hutton was killed, and Baraka spoke at his funeral, claiming, "we want to build a black nation to benefit black people" (158). Cleaver, meanwhile, was jailed and wrote his memoirs from behind bars.

Cleaver's *Soul on Ice* (1968) is a scathing social critique/memoir deeply influenced by the tenets and methods of the Black Arts Movement. It is a collection of essays written at different times and about different subjects, but always with race in the foreground. Cleaver's voice is consistently forceful, clear, loud, and angry. It is one of the most honest sustained meditations on the intersection of the prison experience and black urban life in the late 1960s. He discusses his motivations for raping women, which was one of the crimes for which he was jailed, as nearly a political act, or at least an act of revenge against the forces that had oppressed him. After he returns to prison, he meditates on his criminal actions: "Even though I had some insight into my own motivations, I did not feel justified. I lost my self-respect. My pride as a man dissolved and my whole fragile moral structure seemed to collapse, completely shattered. That is why I started to write. To save myself" (34).

Writing is not only a means of personal salvation for Cleaver, but also a way to examine his own rage out loud, and, more importantly, to monitor his own growth. He writes: "I was very familiar with the Eldridge who came to prison, but that Eldridge no longer exists. And the one I am now is in some ways a stranger to me. You may find this difficult to understand but it is very easy for one in prison to lose his sense of self" (35). Writing is a means to find or even to forge that new self. His model is, not surprisingly, Malcolm X, whose capacity for transformation is the substance of his identity. In the aftermath of the assassination Cleaver courageously declares that he has thoroughly converted to Malcolm X's final message of racial cooperation. He takes down a picture of Elijah Muhammad from his prison cell and replaces it with an image of Malcolm X. The other Black Muslims in prison see this act as a betrayal, but Cleaver defends his position, and gradually describes himself as a "former Black Muslim" who becomes dedicated to Malcolm's ultimate belief rather than to his association with the Nation of Islam: "there were those of us who were glad to be liberated from the doctrine of hate and racial supremacy. The onus of teaching racial supremacy and hate, which is the white man's burden, is pretty hard to bear" (79). Malcolm X represents the powerful individual who gives voice to the concerns of the masses rather than a spokesman for any organization: "The Black Muslim movement was destroyed the moment Elijah cracked the whip over Malcolm's head, because it was not the Black Muslim movement itself that was so irresistibly appealing to the true believers. It was the awakening into self-consciousness of twenty million Negroes which was so compelling. Malcolm X articulated their aspirations better than any other man of our time" (82). Consistent with the leading figures of the Black Arts Movement, Cleaver recognizes oppression as global rather than specifically racial and national, and expresses solidarity with white and Mexican-American convicts just as Baraka sees a connection between African Americans and those who struggle in third-world conditions for power and dignity. He is vocal against American military involvement in Vietnam and puts a great deal of faith in politically minded American youth of all races, including whites, who "have begun to react to the fact that the 'American Way of Life' is a fossil of history" (105).

Despite its insights, *Soul on Ice* reveals some of the limitations of the thinking and vision associated with the Black Arts Movement. Cleaver's claim to the possibilities of racial cooperation is offset by pronouncements that sound essentialist, reinforcing the animosity that led to his historical moment rather than trying to break through it. Perhaps more troubling, though, is a tendency toward homophobia and misogyny that plagued many male Black Arts Movement writers. His homophobia rears its ugly head in a direct attack on James Baldwin in the essay "Notes on a Native Son." Part of his rejection stems from Baldwin's own fraught relationship with Richard Wright, a figure whom Black Arts Movement writers hold as sacred; Cleaver writes, "Of all black American novelists, and indeed of all American novelists of any hue, Richard Wright reigns supreme for his profound political, economic, and social reference" (134). He interprets Baldwin's "Many Thousands Gone" this way: "Baldwin's essay on Richard Wright reveals that he despised – not Richard Wright, but his masculinity. He cannot confront the stud in others" (135). Initially acknowledging Baldwin's "fascinating, brilliant talent," Cleaver gradually sours on the elder author, and it is clear that his change of heart is due to his discomfort with the way Baldwin treats homosexuality in his fiction (122). This perspective eventually reveals itself in no uncertain terms: "it seems that many Negro homosexuals, acquiescing in this racial death-wish, are outraged and frustrated because in their sickness they are unable to have a baby by a white man" (127–128). Of the damaged protagonist of *Another Country* (1961), Cleaver writes, "Rufus Scott, a pathetic wretch who indulged in the white man's pastime of committing suicide, who let a white bisexual homosexual fuck him in the ass, and who took a Southern Jezebel for his woman, with all that these tortured relationships imply, was the epitome of a black eunuch who has completely submitted to the white man" (132). Such rhetoric is evidence of the intolerance and macho posturing that cannot be fully extricated from the Black Arts Movement as a whole. Cleaver's treatment of women in *Soul on Ice* is similarly troubled, as few women rise above the status of sex objects, and his near obsession with the perils of interracial sex between black men and white women is dated and problematic. Baraka and Bullins have faced similar criticism. The liberation and struggle for equality within the Black Arts Movement clearly had its limitations.

Women and the Black Arts Movement

Black Arts Movement writers faced charges not only of homophobia and misogyny, but also racism and anti-Semitism. In his recent book *The Black Arts Movement* James Smethurst argues persuasively that such judgments are limiting, and that they prevent us from seeing how the Black Arts Movement was fundamentally linked to other grass-roots movements expressing the concerns of ethnic minorities. Smethurst also argues that the Black Arts Movement opened up enormous academic interest in minority folk culture, spawning professorships and departments in subjects like Latino literature and culture that flourish in the twenty-first century. Nevertheless, controversies over the less-than-inclusive politics of the Black Arts Movement persist.

Although women writers were a part of the Black Arts Movement, their position in it was not necessarily central. Cheryl Clarke argues, "Wherever they stood in relation to the Black Arts Movement, most black women writers of that time [1968–1978] wrote *because* of it – and still do" (2). It is easy to agree with Clarke given the extraordinary rise of women writers within the African American tradition in the 1970s and 1980s (see Chapter Seven), but the core of the movement, especially in the late 1960s, was dominated by male perspectives and hypermasculine attitudes. Poems by women poets associated with the movement don't always challenge gender roles, as in Sonia Sanchez's "blk / wooooomen / chant":

            blk/men
    u gon pro tect us
    treat us rite [...]
                    yo blk/bitches/queens/
            nigger wooooomen
                waaaiten for you.
                    (5–7, 11–13)

Although the poem ends with a proclamation of power ("yo/hi/voltage/woooo-menNNN" [32–33]), there is still a sense that male and female realms are separate, and that one has considerable power over the other. The volume in which this poem appeared is dedicated to a long list of black women, "the only queens of the universe," and yet one idea is consistent throughout the volume: that the kings are the ruling monarchs within this developing nation (5). The rhetorical excesses of the Black Arts Movement have much to do with the fact that the movement spoke in broad generalizations. Black individuals were expected to speak in terms of black nationhood, and it followed that women and men could be similarly placed into broad categories.

The poet Nikki Giovanni's first two collections of poetry, *Black Feeling Black Talk* and *Black Judgement*, both published in 1968, are poetic reports from the front lines of the revolution, overtly discussing rallies, black leaders such as H. Rap Brown, the Vietnam War, and of course Malcolm X. These poems denigrate white "honkies" and call loudly to black people to empower themselves, sometimes indulging in violent excess: "Nigger / Can you kill / …Can you piss on a blond head / Can you cut it off" ("The True Import of Present Dialogue, Black vs. Negro," 1–2, 18–19). Railing against Lyndon Johnson, she claims, "a negro needs to kill / something / trying to record / that this country must be / destroyed / if we are to live" ("Records," 38–43). Her poetry has always been topical, but since the end of the 1960s it has moved away from its emphasis on activism. Her clear voice has never lost its poignancy and force, though her strident calls for revolution in the early poems was clearly a product of the mood surrounding her formative years as a poet.

The perspectives of both Sanchez and Giovanni in their earliest collections are motivated, like the works of their male counterparts, by nation-building. Readers looking for a strong feminist message in these works are likely to be disappointed, as female empowerment takes a distant backseat to the party-line racial concerns of the movement. As the movement waned, both poets found their way toward more personal, less bombastic means of expression. Giovanni feels a division in her life between public and private selves, and makes this division the subject of her poetry. Her seventh collection *My House* (1972) is divided into "The Rooms Inside" and "The Rooms Outside." The house itself is both a place of refuge and evidence of self-creation. In the concluding poem that gives the collection its title, "My House," she writes, "i'm saying it's my house / and i'll make fudge and call / it love and touch my lips / to the chocolate warmth / and smile at old men and call / it revolution" (37–42). The possibility that revolution can be associated with domesticity is striking here, but even more striking is the poet's insistence that she has the right to name and define, to call her efforts both "love" and "revolution."

Sanchez's career demonstrates an interesting tension between the politics of the Nation of Islam (of which she was a member between 1972 and 1975) and feminist ideology, which do not fit together comfortably. In 1974 she continued to write verse that sounded a note of female empowerment: the title of the collection is *A Blues Book for Black Magical Women*, and the lengthy introductory poem is, again, "Queens of the Universe," but the gender roles she describes in it are wholly conventional; women are "the first teachers. nurses, givers of life" (14). Their role is again subservient to that of their male counterparts: "we must return to Black men / his children full of our women / love / tenderness / sweet / Blackness full of pride / so they can / shape the male children into young warriors" (15). Later in her career, however, the tone, subject matter, and ideology of her poetry change dramatically. She does not compromise her commitment to black solidarity, but her solidarity with women, both alive and deceased, takes on more prominence in these later poems, which are also considerably more lyrical and inventive than her works of the late 1960s and early 1970s. For instance, in "Present" (1978) she writes, "i dance my / creation and my grandmothers gathering / from my bones like great wooden birds / spread their wings / while their long / legged / laughter / stretches the night" (34–41). Even her more didactic poems have a different tone and focus in later years, as in "Poem for July 4, 1994" where she proclaims, "This is the time for the creative / Man. Woman. Who must decide / that She. He. Can live in peace. / Racial and sexual justice on / this earth" (17–21).

In terms of drama, the other prominent genre of the Black Arts Movement, Adrienne Kennedy wrote a number of plays that both borrow from the spirit of the movement and depart from it. "Funnyhouse of a Negro" is arguably her most enduring. It takes place in the room of its central character, Negro-Sarah, and all of the other characters are her projections, including the real-life African revolutionary Patrice Lumumba. The play has a nightmarish quality as the menacing projections of Sarah's damaged personality confront her in the sanctuary of her room. The conflicts dramatized in the play have to do with racial identity, with looking and acting either black or white. Hair in particular is symbolic of racial identity, and the image of a bald head, sometimes disembodied, recurs in the play as a symbol of racial neutrality and the robotic condition that term implies. Sarah herself is the product of an interracial marriage, though a troubled one in which her conception is intertwined with rape. Her white mother went insane and her black father, rejected because of his race, committed suicide. Sarah herself is destined to inherit both her father's suicidal tendencies and her mother's insanity, which are the unfortunate products of the violent, bloody history that is associated with European and African contact. The set of the play bears this out as the worn-out relics of European domestic worlds are juxtaposed with the vibrant but menacing world of the jungle. Also relevant is the so-called war between the sexes, with men consistently in the role of aggressor. The play's surrealism and symbolic content put

"Funnyhouse of a Negro" in line with plays by Black Arts Movement writers such as Bullins and Baraka, but Kennedy's concerns are not limited to those of the movement. Hers is a rich, expansive vision, and although she has historically not received the same critical attention as some other black writers from the 1960s, critics and students have begun to revisit her in recent years.

Postmodernism Meets the Black Arts Movement: Neo-HooDoo Aesthetics

Not every black writer in the 1960s can productively be considered part of the Black Arts Movement, despite its predominance. The general spirit of the movement was undeniably influential over the range of African American authors at the time, but there were traditions evolving separately from it. The core of the Black Arts Movement was urban and northern in terms of its origins and geographical foci, and it was radical, experimental, and revolutionary in aesthetic terms. The seeds planted by writers like Ernest J. Gaines and Maya Angelou (discussed in Chapter Seven) in the late 1960s developed in a direction that bore fruit in the 1970s and 1980s. Adrienne Kennedy develops from a tradition of black intellectual expatriates (like Baldwin) as does the novelist John A. Williams, who is sometimes discussed as a Black Arts Movement writer, but whose novels such as *The Man Who Cried I Am* (1967) – his most famous, an international intrigue novel set largely in Europe and Africa – do not fit as comfortably into definitions of the Black Arts Movement tenets as do the central figures discussed above.

In the immediate aftermath of the peak years of the Black Arts Movement, black writers delved into the same serious themes that had become common fare during the movement, yet they were also discovering a more playful, experimental approach to their art in conjunction with the broader literary phenomenon known as postmodernism. Beginning in the 1970s with the establishment of Black Studies departments at colleges and universities nationwide, there was a new spirit among black writers who knew they would be taken seriously and rewarded for pushing the boundaries in many ways, not just the ways dictated by the Black Arts Movement. The rise of English-speaking African writers on the global literary stage – Chinua Achebe, Wole Soyinka, and Ngũgĩ wa Thiong'o, to name a few – provided inspiration to African American writers who were motivated by their African heritage and by the extraordinary achievements of these practitioners. All were working under the system of colonial occupation, which is historically intertwined with slavery, and all wrote of the threat to traditional African folk culture posed by a dominant European presence. Moreover, these African writers were public intellectuals with expansive insights into both folk culture and the minds of those who would oppress them.

Ishmael Reed is heir to this postcolonial intellectual tradition as well as to the Black Arts Movement and to postmodernism. Prolific as a poet, novelist, and essayist, Reed can perhaps best be described as a satirist or a trickster. His roots are in the Black Arts Movement, but he developed a unique perspective that situates him outside the movement, if not quite in opposition to it. He does share with the

Black Arts Movement an insistence on championing independent, underground work, especially through his organization the Before Columbus Foundation, which is dedicated to viewing American culture and history from non-Western vantage points. A good introduction to his work can be found in his "Neo-HooDoo Manifesto" (1972). In this essay he digs just below the surface of mainstream American culture to discover the black influence that has been suppressed, over-looked, or dismissed. He sifts back through African American culture to lift up his heroes: Ralph Ellison, Zora Neale Hurston, and dozens of musicians from Louis Armstrong through to Jimi Hendrix. Neo-HooDoo is a "church" that is anti-hierarchical: "every man is an artist and every artist a priest" (21). Its spirits or "loa" come from Africa, though it flourishes in the New World. It is against the very Western spirit, not to mention the Western God, which Reed dismisses as "a dangerous paranoid pain-in-the-neck a CopGod" (24). He believes that Western culture at its worst is exclusive, judgmental, and ignorant. By contrast, "A Neo-HooDoo celebration will involve the dance music / and poetry of Neo-HooDoo and whatever / ideas the participating artists might add" (25). Honoring the funky and the folky, Reed's aesthetic is also deeply informed by the patterns of history, including the cyclical patterns caused by revolutions.

Sifting through a considerable amount of official history and folk legend, Reed comes up with (and invents) heroes in the tradition of the trickster, that shape-shifter from African tales who could get away with fooling or making fun of those in power. In his poem "Railroad Bill, A Conjure Man" he extols one such figure: "Railroad Bill was a conjure man he / Could change hisself to a song. He / Could change hisself to some blues / Some reds he could be what he wanted / To be" (62–66). The legendary figure from song resists all forms of oppression and even outwits death, but in contemporary times he has to dodge new, insidious forms of social control: an Ivy League professor, a psychiatrist, and Hollywood. In all cases he manages to slip away from others' attempts to fix his identity or to use him, and the poet triumphantly declares, "Railroad Bill was free" (191). The poem is sub-titled "A HooDoo Suite," and it reflects not only Reed's Neo-HooDoo aesthetic, but also reflects his fascination with history's unlikely heroes.

The forces at work in Reed's most celebrated work, *Mumbo Jumbo* (1972), are consistent with the iconoclasm of the late 1960s and early 1970s. The elaborate plot mixes mystery-novel intrigue with postmodern whimsy as Western civilization attempts to subjugate the defenders of "Jes Grew," the underground ancient mysteries akin to Neo-HooDoo (4). The protagonist, PaPa LaBas, attempts to find and bring to light a document known as the Text that will demonstrate how Jes Grew is the essential force in American culture. "Jes Grew" is a phrase used to explain the development of jazz in the 1920s, which is the setting for the novel. The book is obviously complex, like all of Reed's work, and to summarize it in the brief space here is less productive than to focus on its main thrusts: the quest (for the Text) and the quester (PaPa LaBas). To understand them is to appreciate the redefinitions of art and religion that are at the heart of the Neo-HooDoo aesthetic. What Reed salvaged and developed from the Black Arts Movement was a desire to resist accepted standards and to replace them with something fresh. This impulse is reproduced in both the content and the form of *Mumbo Jumbo*.

Reed's 1976 novel *Flight To Canada* is another important work that freely blends past and present as well as historical and fictional elements. Its main plot is dense and complex, involving parallels between the 1860s and the 1960s. Abraham Lincoln and Stowe's novel *Uncle Tom's Cabin* provide the historical and literary impetus for the tale, which centers around the flight from slavery of Raven Quickskill, a poet who uses literacy as a kind of voodoo. His escape provides a counterpoint to the behavior of another slave, Uncle Robin, who stays on the plantation and who manipulates the obsessed slave owner Swille. When Lincoln discovers a missing bag of gold, he doubts that Robin, whom he describes as a "poor submissive creature," could have taken it (50). After Swille's death, Robin inherits his "castle" and land since he has manipulated the will, dictated to him by the illiterate Swille (167). Raven, the poet, has set out for Canada, which becomes in the novel less an actual place than an invention of individual minds. The novel posits the persistence of slavery in economic terms and suggests that the white man's only god is power, whereas black men have many gods available to them. The question that remains is how best to resist or undermine that power. Robin compares himself to Nat Turner, the leader of the infamous slave rebellion: "Now Nat's dead and gone for these many years, and here I am master of a dead man's house. Which one is the fool? One who has been dead for these many years or a master in a dead man's house. I'll bet they'll be trying to figure that one out for a long time" (178). The invention of a utopian place ("Canada") outside of racist America may initially serve to lift African Americans out of their circumstances, but they ultimately have to find inventive ways to deal with the world they inhabit.

Another postmodern writer to emerge from the Black Arts Movement is Clarence Major. Although he has also written poetry (and edited an important collection, *The New Black Poetry*, in 1969), Major's reputation rests largely on his experimental fiction. In interviews he consistently identifies elements that would help to label his work as American or avant-garde rather than to link them specifically to a black tradition, in spite of the fact that he began his career with a manifesto calling all black writers to break from Western literary conventions. In a 1973 interview he corrects his position: "I now find repulsive the idea of calling for black writers to do anything other than what they each choose to do" (Bunge, 11). What Major chooses to do is rarely the same thing twice. His 1979 *Emergency Exit* is a delightful miscellany including snippets of recognizable stories interspersed with original art-work, lists, seemingly random quotations, and even a self-conscious direct address ("Well, dear reader, how do you feel about it?") printed in the middle of a page toward the end of the book. It is dedicated "To the people whose stories do not hold together," making the reader work very hard to find a coherent statement in it about race or anything at all (vii).

A historical novel that merges a deep reconsideration of history with Reed's or Major's postmodern playfulness is Charles Johnson's *Middle Passage* (1990). Its narrator and protagonist, Rutheford Calhoun, is a scoundrel who was recently freed from slavery. He finds gambling and burglarizing pleasant, so much so that he is unfit for a conventional life, and he stows away on a ship partly to avoid marriage. The ship, as the title indicates, is a slaver, and the less-than-serious Calhoun is forced into a deeper understanding of the world and his place in it. Though it is peppered with anachronisms, the novel reads like a nineteenth-century work, especially one written by Melville. Its primary intent is to create a narrative on the scaffold of philosophy. Reflecting on slavery and class, Calhoun describes the "*either/or* agony created by a sorghum biscuit" as he must either keep it for himself and live with the guilt of depriving his brother of nourishment, or starve: "This was the daily, debilitating side of poverty that no one speaks of, the perpetual scarcity that, at every turn, makes the simplest act a moral dilemma" (47).

If simple acts are moral dilemmas, the more complex milieu he finds himself in – a free black man on a ship carrying slaves – is a grotesque nightmare. Calhoun garners special favor from the ship's maniacal captain, and he is confused about how to proceed when the slaves and crew stage a mutiny. In a world fueled by binary opposites (such as master and slave, black and white, African and American), Calhoun consistently finds himself in an in-between position. He feels paralyzed and without agency throughout much of the narrative. He learns that the captain has captured a shape-shifting African god, one that is responsible for creating chaotic reversals in human affairs, and his experience on the ship seems to be dictated by such reversals. The absurdity of the situation indicates the absurdity of a world in which slavery is a reality: "Could it be that in a dimension alongside this one I was a dwarf sitting in a Chinese robe, telling a white mate I had captured a European god and, below us, the hold was crammed with white chattel? Preposterous!" (102). Calhoun's journey is one of profound transformation, not in the circumstances of the world, but in the way he perceives it: "The voyage had irreversibly changed my seeing, made of me a cultural mongrel, and transformed the world into a fleeting shadow play I felt no need to possess or dominate, only appreciate in the ever extended present" (187). A similar principle applies to history in these works: it is not something to be possessed or dominated, but rather reimagined.

Conclusion

The 1960s in America are generally associated with revolution, and the way that decade affected the trajectory of African American literature is no exception. The Black Arts Movement was brash and insistent: poems and plays had to incite readers and viewers to action or they were not doing their job. Anger and frustration were the keynotes. Writers associated with this movement reached back to Frederick Douglass and Richard Wright as their literary precursors, and used the assassination of Malcolm X as a rallying cry. The emphasis on the individual in the great works of the 1950s by Ralph Ellison, Gwendolyn Brooks, and James Baldwin was replaced by a clear preference for the collective. Racial oppression was the theme, and the literary response was to fight back with violent insistence. Although some of the works of the Black Arts Movement now seem like products of their time rather than timeless works of literature, it is important to understand the movement's radical insistence that black literature had a specific political obligation. Students of the tradition can choose to agree or to disagree, but they cannot ignore the movement's historical significance.

Suggestions for Further Reading

Collins, Lisa Gail and Margo Natalie Crawford. *New Thoughts on the Black Arts Movement*. New Brunswick, NJ: Rutgers University Press, 2006. Print.

Gayle, Addison, Jr. *The Addison Gayle Jr. Reader*. Urbana, IL: University of Illinois Press, 2009. Print.

Neal, Larry. *Visions of a Liberated Future: Black Arts Movement Writing: Poetry and Prose*. New York, NY: Thunder's Mouth Press, 1989. Print.

Terrill, Robert E., ed. *The Cambridge Companion to Malcolm X*. Cambridge: Cambridge University Press, 2010. Print.

Watts, Jerry Gafio. *Amiri Baraka: The Politics and Art of a Black Intellectual*. New York, NY: New York University Press, 2001. Print.

7

1970–2000: THE FLOURISHING OF BLACK WOMEN WRITERS AND THE RETURN TO BLACK HISTORY

The effect of the Black Arts Movement was not simply to "radicalize" African American literature by asserting that it had a political obligation, but also to refocus the tradition and to open it up to new possibilities for free expression. The major works of the 1960s were based firmly in folk culture and black vernacular speech, and many were published by small or alternative presses that were considered marginal or underground. Works that might have been dismissed as bitter, angry, or offensive at the beginning of that decade nearly became the norm, and any literary work that did not rail against racial injustice was likely to be overlooked. This expectation was not to last indefinitely, and there is currently vigorous debate about whether or not black literature in the twenty-first century has the same political obligations it had in the 1960s and early 1970s. Still, the Black Arts Movement has had one lasting effect: African American literature has garnered more attention and produced more debate in the past half-century than ever before.

Moreover, in the aftermath of the Black Arts Movement, which was weighted toward male writers and a conventionally masculine sensibility, black women writers rose to the foreground in the 1970s and 1980s, a trend which reached a crescendo (if not an apex) when Toni Morrison received the Nobel Prize in Literature in 1993, the first and currently only African American writer to earn this prestigious award. It could be argued that fiction writers Morrison, Toni Cade Bambara, Alice Walker, and Gloria Naylor, poets Nikki Giovanni, Audre Lorde, and Lucille Clifton, and playwright Ntozake Shange were influenced simultaneously by the radical politics of both the Black Arts Movement and of second-wave feminism. At the same time, these writers incorporated other traditions, infusing their work with folklore, mythology, history, and individual self-expression. Building on the achievements of a group called the Combahee River Collective, whose essay "A Black Feminist Statement" (1977) was a foundational document in the movement to empower black feminists, Walker coined the term "womanism" to apply feminist principles to African American women's writing, arguing that "feminism" did not address the particular concerns of black women. Morrison, for her part, has claimed that she doesn't want to be held to any ideology or "ism." Both writers assert their individuality and their distinctiveness through these positions.

It is clear that not all black writers, male or female, shared the same concerns or perspectives in the years following the decline of the Black Arts Movement. What is also clear is that the period saw an extraordinary, sustained display of talent and artistic genius that brought African American literature to new heights. In addition to the rise of black feminism, this period also engaged deeply with history in literary contexts. Both of these trends have had long-term effects on the trajectory of black writing.

The 1970s and the Proliferation of Black Women Writers

The second wave of feminism in the late 1960s evolved along with the Black Arts Movement with similar energy and equally radical goals. Black women writers like Sonia Sanchez and Nikki Giovanni (discussed in Chapter Six) were initially associated with the Black Arts Movement, but later demonstrated how their poems could accommodate feminist concerns. Other writers seemed equally influenced by both movements at the same time. 1970 saw the publication of *The Black Woman*, edited by Toni Cade Bambara, the first anthology to focus exclusively on African American women's writing.

Bambara is remembered as a fiction writer, particularly for the 1972 story collection *Gorilla, My Love*, though her contributions were far-ranging as an activist, educator, and filmmaker as well. The stories in *Gorilla, My Love* tend to be upbeat, despite the fact that they emerged from the blighted inner cities of the late 1960s and 1970s. Bambara's gift is to render speech into writing in a way that is compelling without resorting to the historic traits of black dialect in print. Her characters are often feisty women who are both street-wise and caring. Her story "The Lesson" highlights obscene class disparity, as a group of schoolchildren travel to an expensive toy store as a sort of unofficial field trip. "My Man Bovanne" is the most frequently anthologized of her stories. Hazel, the story's narrator, dances with an elderly blind man named Bovanne, and her children drag her off the dance floor telling her that she is embarrassing them. She defies them and continues to dance with Bovanne, planning to treat him with dignity by cooking for him and asking him to help around her house, "Cause you gots to take care of the older folks… old folks is the nation" (9–10). The story responds to a possible breakdown of the black community caused by a lack of respect for one's heritage as the younger generation gets caught up in cultural change.

Ntozake Shange's play *for colored girls who have considered suicide when the rainbow is enuf* (first performed in 1974), like Bambara's "The Lesson," highlights the stories of the underprivileged. This "choreopoem" grew directly out of the Black Arts Movement aesthetic – "creative misspellings" based not only on black vernacular speech, but on a conscious resistance to white standardization of the conventions of written language, disruption of traditional form and genre, and attention to poetry and drama as the most relevant literary forms because of their ability to bond audiences. As discussed in Chapter Six, the Black Arts Movement spawned some writings that have faced charges of misogyny. *for colored girls…* corrects this trend by giving voice to the victims of rape, to women in abusive relationships, to women who become despondent upon realizing "i waz capable of debasin my self for the love of another" (14). The suicidal women who are the subjects of the play are equally oppressed by gender and by disadvantages related to race.

Shange's play features seven women identified only by the color they are wearing. Each delivers a fragmented story, written in verse and in a black vernacular dialect. The effect of their stories is to provide a collective vision of their lives, one filled not only with despair, but ultimately with some sense of hope. They sometimes regard their racial identity as a gift; the lady in blue says, "we deal wit emotion too much so why dont we go on ahead & be white then / & make everythin dry & abstract wit no rhythm & no reelin for sheer sensual pleasure" (44). Through their woeful tales and confessions, these women, who speak with each other but never really *to* one another, all take up a single line at the play's end: "i found god in myself & i loved her / i loved her fiercely" (63). Each of the women repeats this line, then they all chant it together until it becomes "a song of joy" accompanied by a celebratory dance (63). The theme of Shange's work is clearly black female empowerment and the evolution of community beginning with individual self-expression.

That same description could be applied to Alice Walker. Her most notable achievement is the Pulitzer Prize-winning novel *The Color Purple* (1982), made into a successful Hollywood film. From that point on, Walker's readership has diminished as critics faulted her subsequent fiction as overly polemical. Unconcerned with this popular decline, she has continued to publish prolifically in multiple genres. Walker grew out of the Civil Rights Movement as a devoted follower of Martin Luther King, Jr. She was initially married to a white civil rights lawyer and they were the first interracial married couple in Jackson, Mississippi. This relationship was the basis for "Laurel," one of her more famous short stories, and her work in the Civil Rights Movement is reflected in her 1976 novel *Meridian*. Another frequently anthologized story is "Everyday Use" (1973), which celebrates the folk achievements of black women and which displays wariness toward the trendy whims of young black people who either denigrate or fetishize the folkways of their families rather than to honor them properly, a theme also evident in Bambara's "My Man Bovanne." This sensibility led Walker to seek out and champion forgotten black women artists, especially in her famous essay "In Search of Our Mothers' Gardens" (1974), which recovered Phillis Wheatley. It also led to her more ardent recovery of Hurston. The essay "Looking for Zora" (1975) was instrumental not only in securing Hurston's place as a major figure in the African American canon, but also in advancing the project of revising all literary canons to include writers overlooked because of their gender, race, or class. Walker's efforts to shine a light on Hurston's achievements established a more diverse and inclusive body of writers that has become standard in our era.

The Color Purple is an epistolary novel told mostly from the point of view of Celie, a poor black girl who grows into womanhood during the course of the narrative. The novel takes place in the rural South during the Great Depression, consistent with many other works during this time that turned their attention to forgotten history. A useful inroad can be found in the introductory paragraph of Walker's essay "In Search of Our Mother's Gardens" which describes black southern women of the 1920s this way: "They stumbled blindly through their lives: creatures so abused and mutilated in body, so dimmed and confused by pain that they considered themselves unworthy even of hope" (232). Celie tries to respond to her pain and bewilderment by writing letters. She initially addresses them to God, but gradually switches her addressee to Nettie, the sister who was lost to her in youth when Celie was essentially sold into marriage by her stepfather who repeatedly raped her and impregnated her twice. Nettie's letters responding to Celie comprise a significant portion of the novel. They are written in educated Standard English, in marked contrast to Celie's letters.

Celie marries a man named Albert, whom she refers to as Mr. _____ throughout the book, and is forced to raise his children, to manage his chaotic house, and to submit to his sexual urges. The book's main concerns are not disguised: Walker's primary subjects are female sexuality (including homosexuality), conflicts between the sexes, racial oppression, the dangers of anthropomorphizing God as a powerful white man, and the role of Africa in African American identity formation. Celie is naïve and occasionally makes dubious decisions, as when she encourages Mr. _____'s son Harpo to beat his wife Sofia. (She admires the way Sofia fights back against Harpo and eventually discovers in herself the spirit to fight back against her own husband, but in the meantime Sofia's belligerence leaves her wounded and eventually lands her in jail as she is unable to control her rage.) Celie gradually forms a sense of community and solidarity with Sofia and with Squeak, another young woman in the household.

Part of her ability to forge such healthy relationships comes from her transformation from an abused victim with tragically low self-esteem into a woman who believes in her own worth. This is a hard-fought transformation, and it stems from an unlikely source: a sexually promiscuous, hard-drinking singer named Shug Avery. Shug sleeps with Mr. _____, leaves him for another man named Grady whom she brings back into Mr. _____'s household, forsakes both of them to act as Celie's mentor in the field of same-sex love, and leaves Celie for a teenage boy. Celie feels a strong sexual attraction to Shug before she even meets her, and it intensifies as they grow closer. But more importantly, Shug acts as a spiritual guide to Celie, suggesting that God might be a spirit found in nature and within people rather than an aloof deity. This idea enables Celie to accept the conceptions of God that her missionary sister articulates after traveling to Africa: "God is different to us now….More spirit than ever before, and more internal" (264). Shug also gives Celie practical advice about how to deal with

Mr. _____, and she protects Celie as a way of teaching her how to protect and defend herself. In the dramatic scene in which she finally stands up to her abusive husband, Celie loudly proclaims, "I'm pore, I'm black, I may be ugly and can't cook….But I'm here" (214). This declaration of survival and self-affirmation overtly states the novel's moral.

Celie's journey illustrates what Walker termed "womanism." The term was a conscious variation on feminism which had productively fought for gender equality, but perhaps without sufficiently addressing the unique struggles of black and poor women. It was earlier referred to as black feminism, as in a foundational 1977 article by Barbara Smith, "Toward a Black Feminist Criticism:" "A black feminist approach to literature that embodies the realization that the politics of sex as well as the politics of race and class are crucially interlocking factors in the works of black women writers is an absolute necessity" (164). Smith cites a number of critics who seem to regard "black" and "feminist" as mutually exclusive terms, and her project is to unite them in a way that will allow readers to see underappreciated writers in a new light. The womanist movement was not just political, but deeply spiritual and committed to moral and social values that can heal ruptured communities such as those depicted in *The Color Purple.*

A strongly spiritual impulse dominates Walker's work and that of her contemporaries, who tend to champion the domestic folk arts such as quilting and gardening. There is during this period an ardent search for female sacred spaces, physical as well as psychological. Audre Lorde is a poet who exemplifies the womanist ideology Walker and others identified in the late 1970s and 1980s. In her essay "Poetry is Not a Luxury" (1977) she writes, "For each of us as women, there is a dark place within, where hidden and growing our true spirit rises…as we come more into touch with our own ancient, noneuropean consciousness of living as a situation to be experienced and interacted with, we learn more and more to cherish our feelings, and to respect those hidden sources of our power from where true knowledge and, therefore, lasting action comes" (36–37). Lorde resists the accepted wisdom of the white Western male-dominated poetic tradition: "I speak here of poetry as a revelatory distillation of experience, not the sterile word play that, too often, the white fathers distorted the word *poetry* to mean" (37). Poetry itself has the potential to be one of the sacred spaces women of color need to embrace, "a safe-house for that difference so necessary to change and the conceptualization of any meaningful action" (37). In her essay "The Master's Tools Will Never Dismantle the Master's House" (1979) Lorde argues passionately for "the creative function of difference in [women's] lives," particularly women who "stand outside the circle of this society's definition of acceptable women; those of us who…are poor, who are lesbians, who are Black, who are older" (90–91). This belief is reflected in her poetry, as in the conclusion to the poem "Stations:" "Some women wait for something / to change and nothing / does change / so they change / themselves" (41–45).

The long, varied career of Lucille Clifton provides another example of the way the Black Arts Movement gave rise to new sensibilities. Her earliest poems in the

1960s and 1970s focused on some of the important figures of the time: she published works about Eldridge Cleaver, Malcolm X, Bobby Seale, and Angela Davis. Her style and tone did not necessarily align with other writers associated with the movement, though, and her focus was always on individual people rather than on social trends. The importance of family in particular is a recurrent touchstone. In her collection *Good Times* (1969) she celebrates the circumstances of her people: "we hang on to our no place / happy to be alive / and in the inner city / or / like we call it / home" (31–36). Family supplants the imperative for forging black nationhood in her work, and there is a special emphasis on connecting the present to the past against the background of domesticity. In her poem "i am accused of tending to the past" she envisions history as a "monstrous unnamed baby" that she discovers, nurses, and names, but it was not her baby to begin with (7). In her hands, though, the baby called History matures: "she is more human now, / learning language everyday, / remembering faces, names and dates. / when she is strong enough to travel / on her own, beware, she will" (49–53). The fact that this poem appears in a collection entitled *Quilting* (1991) coupled with the notion that Clifton casts history as female indicates her participation in both of the main themes of this period in equal measure: a burgeoning interest in women's ways of knowing and deep attention to neglected instances of historical significance.

The Historical Impulse and the Rise of Toni Morrison

In addition to the proliferation of female voices, a major theme in African American literature beginning in the early 1970s was the turn toward history. The Black Arts Movement, although sensitive to history, was focused on the present, on the radical need to establish black nationhood, but not all writers were engaged in this project. Two important writers of the late 1960s and early 1970s – Maya Angelou and Ernest J. Gaines – focus on history and the South more than on the revolutionary present in America's urban centers. Angelou's famous memoir *I Know Why the Caged Bird Sings* (1970) traces the author's maturing from her early years in the Great Depression to adulthood. The rural South of her youth is humble and crude, where black people are still employed as cotton pickers, where the Christian church is central to the social and spiritual lives of virtually all residents, and where segregation is absolute. The young Angelou's insecurity derives from her sense of racial persecution, and the fact that her mother's lover raped her at a young age sends her to the brink of insanity, causing her to lose her voice temporarily. During her early teens Angelou leaves Arkansas with her family to seek success in California while World War II rages overseas. After a series of inspirational moments and setbacks, Angelou becomes pregnant and gives birth at the age of sixteen. The narrative ends with her sleeping next to her newborn son, unsure of her future but certain of the role she has taken on as protector.

Angelou's memoir – the first volume of a five-part autobiography – reveals the impulse to confess: to expose the wounds of the past that may have been buried. The turbulence of the 1960s that resulted in such a potent unleashing of experimental techniques and raw language in Black Arts Movement poems and plays is not evident in Angelou's work. Rather, she draws her power from her heritage, largely transmitted through her family, and through her own personal perseverance. Her perspective is informed by her interpretation of her place in the world on three levels: "The Black female is assaulted in her tender years by all those common forces of nature at the same time that she is caught in the tripartite cross fire of masculine prejudice, white illogical hate and Black lack of power" (272). Her own power can be understood in the context of her book's title: she is a caged bird who *sings*, converting oppression into beautiful communication.

Ernest J. Gaines's *The Autobiography of Miss Jane Pittman* (1971) is a historical novel that traces the life of the fictional protagonist from her birth in slavery through to the present, as she witnesses the unfolding of the Civil Rights Movement in the 1960s. The narrator tells briefly of her early years on the plantation, but the story essentially begins with emancipation. Her name was Ticey, but she renames herself Jane when a friendly northern officer suggests that "Ticey is a slave name, and I don't like slavery. I'm go'n call you Jane" (8). She embraces her new name along with the soldier's last name (Brown), but she soon finds herself battling with her fellow ex-slaves who all clamor to rename themselves, usually after Lincoln, but also "Brown" following emancipation. This petty division in their community indicates an urgent need for cooperation rather than individual vanity.

Jane must grow up quickly without guidance or assistance following slavery. She does not follow the typical path from the racially oppressive South to the benevolent North, but rather finds herself returning to the South to grow and develop, both as an individual with strong ties to her community and as a witness to history. Jane is a complex character – a lover, a wife, a nurturing mother figure, a survivor, and a pragmatist. She is less a symbol or a fictionalized heroine than she is a believable, fully rounded character, neither content to accept a prescribed fate nor ambitious to reach beyond the boundaries of her somewhat humble life to make a grand impact. She is over one hundred years old at the time of narration, and has been a witness to and participant in history, from slavery through to the end of segregation. Yet what makes the story so appealing is the authenticity of her voice. The aesthetic and actual revolutions that dominated black literature in the 1960s were a dramatic part of the evolution of the African American literary tradition. Quieter, but equally compelling, were narratives such as those of Angelou and Gaines that chronicled the past through the stories of lived lives. These stories did not shy away from the negative effects of the persistence of racism, but they were content to consider those effects in subtler ways and more traditional methods than those employed by the Black Arts Movement.

1976 saw the publication of Alex Haley's novel *Roots*, a family history novel based on genealogical research that reaches back to the moment of enslavement in Gambia in the eighteenth century. This sprawling saga, many years in the making, became a sensation and, along with his role as co-author of *The Autobiography of Malcolm X*, led to Haley becoming the best-selling African American author in history. The novel was made into a TV series that reached a record number of viewers. It concludes with the death of the author's father, who joins the rest of his ancestors in the afterlife: "I feel that they *do* watch and guide, and I also feel that they join me in the hope that this story of our people can help to alleviate the legacies of the fact that preponderantly the histories have been written by the winners" (587). *Roots* is accessible and compelling, but its legacy has been damaged by charges of plagiarism brought by Harold Courlander, who claimed that Haley copied multiple passages from his novel *The African* (1967). Genealogists also disputed the authenticity of Haley's research into his family's roots, despite the fact that the book is a novel. Its tarnished legacy is perhaps less important than what it represented at the time: a fresh look at history and at the deep ancestral connections that became a primary literary focus in the 1970s and 1980s. Lucille Clifton's memoir *Generations,* also published in 1976, is another significant example of a burgeoning interest in African American family history. This trend built on Gaines's *The Autobiography of Miss Jane Pittman,* but *Roots* and *Generations* represented a flowering of the tendency to reexamine the past, to reconnect sundered family ties, and to shift attention from the plight of the ghetto to the expansive landscape of history.

Cheryl Wall argues persuasively that the rise to prominence of black women writers in the 1970s and 1980s and the interest in genealogy and history at that time was no coincidence; she writes, "To a great extent, the urgent preoccupation with history in the writings of black women in the 1970s and 1980s registered alarm at the potential loss of a history that had never been accurately recorded" (7). Black women's writing, particularly during this period, proved less concerned with interracial conflict than with "those intimate relationships in which the most painful consequences of racism are played out," including love relationships, family bonds, and friendships (6). The simultaneous turn to history and ascendancy of women writers during that era was a widespread phenomenon, but one central figure should be singled out for deeper consideration. Toni Morrison is by almost any measure the most important American novelist of the late twentieth century. Her fiction – complex, tough, mesmerizing – has received more critical scrutiny than any other black writer in recent history. Her output has been patient rather than prolific, and it is difficult to select the novels to discuss in this introductory context. Most critics would agree that *Song of Solomon* (1977) and *Beloved* (1987) are at the center of her magisterial *oeuvre,* and both underscore the prominence of family history and history more generally in African American fiction of this era.

Morrison began as an editor at Random House, helping to promote the careers of important members of her cohort such as Gayl Jones and Toni Cade Bambara. She also curated and co-edited *The Black Book* (1974), an illustrated history of the African American experience that foretells her emphasis on folk history in her fiction. The themes of Morrison's writing are too complex to merit a quick summary, but a few prominent motifs recur: violence and love are always intertwined in her work, human sacrifice is both a necessary and random component of societies, material values are the primary threat to higher spiritual values, and growth is impossible without pain and effort. Her characters tend to be damaged both physically and psychically. Their worth depends not upon what has happened to them, through their own fault or through circumstance, but on how they cope or fail to cope with it. Her focus is largely (but not exclusively) on the experiences of black women. The truly heroic characters in her work are unlikely mentors and spiritual guides, frequently outcasts rather than pillars of their community. The majority of her novels are historical. Critics have noted the influence on her style of Virginia Woolf and William Faulkner – the subjects of her Master's thesis – and also of the late-twentieth-century mode of magical realism that originated in Latin America.

Many readers encounter Morrison's first two novels, *The Bluest Eye* (1970) and *Sula* (1973), in high school or in introductory college courses, but this selection may have to do with the relative brevity and accessibility of these works. Morrison has only published one short story, "Recitatif" (1983), which is frequently anthologized. All three of these works are about the relationships between damaged young women. Pecola Breedlove, the tragic central figure of *The Bluest Eye*, is the victim of incest who converts her devastation into a longing to achieve the impossible: blue eyes, the source of beauty in countless representations she sees in white popular culture. Her community treats her as a scapegoat: the sacrificial victim for a people struggling to move beyond the wounds of the past even as they inflict new wounds upon themselves and each other. *Sula* tells the story of two best friends, the title character and Nel, who are also members of a community insistent on ritual sacrifice and scapegoating. The black residents of a town at the infertile highland ironically known as "The Bottom" perpetuate a ritual called National Suicide Day, initiated by a shell-shocked veteran of World War I. The friends unconsciously participate in this ritual when they throw a young boy into a river, where he drowns. Sula later becomes the community's scapegoat because of her promiscuity and unconventional lifestyle. These best friends grow apart and are unable to reconcile their differences, and the gap between them symbolizes the community's larger inability to accept difference. "Recitatif" touches on many of the same themes. Two friends, Twyla and Roberta, are placed in a school for wayward children because their mothers are deemed unfit. They, too, grow apart over time. The game Morrison plays in "Recitatif" is to make the reader aware that one of these two girls is black and the other white, but she constantly confounds our ability to determine which is which. Their relationship is interdependent, to the point that they become confused and unmoored as they grow apart, reflecting the confusion of a desegregated America that has not fully come to terms with the wounds of its past or the persistence of those wounds in the present.

Morrison's deep understanding of mythology and history as they intersect with the African American experience reaches a pinnacle in *Song of Solomon*. Here again are two childhood friends who grow apart – Milkman Dead and Guitar Bains – and they follow the pattern of class division that permeates Morrison's earlier work. The decided emphasis here is on genealogy, though, as Milkman eventually builds his identity on stories of his ancestral past rather than on the petty tribulations of his present. The story opens with an attempt at flight that is actually a suicide, echoing the National Suicide Day ritual in *Sula*. An insurance agent named Robert Smith jumps from the roof of Mercy Hospital the day before the protagonist, Milkman, becomes the first black baby to be born there. Milkman's life is connected to the fate of Robert Smith in myriad ways. Symbolically, Milkman is driven by a desire to fly, coupled with the knowledge that he can't. He spends his youth passively, opting for an unfulfilled existence devoid of deeper meaning. His nickname derives from his mother Ruth's insistence that he submit to breastfeeding at an inappropriate age. When they are caught during one of these nursing sessions, his mother stands abruptly, dropping Milkman to the ground, "confirming for him what he had begun to suspect – that these afternoons were strange and wrong" (14). His name is redolent with shame and produces in him a lifelong confusion between bodily gratification and love.

This is only the first of many incidents of twisted love in the novel. Ruth had insisted that her father kiss her goodnight on the lips when she was too old for such treatment, and his rejection of her created a void that stunts her emotional growth and infects her marriage to Milkman's father Macon. Macon and Ruth's sex life is unhealthy, and their inability to love properly is transferred to Milkman when he becomes romantically involved with his second cousin Hagar. When Hagar feels used and neglected by him, she seeks to win him back by attempting (and failing) to murder him every month. This pathetic cry for attention is brought about by neglect, as Milkman (like his parents) is selfish in his attempts to love and unwilling to separate his own gratification from others' needs.

The sickness of romantic love has its parallel in the troubled friendship of Milkman and Guitar, but also operates as a metaphor for troubled race relations in *Song of Solomon*. The main events of the book take place around the most catastrophic events of the Civil Rights era, notably the murder of Emmett Till (discussed in Chapter Six) and the bombing of the Birmingham church that killed four young black girls. In response to such events, Guitar becomes involved in a secretive group called "The Seven Days." Their mission is to seek revenge against the white race whenever there is a race-based murder. The Seven Days are sworn to secrecy and celibacy. They randomly select a white victim to murder on the same day of the week the crime against a black person occurred. Guitar explains the philosophy of the group to Milkman who reacts with horror, saying "There's no love in it." Guitar reacts strongly: "No love? Didn't you hear me? What I'm doing ain't about hating white people. It's about loving us. About loving you. My whole life is love" (159). This justification of violence through love is consistent with the rest of the novel, such as Hagar's feeble attempts to kill Milkman. There is a deep sickness at the heart of this community that affects virtually all of its characters except one: Milkman's Aunt Pilate.

Pilate is Milkman's spiritual guide away from the materialistic values of his father. Macon is consumed by his twisted code: "Own things. And let the things you own own other things. Then you'll own yourself and other people too" (55). He gives this advice to Milkman without realizing that it evokes slavery. Pilate, by contrast, is motivated by generosity, by catering to the needs of others. Macon forbids Milkman from going to Pilate's house because he associates it with sin, disorder, and a lack of respectability, but Milkman disobeys his father and develops with Pilate the only healthy relationship he has ever had. Both Pilate and Macon witnessed their father being shot for attempting to stay on his land in the South, and they unintentionally murder a man afterwards, a man in possession of gold. Macon believes that this money can replace his father, but Pilate honors her father's life by carrying his bones with her wherever she moves, indicating their separate set of values in the material and spiritual worlds, respectively. The second half of the novel has Milkman attempting to find the missing gold his father yearns for, but he is actually in search of his origins.

In his journey south, Milkman must eventually shed his father's materialistic values in favor of the more spiritual values professed by Pilate. On his journey, he has to learn how to listen to others and to trust them. He undergoes stereotypical rituals of manhood – fighting and hunting – and has a revelatory moment in the woods during the hunt, listening to the communication between men and dogs: "It was all language....No, it was not language; it was what there was before language. Before things were written down" (278). During his journey Milkman is not able to rely on signs or written language and instead has to listen carefully to stories and to develop his own instincts.

This revelation in the woods sets up the novel's conclusion in which Milkman pieces together the legend of his people from a series of clues in the stories he hears as well as a children's playground song. The Solomon of the title is his ancestor, one of a tribe of Africans who escaped slavery by flying, according to legend. Milkman and Pilate travel back to their ancestral homeland to bury Pilate's father's remains as a way of reconciling with a troubled past. This journey sets up one final confrontation between Milkman and Guitar, with Pilate becoming another sacrificial victim. Milkman holds Pilate up as the ideal woman, the heaven-going counterpart to his newly discovered soul: "Without ever leaving the ground, she could fly. 'There must be another one like you,' he whispered to her" (336). Despite the ambiguity of the final confrontation between Milkman and Guitar, it is clear that the novel's impulses are toward growth and transcendence. The sick society that Milkman is born into is capable of some kind of redemption, but only through the cooperative efforts of individuals.

Song of Solomon clearly announced Morrison as a truly major author, but it was the publication of her fifth novel, *Beloved*, that finally made her a household name. *Beloved* won the Pulitzer Prize and was named the best work of American fiction published in the past twenty-five years by *The New York Times Book Review* in 2006. The novel continues the impulse of the era to reexamine history and to confront the ghosts of slavery, not to bury them properly, but to suggest that they still walk among us.

Beloved was inspired by the infamous historical story of a slave named Margaret Garner who, after escaping slavery with her family, murdered her own child rather than allowing her to return to slavery. Garner's story reveals the limited choices of slaves and draws attention to the desperation that ranks violent death above a life under slavery. Although slavery is the context, the novel also develops themes found in Morrison's earlier works: the challenges of familial love, the costs of separate gender spheres, the importance of place and naming to identity, and the interplay of memory and history, to name a few. The story's heroine, Sethe, had four children, including her daughter Beloved, whom she murders. Her two sons ran away; her daughter Denver remains with her. The novel opens seventeen years after the bloody event with Sethe still shocked by what she has done. Paul D, who had known her on the plantation, returns to her for love and companionship, but discovers that her house is haunted. The invisible ghost becomes incarnate as a young girl enters their house and attempts to drive the fragile family apart by demanding the affection of each of them.

As in *Song of Solomon*, there are many ancillary characters in *Beloved* who are an integral part of the story, notably Sethe's mother-in-law, Baby Suggs, who helps escaped slaves by conducting spiritual services in a church-in-nature known as "the clearing," and the antagonist, Schoolteacher, a white man who conducts pseudo-scientific experiments on Sethe to prove his theory that slaves are closer to animals than to people. The horrors of slavery are manifold, but the breaking point for Sethe is when Schoolteacher allows his nephews to nurse from her breasts, stealing milk intended for her own child.

Sethe's challenge is twofold: to heal, and to assemble the fragments of the past that slavery has scattered. As in *Song of Solomon*, telling the truth by piecing together bits of a story from various sources is in fact what leads to healing. The novel opens with Sethe's declaration of her physical and psychological pain; she tells Paul D, "I got a tree on my back and a haint in my house, and nothing in between but the daughter I am holding in my arms" (18). The tree on her back, part of the tree imagery that permeates the novel, is scar tissue caused by the whippings she received as a slave. The "haint" is the ghost of Beloved, a spirit described as "spiteful" in the novel's opening line, and "not evil, just sad" by Sethe (1, 10). The daughter is Denver, Sethe's only remaining child, who is socially isolated as a result of her mother's overprotection. Paul D immediately tries to drive out the spirit and to heal Sethe's scarred back by making love to her, but the gesture actually summons the ghost of Beloved.

The ghost, "a fully dressed woman," crawls out of the water, suggesting not only childbirth, but a reincarnation of the slaves who died by falling or jumping overboard during the leg of slave transport known as the "middle passage" (60). (The novel's epigraph, "*Sixty Million and more*," includes not only the staggering number of slaves brought to the New World, but details those who died during transport). The introduction of this stranger destroys any hope for a harmonious domestic future. Sethe becomes so smitten with Beloved, so intent on nurturing her and spending time with her to atone for her crime, that her love quickly turns to an unhealthy obsession. After initially wanting to start a new family with Sethe, Paul D observes, "For a used-to-be-slave woman to love anything that much was dangerous, especially if it was her children she had settled on to love" and later develops this idea: "unless carefree, motherlove was a killer" (54, 155). Sethe, needless to say, is incapable of carefree love. For Denver, Beloved becomes her first playmate, though it is clear that Beloved is more of a parasite, feeding off the information Denver has of the past: "she anticipated the questions by giving blood to the scraps her mother and grandmother had told her....Denver nursing Beloved's interest like a lover whose pleasure was to overfeed the loved" (92). Paul D, whose first response to the ghost of Beloved is the stereotypically masculine one of driving it out with a display of violence, suffers by burying his richest emotions in a metaphorical tin box in his chest. Beloved seduces him, causing him to confront his past more deeply, and simultaneously drawing him away from Sethe. The rift between them widens considerably when Paul D learns the truth of what Sethe did to her infant girl. He tells her, "Your love is too thick" to which she replies, "Thin love ain't love at all" (193, 194). He tells her that her actions were wrong, and punctuates his judgment with the statement, "You got two feet, Sethe, not four" (194). In doing so, he evokes the experiments that Schoolteacher conducted in which he separates Sethe's human characteristics from her animal characteristics. The budding love they had is all but destroyed at this moment, and the two retreat from one another.

It takes the intervention of the community to rescue Denver, Sethe, and Paul D from eternal isolation. The character who helped to ferry slaves to freedom, Stamp Paid, is the one who originally told Paul D that Sethe murdered Beloved, but he is also the one who lifts Paul D from despair, arguing that Sethe deserves his compassion: "She ain't crazy. She love those children. She was trying to out-hurt the hurter" (276). Paul D asks, "How much is a nigger supposed to take?" and Stamp Paid replies, "All he can" (277). This advice seems ironic in a novel containing multiple instances of black slaves and ex-slaves who are pushed to the point where they can't take any more, but it connotes survival, the first step to healing and strengthening. Denver finally breaks the cycle of unhealthy love that has dominated her household, realizing, "She would have to leave the yard; step off the edge of the world, leave the two behind and go ask somebody for help" (286). The women that Denver finds understand that Beloved is destroying her mother, which is no way to atone for Sethe's destruction of her daughter. They intervene, and drive Beloved back into the woods from where she came. After the true exorcism of Beloved, Paul D finds it safe to return, to convince Sethe of her own self-worth and to allow for their mutual growth along with Denver's long-delayed maturity. Their love story, such as it is, is filled with the violent intervention of the past in the form of Beloved. This violence is necessary for healing. When Sethe initially escaped slavery, pregnant with Denver, a white woman massaged her damaged, swollen feet and legs, bringing tears to Sethe's eyes; she says, "It's gonna hurt....Anything dead coming back to life hurts" (42). This maxim is a truth that underpins the novel and accounts for its broader theme: America's collective memory of slavery is painful and difficult to confront, but if healing is to happen – if scarred souls are to come back to life – that pain is inevitable. This pain is softened somewhat by the understanding that it is collective.

Black Women Writers after Morrison

This motif was clearly one of the inspirations for Gloria Naylor, the heir to the achievements of both Morrison and Walker. Naylor has been overshadowed by both of her mentors, but she has earned a place alongside them. Her gift is in developing characters within a specific setting, indicated by the titles of many of her works: *The Women of Brewster Place* (1982), *Linden Hills* (1985), *Bailey's Café* (1992), and *The Men of Brewster Place* (1998). These interrelated works also connect to *Mama Day* (1988), the pinnacle of her achievement, and a novel that certainly would have achieved more notoriety if it had been published any other time than in the wake of *Beloved*.

Naylor's debut novel, *The Women of Brewster Place*, is actually a series of seven related stories, most of them named after their female protagonists, all of whom live at Brewster Place, a dilapidated housing project on a dead-end street. The women of the novel are unique, but their stories share some common elements. Notably, they are all "fallen" women whose sexual activity often leads to pregnancy. The challenges of raising their children on their own provide the novel's rising tension, leading to some grotesque episodes such as a rat biting one baby in a crib, or a neglected child dying when she sticks a knife into an electrical socket. Frequently, these women are exiled from their families, providing more tension as they struggle with independence. One has come to Brewster Place to get away from her mother's bourgeois ways as she participates in a familiar revolution. She screams at her mother that she is "Trying to be proud of my heritage and the fact that I was of African descent....I'd rather be dead than be like you – a white man's nigger who's ashamed of being black!" (85). Her mother retorts: "I am alive because of the blood of proud people who never scraped or begged or apologized for what they were. They lived asking only one thing of this world – to be allowed to be. And I learned through the blood of these people that black isn't beautiful and it isn't ugly – black is!" (86). The tensions between dreams and reality that fuel the novel come to a head here, and aren't easily resolved. The women of Brewster Place derive their strength not from escaping the sometimes unpleasant facts of their lives, but from learning how to cope with them. *Linden Hills* represents a more troubled allegory, with direct parallels to Dante's *Inferno*, as materialistic black women attempt to escape from their own histories and wind up in a kind of hell.

The very definite locations of these novels give way to the no-place of *Mama Day*, an island called Willow Springs that is in no state as it belongs to neither Georgia nor South Carolina. The paratextual elements at the beginning of the novel include a map and a family tree, indicating the setting's separateness from America (in the direction of Africa) and the importance of genealogy. The story of the star-crossed lovers Cocoa and George in the present connects to the history of Sapphira Wade, a slave brought to the island who became free before the Civil War. Employing the mode of magical realism, Naylor encourages the reader to believe that which Western, patriarchal culture deems "irrational" just as *Beloved* causes the reader to suppose that ghosts are not just psychological phenomena. The figure of the conjure woman, made powerful through African-based belief systems, is at the heart of *Mama Day*. The title character, Cocoa's grandmother, has the ability to alter the weather, among other powers. The reader is initially fooled into thinking that the novel is a love story between George and Cocoa, but its impulses are toward Cocoa's own growth, not through romance or through appropriating George's mainland/capitalist values, but through returning to her ancestral past through gaining the ability to narrate it. *Mama Day* is an important contribution to the general trends of the 1970s and 1980s: the increasing volume of women's voices, a turn toward folklore and oral history as a potent source of wisdom, and a fascination with genealogy and family history.

A noteworthy variation on this theme is represented in the novels of Octavia Butler, whose work has been defined as speculative fiction, involving genetic mutation, immortality, interplanetary travel, and vampires. Her most famous work, the 1979 novel *Kindred*, might more accurately be described as paranormal fiction, and it is consistent with much of the fiction discussed in this chapter in its interest in history, particularly the history of slavery. *Kindred* is the story of Dana Franklin, a writer in her twenties living in contemporary (1976) California. On her birthday she experiences a dizzy spell and wakes up in Maryland in the early nineteenth century. This is the first of a series of journeys she takes, against her will, to the antebellum South. In each case she is summoned by the son of a plantation owner, Rufus Weylin, who seems to need her at times of crisis. In Dana's first journey, Rufus is a young child drowning in a river; in the second he is slightly older and has started a fire in his house. Whenever Dana returns to 1976, very little time has elapsed in the present, but her time in the past lasts days or months, and she is forced to assimilate to the ways of slavery, frequently through brutal beatings. When she fears for her life, she is transported back to the present, but she becomes less fearful with each visit, ironically increasing the length of time she spends as a slave.

The plot becomes even more complex when Kevin, Dana's white husband, accompanies her on a journey to the past because he happens to be holding her hand when she is transported. She returns to the present alone, and when she finally finds him on her next visit, he has aged considerably. He finds the present disorienting upon his return and their relationship sours. With each journey to the past, Dana finds it easier to act like a slave, putting up with verbal and physical abuse and acting submissive, especially to the increasingly manipulative Rufus. Her motivation for enduring this abuse stems from the fact that Rufus is her family: she knows her genealogy well and understands that Rufus and his slave Alice will eventually have a child named Hagar who is an important figure in her family tree. Essentially, she must preserve the despicable Rufus and ensure the wellbeing of Alice in order to secure her own existence.

Dana's confrontation with the past provides much psychological intrigue. She is an anachronism: an enlightened, educated, and opinionated black woman, thrust into a time when all of these qualities are liabilities. She speaks and dresses differently from everyone she encounters. She is only partly able to gain power within this world, though. She initially bristles at Rufus's use of the word "nigger," but submits to his demand that she call him "master" in front of others so as not to arouse suspicion. She knows a great deal about slavery from books, but this knowledge does not prevent her from having to witness first-hand – and even to experience – all of the horrors of slavery. She returns to the present with physical wounds as well as psychological ones. She surprises herself by developing empathy for the people she encounters in the past – including the underhanded Rufus – and yet she is alienated from her fellow slaves who repeatedly accuse her of being "more white than black" (224).

Kindred is a rich novel in terms of the number of subjects it takes on and the original way it approaches them. One of those subjects is history itself. At one point Dana tries to convince Rufus that slavery will end sooner than he thinks, and she shows him a book she has brought from the present. He declares it "abolitionist trash." She tells him, "That's history. It happened whether it offends you or not. Quite a bit of it offends me, but there's nothing I can do about it" (140). Dana understands that history is factual, and yet the mysterious circumstances that lead her into the past force her to confront it personally so that it cannot become abstract. Dana's violent confrontations with the past encourage the reader to consider slavery from a new vantage point. There are dangers to romanticizing anything about the period: her husband Kevin, for instance, is seduced by the past without realizing initially his position of privilege; he says, "This could be a great time to live in…I keep thinking what an experience it would be to stay in it – go West and watch the building of the country, see how much of the Old West mythology is true" (97). This is the beginning of the schism that threatens to drive Kevin and Dana apart. Their relationship, whether they want to admit it or not, is troubled by slavery, just as Dana's mixed-race identity renders her unstable in ways she has not come to terms with. Although the reasons behind her involuntary journeys to the past are not spelled out, it is clear, as in *Beloved*, that survival and true growth cannot occur when suffering is ignored.

African American poetry from this period has similar thematic concerns. In 1987 Rita Dove became the second African American to win the Pulitzer Prize for poetry (after Gwendolyn Brooks). She was also the first African American to be named Poet Laureate of the United States. Although much of Dove's poetry is lyrical, a significant portion of it, consistent with much African American literature from the late twentieth century, focuses on history. The third section of her first volume of poetry, *The Yellow House on the Corner* (1980), initiates this trend as Dove focuses on historical figures from the era of slavery, including David Walker, whose famous 1829 appeal was a landmark work of abolitionist literature. The fragility of his figure at the end of the poem raises poignant questions about historical significance: "A month – / his person (is that all?) found face-down / in the doorway at Brattle Street, / his frame slighter than friends remembered" (28–31). Like Morrison, Dove does not look away from the physical or psychological horrors of slavery, but attempts to contextualize them by putting voices in conversation within her verse.

Dove's Pulitzer Prize-winning collection *Thomas and Beulah* (1986) is also based in family history, as it tells the story of the poet's maternal grandparents. The first section, "Mandolin," focuses on her grandfather and the second, "Canary in Bloom," on her grandmother. It is both a family story and a collective story, like Alex Haley's *Roots* on a more concentrated scale, in poetic language. Thomas migrates from the South with a mandolin, landing in Akron, Ohio in 1921, and thus is part of the Great Migration. *Thomas and Beulah*'s primary focus is narration, as it tells the story of these two lovers, and its voice is restrained, allowing the poet to build characters through focusing on images, such as a mandolin, cars, scenes from factories and other workplaces, and the choir in the local AME (African Methodist Episcopal) church. It ends with a chronology, containing significant events in the family history as well as in national history (such as the March on Washington, which occurs just after Thomas's death). The collection is impressionistic, as if the poet were thumbing through a family photo album, and yet the overall effect is to bring the reader deeper into the somewhat unremarkable lives of Dove's ancestors. There is a fascinating interplay of the two stories as certain moments are told from each perspective. For instance, in "Courtship," in Thomas's section, he is described this way: "King of the Crawfish / in his yellow scarf, / mandolin belly pressed tight / to his hounds-tooth vest –" (12–15). In "Courtship, Diligence," in Beulah's section, we see him from her perspective: "A yellow scarf runs through his fingers / as if it were melting....She'd much prefer a pianola [to his mandolin]....Not that scarf, bright as butter. / Not his hands, cool as dimes" (1–2, 10, 12–13). Their lives are full of such discrepancies, and Dove neither romanticizes them nor the history that surrounds them.

The poet Ai (whose name means "love" in Japanese) marks the beginning of a trend toward more expansive definitions or understandings of ethnic identification in late-twentieth- and early-twenty-first-century America. Ai's poems are often dramatic monologues. The speakers are sometimes familiar historical figures or those close to them: the reader encounters the perspectives of, for example, John and Bobby Kennedy, General Custer, the provocative 1950s comedian Lenny Bruce, the daughter of Marilyn Monroe, the legendary labor leader Jimmy Hoffa, and the anti-communist senator Joseph McCarthy. These characters are all public figures who died prematurely, and they collectively represent Ai's empathetic stance and her interest in the people who have both created history and been defined by it. She is also concerned with the disenfranchised who have been forgotten by history, and when she does take the collective African American experience as her subject, the poetic result is sometimes jarring, as in her poem about the Rodney King riots, "Riot Act, April 29, 1992," from her 1993 collection entitled *Greed*. She assumes the voice of one of the many looters who took to the streets of Los Angeles following the acquittal of white police officers who were videotaped beating King, a defenseless black motorist. Rather than an act of empowerment or civil disobedience, this riot is depicted as a desperate act by those who do not understand the true differences between the fantasies they see on television and the reality they live in; the speaker says, "I'm going out and get something. / I don't know what. / I don't care" (1–3). This desire for material gain for its own sake is born not of a desire for freedom or empowerment, but of a simple misunderstanding of what is valuable in the world, which breeds the nihilism that had devastating effects on black urban communities in the 1980s; the speaker says, "if I destroy myself / and my neighborhood / 'ain't nobody's business, if I do'" (49–51). The final line, an echo from an old Jamaican folk song, strikes a sinister note here as the speaker's disregard for himself and his community indicates the rise of black-on-black crime in the late twentieth century.

Black Drama of the 1980s: Representing History Anew

The concern with history also affected African American drama in the 1980s. Charles Fuller won the Pulitzer Prize for drama for *A Soldier's Play* (1981) about a soldier's murder outside a segregated army camp in Louisiana. Fuller's triumph led to the grand achievement of August Wilson, who penned a ten-play cycle chronicling the African American experience of the twentieth century, decade by decade, including two that won the Pulitzer Prize: *Fences* (1987) and *The Piano Lesson* (1990). Nearly all of these plays are set in Pittsburgh, providing a continuity of spatial setting in contrast with the variability of historical setting. (The exception is *Ma Rainey's Black Bottom* [1984], set in Chicago). These plays were not published in chronological order according to the decades they depict, but they may productively be read that way, beginning with *Gem of the Ocean* (2003) and ending with *Radio Golf* (2005). Characters and character types recur, and many themes replay throughout the cycle. They may also be read individually: each stands alone as a complete play and a fair inroad into Wilson's work. One excellent starting point is the first play from the cycle that won the Pulitzer Prize, *Fences*, which economically presents the concerns of the cycle overall: frustration over the disparity between the ostensible American Dream and the African American experience, concern over the disconnections between the African past (or the past in general) and the present, and finally the potential for a specific form of African American cultural expression – the blues – to address the wounds laid open by the first two concerns.

Wilson was initially influenced by Amiri Baraka, though his plays resemble realistic drama to a much greater degree than Baraka's do. But there is a revolutionary impulse at their core as Wilson shares with Baraka the belief that the theater is the proper place for African Americans to dramatize and examine their history, basing it largely in oral traditions. Wilson's characters tell stories, sometimes in lengthy monologues, and sometimes building upon or even contradicting other versions of stories. He also borrows from the Black Arts Movement a reliance on symbols and recurrent motifs as a way of both determining and destabilizing meaning on stage. The title of *Fences* calls attention to its central symbol.

Fences, which takes place in the 1950s, tells the story of Troy Maxson, an ex-convict, ex-baseball great, and well-meaning yet terrifying patriarch who builds a fence around his shabby brick house in Pittsburgh. He also builds psychological fences that separate him from the ones he loves, out of impulses to contain his chaotic experience and to protect his fragile core. Troy's flaws are evident, but the audience is also likely to feel for him because his well-defined dreams seem to be attainable. Still, he is not kind to his wife, his friends, or his sons. His brother Gabriel – delusional after suffering from post-traumatic stress following his stint in the Second World War – is a particularly pathetic victim of Troy's manipulative ways. Troy takes his brother's meager military pension and uses it to make ends meet. By the end of the play Troy has committed Gabriel to a mental hospital. He has also been unfaithful to his wife and unsupportive of his two sons.

On a very basic level, *Fences* can be viewed as a family drama, perhaps most directly in the tradition of Hansberry's *A Raisin in the Sun* (1959) (see Chapter Five) in which the pressures of discrimination weigh on the internal family dynamic. Much of the play is concerned with material ethics, such as the value of honest work and the importance of paying what you owe. (Troy constantly browbeats his son Lyons, for instance, for only coming around to borrow money when in fact Lyons has returned to repay his father). The value of familial responsibility is under scrutiny in this play. Troy feels as though he has fulfilled his duty to his son Cory, who aspires to play football – a dream that Troy denies, even while exaggerating his own thwarted dreams to play baseball. When Cory asks him, "How come you ain't never liked me?" Troy goes on a tirade: "Don't you eat every day?....Got a roof over your head....Got clothes on your back....Like you? I go out of here every morning...bust my butt...putting up with them crackers every day...cause I like you? You about the biggest fool I ever saw. It's my job. It's my responsibility! You understand that? A man got to take care of his family" (37–38). The cool nobility of this position is one-dimensional, and Troy seems oblivious to the non-material needs of his family. Cory, for instance, needs the support of his father to nurture his dreams, but Troy insists that his son work a wage job instead of speaking to a football recruiter. Troy also does not honor his wife's need for a faithful partner who loves her and accepts her. She recognizes the pathos of his situation as a man who cannot adapt to a world in which opportunities are opening up; she tells him, "The world's changing around you and you can't even see it" (40). When he replies, "I do the best I can do," the audience can only partly agree (40). It's true that Troy tries hard, but he is in fact fenced in by the past, and by a worldview that bluntly substitutes control over one's small environment for true power.

Following Troy's death, the family gathers for his funeral and the play posits a catharsis that comes not from any false eulogies, but rather from the blues. Cory and Raynell, Troy's illegitimate daughter, sing the blues song that Troy had always sung, memorializing his life but also honoring the tradition that underpinned it. It is a song about a faithful dog named, fittingly, "Old Blue," who "laid down and died like a man" (99). The dog is praised for his goodness and moves on to a blissful afterlife, presumably in contrast with the unfaithful and not always good protagonist of the play. Nevertheless, the blues help to purge the demons of Troy's life. Gabriel, Troy's mentally challenged brother who believes that he is the angel Gabriel from the Bible, attempts to blow a trumpet to announce Troy's arrival in heaven, but the instrument lacks a mouthpiece and produces no sound. The final stage directions read, "*There is a weight of impossible description that falls away and leaves him bare and exposed to a frightful realization. It is a trauma that a sane and normal mind would be unable to withstand. He begins to dance. A slow, strange dance, eerie and life-giving. A dance of atavistic signature and ritual"* (101). This dance, following the spontaneous rendition of Troy's blues song, offers the possibility of connection to African rituals, the source of comfort that predates Troy's materialistic dreams or Gabriel's Christian definitions of an afterlife. The deep roots of the Maxson family tree are evoked for their possible healing powers for future generations.

In a different way, a look back to literary history produced one of the first overt parodies of the African American literary tradition as the irreverent genius George C. Wolfe penned *The Colored Museum* (1986), a parody that represents a newfound confidence to question the sacred achievements in African American drama. Wilson's plays have a basically serious intent, even though they may be punctuated by light moments of comic relief. *The Colored Museum* also has a serious intent, but it is achieved through wildly comic and frequently uncomfortable satire. In the mode of Ishmael Reed, Wolfe curates a museum of myths, legends, and stereotypes that blend the past and the present to formulate a critique, not only of culture, but also of how we approach culture. The audience of the play is encouraged to participate, sometimes as a way of demonstrating how the very real and sometimes painful experiences of African Americans are converted into cheap entertainment. It is a play intended to push the buttons of anyone who feels they have a grasp on African American culture, history, and literary history.

The Colored Museum takes the form of a number of vignettes, beginning with "Git on Board," which uses the conceit of an airplane ride to evoke the "middle passage" of slavery. A character dressed as a flight attendant tries to control the behavior of the audience, which becomes more difficult as the plane passes through a time warp with considerable turbulence; she implores, "Stop playing those drums!....You can't turn back the clock! (*To the audience.*) Repeat after me, I don't hear any drums! I will not rebel!" (5). Captive in their seats watching a performance, the audience is limited by social conventions and decorum at a theater. Wolfe uses this tactic to increase the audience's discomfort and to make them realize their possible complicity in the perpetuation of African American stereotypes. The next vignette has a character named Aunt Ethel in a parody of a cooking show, singing in a loud gut-bucket blues such lines as, "NOW YA STIR IN SOME PRE-OCCUPATION / WITH THE TEXTURE OF YOUR HAIR" and "AND NOW A WHOLE LOT OF HUMOR / SALTY LANGUAGE, MIXED WITH SADNESS" (7, 8). At the end she tells the audience, "YOU HAVE BAKED / BAKED YOURSELF A BATCH OF NEGROES" and adds, "But don't ask me what to do with 'em now that got 'em, 'cause child, that's your problem" (8).

Perhaps the most uncomfortable part of the play is the vignette entitled "The Last Mama-on-the-Couch Play," as it satirizes two major works from the tradition of African American drama: Hansberry's *A Raisin in the Sun* and Shange's *for colored girls who have considered suicide* (discussed in Chapter Five and this chapter, respectively). There are also echoes of Baldwin's *Blues for Mister Charlie* (1964) (discussed in Chapter Six), and Wilson's plays might have been considered part of the subject of this parody, but many were published after Wolfe's play. In this domestic drama, an onstage narrator describes Walter-Lee-Beau-Willie in this way: "His brow is heavy from three hundred years of oppression" (24). His mother rules this space, though, and feels compelled to beat him down for his blasphemy against God, and also because he refuses to wipe his feet. His wife, "The Lady in Plaid," enters speaking English that is so formal as to be stilted and archaic. The narrator gives each of them an award for their performances, but Walter-Lee-Beau-Willie is summoned to a window by the voice of a man that says, "You have been convicted of overacting. Come out with your hands up" (29). He is shot, but revives onstage after Mama sings a gospel song that begins, "OH WHY COULDN'T HE / BE BORN / INTO A SHOW WITH LOTS OF SINGING / AND DANCING" (29). Clearly Wolfe is not attempting to destroy the idols of his tradition so much as to use them to make space for new traditions to flourish.

Toward the Twenty-First Century

The trend in African American literature from 1970–2000 was to focus on history as a way of situating, reimagining, and revising the black experience. Some of the writers discussed in this chapter (such as Toni Morrison and Alice Walker) continue to write, but their later works do not have the same cultural impact or cachet as their novels of the 1970s and 1980s. Many of the trends they initiated have continued, though, such as a focus on personal or familial stories to indicate wide-ranging cultural/historical trends. Some writers who became famous at the same time Morrison and Walker rose to prominence can be seen as heirs to both the Black Arts Movement and the school of writing that situates family stories against a broader cultural background. John Edgar Wideman is one such author. An enduring writer who pushes the boundaries of genre to produce original, densely packed, and challenging works, Wideman is among the most important black literary authors alive. At the same time, he has not been uniformly praised or widely read, partly because his work resists easy classification.

Critics tend to divide Wideman's career into two phases, the first consisting of a trio of early novels published between 1967 and 1973 and the second beginning in 1981, with the publication of the renowned *Homewood Trilogy*. During the eight-year hiatus between these phases Wideman sought to reflect on his career path and his aesthetic in order to reconnect with his black identity. The first phase was marked by a perhaps unconscious flight from the African American literary tradition. As a scholarship student at an Ivy League university (The University of Pennsylvania) who won a Rhodes Scholarship and studied at Oxford, Wideman was influenced initially by the masterpieces of white modernist literature. He had moved a long way, literally and culturally, from his upbringing in blighted 1960s Pittsburgh. He wrote his thesis at Oxford on the eighteenth-century novel and returned to Penn to become the university's first tenured black professor in 1974. When a group of black students asked him to teach a course in African American literature, he replied that he didn't know the field, and their crestfallen response caused him to reform the trajectory of his writing. His works published after 1981 have allowed him to develop a unique voice and to invent new genres. He can be regarded as a bridge between the street-savvy Black Arts Movement writers and the next genera-tion of formally educated authors who allude widely to a vast array of historical, cultural, and literary sources.

Brothers and Keepers (1984) is a work of non-fiction that borrows techniques from Wideman's novels. It tells the story of Wideman's brother, Robby, who has been incarcerated since 1975 when he was involved in a botched robbery. At the time of its publication Wideman was an acclaimed novelist with an endowed pro-fessorship, and the book is an inquiry into the startlingly divergent paths he and his brother have taken. Critics debate whether the work more closely represents a biography or an autobiography, and the way Wideman blends his own voice – highly educated, consistently analytical – with that of his brother, which is marked by street slang, intensifies this blurriness. The title alludes to the biblical story of Cain and Abel, where Cain, having murdered his brother, answers a question about Abel's whereabouts, "Am I to be my brother's keeper?" Wideman clearly experiences guilt about his own success relative to his brother's tragic life, even if he does not feel entirely responsible. The title refers to African American identity (evoking the colloquial term "brothers") as well as literal brotherhood, weighed against the "keepers" of the jail – the enforcers of society's rules and norms who tend to be white. Incarceration has become a prominent subject for Wideman whose son Jacob has also served time in prison.

Central to *Brothers and Keepers,* and to virtually all of Wideman's works, is a deep examination of the workings of stories and their continued importance. He cri-tiques his first draft of *Brothers and Keepers,* faulting himself for editing his brother's story: "The problem with the first draft was my fear. I didn't let Robby speak for himself enough. I didn't have enough confidence in his words, his vision, his insights. I wanted to clean him up" (195). His 2002 work *Hoop Roots,* ostensibly about playground basketball, but actually about a host of subjects ranging from the death of Wideman's grandmother to the history of minstrelsy, is also based on storytelling. In both cases, these works are written in a digressive style. It takes patience and trust for readers of Wideman's works to believe that they will get the point of a given story, for his writing calls on readers to make connections that aren't immediate. His method is to add layer upon layer of context, and to associate freely between subjects that might not immediately seem related. His paragraphs and even sentences mirror this structure. His allusions are far-reaching, causing the reader to understand that any subject is never just about what it superficially seems to be about. This is how his enduring subject – the sometimes-frayed bonds between the members of poor, urban, African American families – connects to the other subjects that inform his work.

The Homewood Trilogy consists of three works published in quick succession: *Hiding Place* (1981), *Damballah* (1981), and *Sent for You Yesterday* (1983). "Home-wood" refers to the neighborhood in Pittsburgh where Wideman grew up, which is the setting of these works. The trilogy brings together a number of prominent trends in late-twentieth- and early-twenty-first-century black writing. The story of his brother Robby recurs in various forms throughout the trilogy in the guise of the character Tommy, and other autobiographical elements are evident as Wideman weaves an intergenerational tapestry, reinforcing the emphasis on ancestry and family history in the late twentieth century. The second volume, *Damballah*, contains "A Begat Chart" and a family tree. Together they provide a genealogy that maps the relationship between various characters. Oral storytelling is deliberately rendered into written literature in these three works as Wideman retells stories, allowing them to blend and recombine gracefully. The character Doot in *Sent for You Yesterday* is a version of Wideman himself who returns from a kind of intellectual exile to live in the Homewood community and to listen to the stories that both ground him and validate his identity. The older generation in Homewood is connected by these stories, and the younger generation, marked by alienation through either intellectual exile or incarceration, needs to hear them in order to feel grounded again.

Ernest J. Gaines's 1993 novel *A Lesson Before Dying* is a landmark work noteworthy for its treatment of religion, masculinity, and the ethics of the death sentence. Even though it is set in the segregated South in the 1940s, the novel has implications for contemporary readers. Its narrator, Grant Wiggins, is a conflicted schoolteacher in the South. It opens with a trial: a local youth named Jefferson is in the wrong place at the wrong time as two delinquents rob a liquor store and kill the owner. Jefferson, the only survivor, is convicted and sentenced to death. His defense attorney argues that there is no sense in capital punishment in this case because the defendant is subhuman; he argues, "I would just as soon put a hog in the electric chair as this" (8). Wiggins's charge, enforced by his aunt and by Jefferson's mother, is to restore some sense of dignity to Jefferson so that he can regard himself as a man before being executed. Part of Wiggins's dilemma is his lack of faith: in God, in justice, and in himself as a teacher or as a man more generally. He laments of his students, "Am I reaching them at all? They are acting exactly as the old men did earlier....Is it just a vicious circle? Am I doing anything?" (62). He initially approaches his task of restoring Jefferson's human dignity with both cynicism and apathy, and Jefferson responds similarly.

Wiggins's impulse is to flee the South and the demands being placed upon him by his aunt, Jefferson's mother, and his lover Vivian, but he remains and eventually effects a change both in Jefferson and himself. He does this by seeking to under-mine the very thinking that has led to white supremacy; he says, "A myth is an old lie that people believe in. White people believe that they're better than anyone else on earth – and that's a myth. The last thing they ever want is to see a black man stand, and think, and show that common humanity that is in us all. It would destroy their myth" (192). These words seem to get through to Jefferson, and they also ignite in Wiggins a spark of anger that leads to nothing more productive than a bar-room brawl, but he has at least tapped into the source of his own nihilism and ends the book with a stronger sense of purpose.

The fiction writer Edward P. Jones, though not prolific, has helped to push outward the boundaries of African American historical fiction established earlier by

Gaines, Haley, Wilson, and Morrison. His story collection *All Aunt Hagar's Children* (2006) focuses on the early-twentieth-century experience of black people in Washington, D.C., and his Pulitzer Prize-winning novel *The Known World* (2003) reexamines slavery, complicating binary notions of race and slavery by examining the relationships between a mixed-race slave owner named Henry Townsend and the slaves he owns. The novel is inventive and broad in scope: many characters' stories emanate from Townsend's unusual situation. The novel is grounded by a wealth of historical information such as census data, much of which Jones invented for artistic effect. Readers are likely to come away from *The Known World* asking important questions about the knowability of the past. There is no such thing as "the *story* of slavery," and our understanding of it depends upon the willingness of authors to continue to generate *stories* of slavery.

Conclusion

The preoccupation with history in the post-Black Arts Movement era is frequently an attempt to come to terms with the past, not to bury it and move on, but rather to exhume it, examine it, and find out how it can benefit artists in the present and the future. A term that became common in the 1970s and 1980s was "revisionist history," which can be seen as a way to correct the way that history has been recorded. Benefiting from the perspective of second-wave feminism, women in these decades were acutely aware of the absence of female voices and stories in the official histories of the past, and the proliferation of black women's voices in literature was not only a way to correct this omission, but to redirect the trajectory of African American literature for the future. The period after the Black Arts Movement involved a notable and important broadening of assumptions about what black literature should be. The emphasis on black empowerment and nation-building in the 1960s became a foundation for more truly diverse and individualized stories thereafter.

Suggestions for Further Reading

Bates, Gerri. *Alice Walker: A Critical Companion*. Westport, CT: Greenwood Press, 2005. Print.

Mitchell, Angelyn and Danille K. Taylor, eds. *The Cambridge Companion to African American Women's Literature*. Cambridge: Cambridge University Press, 2009. Print.

Simawe, Saadi A. *Black Orpheus: Music in African American Fiction from the Harlem Renaissance to Toni Morrison*. New York, NY: Garland, 2000. Print.

Tally, Justine, ed. *The Cambridge Companion to Toni Morrison*. Cambridge: Cambridge University Press, 2007. Print.

Wall, Cheryl A. *Worrying the Line: Black Women Writers, Lineage, and Literary Tradition*. Chapel Hill, NC: University of North Carolina Press, 2005. Print

Wilson, Charles E. *Gloria Naylor: A Critical Companion*. Westport, CT: Greenwood Press, 2001. Print.

8

TWENTY-FIRST-CENTURY WRITING

A Time of Reckoning

Although literature remains potent in contemporary America, its influence has been diminished by the Internet and by popular culture, especially film, television, and music. The last two decades of the twentieth century saw a number of black celebrities rise to superstardom. The rise of Oprah Winfrey as a media figure, businesswoman, and tastemaker was astounding and unprecedented, and continues to be: few contemporary figures match her cultural influence. Black athletes like Michael Jordan and Tiger Woods became ubiquitous for their product endorsements as much as for their athletic prowess. Spike Lee earned a place in the pantheon of great American filmmakers. This trend has continued in the first decades of the twenty-first century. Rap music crossed into the mainstream and hip-hop's most prominent power couple – Jay-Z and Beyoncé – are in the cultural stratosphere. And, of course, the United States elected and reelected its first black president, Barack Obama. The media advances and reinforces the perception that African Americans are no longer denied access to the American dream of prosperity.

These examples of black success tend to mask the harsh realities that continue to plague a high percentage of African Americans. In terms of income, education, and rates of incarceration, there is still a tremendous gap between black and white America. The deaths of a number of black citizens at the hands of white police officers have exacerbated tensions between those groups that have existed since the Civil Rights era (and well before). Contemporary black literature is troubled by the notion (or myth) that America is "post-racial:" that the scars of history have healed and that individuals fail or succeed entirely based on their own merit rather than by social factors related to race. Whether or not black writers are writing for or about an underclass, they often remain sensitive to the plight and existence of that population, perhaps as a way of complicating the narrative that the United States has finally moved past its racist ways into a harmonious, raceless future. At the same time, many contemporary black writers resist writing exclusively about the racial struggle for equality as it was expressed in earlier decades. Now, more than ever before, black writers demonstrate a willingness to write about any subject they wish.

Contemporary African American literature has grown in conjunction with a welcoming and active academic interest in it. The rise of Black Studies programs in the 1970s and 1980s brought forth prominent literary critics like Henry Louis Gates, Jr., Eleanor Traylor, Houston Baker, and Trudier Harris. Literary and cultural icons of earlier literary periods, such as Toni Morrison, Angela Davis, Ishmael Reed, and John Edgar Wideman, have landed positions at wealthy universities. Contemporary black writers tend to be highly educated and intellectual, exacerbating the class distinctions that trouble the world they sometimes write about. The same could be said about African American literary criticism, which took a turn toward the esoteric in the 1980s, along with literary studies more generally, as literary theory ushered in more sophisticated discourse (occasionally at the cost of clarity). Gates, one of the people who steered criticism in that direction, relates a humorous anecdote about a dense lecture he gave to undergraduates at Howard University. It met with silence. Finally a student asked a question: "Yeah, brother, all we want to know is, was Booker T. a Tom or not?" Gates was troubled over "the yawning chasm between our critical discourse and the traditions they discourse on" (*Loose Canons*, 20). The chasm seems to be widening.

Gates's anecdote revives essential questions: what is black literature and who are its various audiences? Kenneth Warren's provocatively titled study *What Was African American Literature?* (2011) argues that the circumstances that produced a body of recognizably African American literature have changed irrevocably, and he goes so far as to suggest that they changed long ago, more than a half-century prior to his study, at the end of the segregation era (from the late nineteenth century through to the 1950s). He writes:

> Whether African American writers of the segregation era acquiesced in or kicked against the label, they knew what was at stake in accepting or contesting their identification as Negro writers. By contrast, the entailments of being regarded or not being regarded as an African American writer at the present moment are comparatively less clear. My argument presumes, then, that African American literature can be treated as a historical designation.
>
> *(9)*

Part of Warren's project is to recenter the African American literary tradition rather than to declare it over, as the book's title implies. Warren believes that the word "literature" connotes more than just a collection of texts, and that black literature existed (pre-1954) to fight against the prevailing racism in America. In a desegregated America, the race of a book's author does not have the same set of connotations it once did; Warren writes, "there is no broadly useful social end served by viewing contemporary black writing as a collective undertaking" (116). The motivations behind the production of African American literature are as varied as the personalities and experiences of its authors, and the subjects they treat may no longer touch on racism, or race at all.

Warren's small book proved controversial, and has been only one of a number of revisions of the meaning and emphasis of black literature. The term "post-racial" has been both popular and unpopular at literary conferences in recent years. One of Amiri Baraka's final gestures before his death in 2014 in an essay entitled "A Post-Racial Anthology?" was to criticize *Angles of Ascent* (2013), a recent anthology of African American poetry edited by Charles Rowell and published by the venerable Norton; Baraka writes, "A sharp class distinction has arisen, producing a mini-class of Blacks who benefited most by the Civil Rights and Black Liberation Movements, thinking and acting as if our historic struggle has been won so that they can become as arrogant and ignorant as the worst examples of white America....This 'new American poetry' is mostly dull as a stick" (172). There is both discomfort with the idea that black literature has changed (or diminished in political intensity) over time and disagreement about whether it has. One thing is clear: that African American literature has become a less predictable and less coherent entity than it had been in any earlier period in history. It is less clear whether that fact is cause for celebration or lament.

Queer Black Writing in the Twenty-first Century

Although there have been gay black writers throughout the tradition, the politics of queer identity is a relatively new phenomenon. During the Harlem Renaissance, Richard Bruce Nugent was unusually candid in his rendering of same-sex desire, but other writers of that era (notably Countee Cullen and Langston Hughes) were closeted, and it would take some creative interpretation to discover evidence of the subject in their poems. James Baldwin wrote overtly of same-sex relationships, more often in his fiction than in his non-fiction, and made no secret of his homosexuality, but declined to ally himself with the gay rights movement when interviewers tried to get him to do so late in his career. As discussed in Chapter Six, he was the subject of a homophobic attack in Eldridge Cleaver's *Soul on Ice*, indicating that there was palpable discomfort with accepting the subject of homosexuality in black writing as recently as 1968. Rita Mae Brown, Alice Walker, Audre Lorde, and Michelle Cliff in the 1970s and 1980s represent four prominent black lesbian writers whose political commitments enhanced their creative work. Black gay writers of the twenty-first century owe a debt to these literary predecessors, but also to the entire gay rights movement that formed after the 1970 Stonewall Riots, the flourishing of activism in response to the AIDS epidemic, and the rise of Queer Theory which seeks to identify a number of trends, including the intersectionality of discrimination based on class, race, gender, and sexuality.

Brian Freeman's play *Civil Sex* (1999) is a clear example of such intersectionality. It centers on the Civil Rights leader Bayard Rustin, who was the principal architect of the 1963 March on Washington (where Martin Luther King, Jr. delivered his "I Have a Dream" speech) among many other important events during the Civil

Rights era. In Freeman's play, Rustin boasts about being arrested twenty-two times in twenty-four years, but one of those arrests was a source of embarrassment rather than testimony to his belief in racial equality. In 1953 Rustin was arrested for sex perversion in California, a euphemism for a homosexual act, which was against the law in most states at the time.

Freeman's play makes use of the passage of time to demonstrate how Rustin's sexuality was in fact a catalyst for his commitment to civil rights, not something that inhibited it, as some of his colleagues believed. Freeman bases his drama on a number of interviews he conducted in the 1990s with people who knew Rustin in the 1950s and 1960s. The play also includes a somewhat campy depiction of James Baldwin, as well as Malcolm X and public figures like A. Philip Randolph and Senator Strom Thurmond, who publicly attacked Rustin just before the March on Washington and dredged up his arrest for homosexuality as a way of defaming his character. Much of the play's effectiveness hinges on the evolution of attitudes toward homosexuality over the half-century between Rustin's arrest and the play's production. In one humorous scene, an African American couple from a popular middlebrow magazine from the 1950s called *Our World* lectures the audience on the topic of homosexuality, suggesting that black families can train their children to be heterosexual through their behavior: "Family rituals. Going to church on Sunday. Having at least one meal together each day. Add to these the warmth and security of a good home and you have a good start!" (124). Rustin's promiscuity is in marked contrast to this heterosexist bullying, and he comes across as someone whose confidence in his identity is linked to his accomplishments for civil rights. The play ends on a triumphant note as Rustin emerges in the 1980s at a gay pride event after a period of retreat, suggesting that his struggle for civil rights was not bounded by race.

The abbreviated career of the poet Essex Hemphill is another study in the intersection of black identity and other concerns, notably sexuality, but also poverty and gender. He is a relentless critic of stereotypical masculinity and the damage it is capable of doing to black communities. His lengthy poem "Heavy Breathing" (1992) showcases some of his main themes. In it, his blackness becomes "a rumpled black suit" (397) and "a scratchy black suit" (399), indicating not only an uncomfortable, ill-fitting garment, but one that can presumably be removed. His black identity isn't his only identity, in other words, and his gay identity presumably provides an alternate suit, though one that can also be scratchy and rumpled. The scenes in this powerful poem shift from very public ones to illicit, private, anonymous encounters between gay men. The poem is characterized by a fascinating interplay between the discourse of civil rights and the discourse of illicit homosexual encounters. As the poem builds in intensity the speaker links these two separate facets of identity through the act of "heavy breathing" – the breathlessness following the public struggle for racial equality and the private encounters he has with lovers. Both are ultimately dissatisfying as something seems missing in his life: "At the end of heavy breathing / the fire quickly diminishes" (404). The speaker notices a post-coital letdown that he also applies to the political struggle of the 1950s and 1960s.

He is concerned about something fundamental absent from each: "At the end of heavy breathing / who will be responsible / for the destruction of human love?" (405). He focuses on the failure of the promise of the Civil Rights era, "the dream deferred / is in a museum / under glass and guard" (408). The landscape around him is marked by destruction, including the devastation of AIDS, as well as violence, poverty, and drug use. "I'm not content / loving my Black life / without question," he states, concluding, "The dream of King / is incomplete" (407, 408). Linking troubled, underground gay encounters to this vision of a still-struggling black America, Hemphill makes crucial observations about the nature of discrimination in many forms, and he takes on these subjects with tremendous candor.

Randall Kenan's treatment of homoeroticism in fiction is subtler than Hemphill's. His short story collection *Let the Dead Bury Their Dead* (1992) garnered attention for its revival of black southern literature, as Kenan creates legends and tales with a strong oral component set in the fictional town of Tims Creek, North Carolina. The fantastic blends with reality in these tales in ways that evoke Chesnutt's tales from a century earlier. The title of the collection suggests that death is the main theme, particularly mysteries surrounding the dead who don't stay buried. But the collection also emphasizes same-sex desire and the way the townspeople of Tims Creek, unaccustomed to homosexuality, attempt to regulate it.

One particularly affecting story in the collection is "The Foundations of the Earth," which is framed by the story of Mrs. Maggie MacGowan Williams and her inner circle, including the local preacher, who are wondering why a man is plowing a nearby field on Sunday, a day reserved for rest and worship. Sitting with them is Maggie's "young, white, special guest," Gabriel, who doesn't understand why they care. The Reverend chides him for not realizing that the Lord's Day is sacred and speculates (correctly) that he was not raised with religion. We learn that Gabriel had been the lover of Maggie's grandson Edward who had died prematurely in a car accident. She had not known that Edward was gay until his death, and when she finds out and meets Gabriel, her response is violent: "Her anger was burning so intensely that she knew if she didn't get out she would tear his heart from his chest, his eyes from their sockets, his testicles from their sac" (57). She has a dream that night that makes her humble, that causes her to dress in bright colors for her grandson's funeral because "Edward would have liked it" (60), and finally to reach out to Gabriel physically and verbally to ask how he is coping with Edward's death.

In conservative Tims Creek, interracial relationships are uncommon. Homosexual relationships are unspeakable. Maggie's response to Gabriel is of supreme importance in a community resistant to change. She realizes that she is being called on to change her way of thinking, but it doesn't come easily. The issues of race and homosexuality intersect when Maggie asks Gabriel first if he wants to be normal ("I *am*. Normal," he replies emphatically), and then if it's hard being gay. Gabriel recalls a conversation with Edward: "He used to say it was harder being black in this country than gay. Gays can always pass for straight; but blacks can't always pass for white" (65). This response, and all of her interactions with Gabriel, cause her to realize that people should allow individual lives to exist without judgment, and without imposing regulations on others. When the Reverend confronts the man on the tractor at the end of the story about working on a Sunday, Maggie dissents and turns her frustration not to those who are different, but to those who enforce sameness. "When, Lord, oh when will we learn? Will we ever? *Respect*, she thought. Oh how complicated" (72). Kenan has written a biography of Baldwin intended for young readers, and edited a collection of Baldwin's uncollected writings. His fiction extends Baldwin's message, but in his own style and in a southern setting, with the same intensity Baldwin employed during a less tolerant era.

The Caribbean: African American Immigrant Writers

One recent trend in American literary studies is an understanding of writers in global rather than strictly national contexts. The move toward transatlantic studies in early American literature has complicated questions of citizenship and African American identity. Afro-Caribbean writers, even those writing in English, are not always considered part of the African American literary tradition. The Caribbean islands are not politically affiliated with the United States, but the cultural influence of the latter over the former, especially through tourism and television, has been increasingly profound, and the very existence of black people in the Caribbean is connected to the existence of black people in the United States through the history of chattel slavery and mercantile exchange.

Some Caribbean writers have immigrated to America, vexing the already unstable definition of whether or not the link between black Americans and the history of slavery in the United States is *essential* to the definition of African American identity. Put bluntly, are recent black immigrants to the United States "African American" in the same way the descendants of slaves are? (Barack Obama, whose mother was white and whose father was Kenyan, has provided a famous illustration of this debate). Three Afro-Caribbean immigrant writers rose to prominence in the 1980s: Michelle Cliff, Jamaica Kincaid, and Derek Walcott. Their separate concerns illustrate how complicated the subject of African American identity and its connection to the African diaspora has become.

Jamaica Kincaid renamed herself from her birth name (Elaine Potter Richardson) as a way of keeping herself associated with the Caribbean (though she was born in Antigua, not Jamaica). Her fiction builds upon fraught relationships, usually between daughters and their mothers and, simultaneously, islanders and their motherland. In her mid-twenties Kincaid moved to New York and was hired in a job typical for young, female immigrants from Caribbean islands: as nanny to a wealthy family. This experience informs much of her fiction, including her novella *Lucy* (1990).

Kincaid, like other contemporary writers discussed in this chapter, is difficult to categorize. Her pieces in *The New Yorker*, such as the frequently anthologized "Girl" (1978), do not resemble traditional fiction in their form or structure. But beyond questions of genre, her work ranges over a wide terrain of subject matter, some of which does not include the traditional topics of African American writing. Her concerns are sometimes more aligned with postcolonial thought, feminism, or aesthetics. Her best-known works are a coming-of-age novella (*Annie John* [1990]) and a searing cultural critique (*A Small Place* [1992]). The early sections of *Annie John* describe the protagonist's youth spent with her protective and domineering mother in Antigua. Annie's mother attempts to transmit heritage and culture to her daughter as they go through a trunk of her belongings, but, as symbolized by the way her mother feeds her – by pre-chewing bits of meat for her to eat – Annie is poised to reject this ancestral identity in favor of forging one of her own. Her journey to adulthood coincides with a literal journey to England, where her liberation and her opportunities to establish her identity are compromised by her realization of her native island's complex relationship to its own motherland. Her language and much of her culture is bound to English custom, and her difficult task is to blaze an individual path that frees her from both England and Antigua. *Lucy* depicts another journey, to the United States, in which the titular character seeks to identify herself apart from her family. She bitterly, and some might say unfairly, rejects the white matriarch of the family, Mariah, for whom she works, who makes the mistake of showing her a field of daffodils and extolling their beauty. Lucy, who had once been forced to recite a poem by Wordsworth about daffodils, associates the flowers with the oppression of her school years, and rejects Mariah's gesture: "I felt sorry that I had cast her beloved daffodils in a scene she had never considered, a scene of conquered and conquests….But nothing could change the fact that where she saw beautiful flowers I saw sorrow and bitterness" (30).

This anecdote is about the way individuals view the world based on divergent cultural perspectives. Kincaid's study *A Small Place* varies this theme by addressing the subject of tourism, asserting "the tourist is an ugly human being" (14). It is a broad indictment of bourgeois Americans and Europeans who frolic in the Caribbean sun, unaware of the history or current situation of many of the island's inhabitants. This critique is largely postcolonial, but it (and others like it) evokes the history of slavery that once fueled the Caribbean economy, just as it once fueled the economy of the United States prior to the Civil War. Books like *A Small Place* or John Edgar Wideman's *The Island: Martinique* (2003) link the history of slavery to current practices of economic exploitation that affect the African diaspora.

Like Kincaid, Jamaican-born Michelle Cliff immigrated to the United States. She was the long-term partner of feminist poet Adrienne Rich, who died in 2012. Cliff has described herself as a "political novelist" (Hoving, 2), though she has published a good deal of poetry and non-fiction in addition to fiction. Her best-known works are her first two novels (*Abeng* [1985] and *No Telephone to Heaven* [1987]) and her powerful long essay *If I Could Write This in Fire, I Would Write This in Fire* (1982). She shares with Kincaid and the younger Haitian novelist Edwidge Danticat (discussed below) the imperative to tell the untold stories of Caribbean history. She is attuned to the politics of language and how the gulf between the "King's English" and the Jamaican *patois* she learned as a youth reveals irreconcilable differences, if not outright animosity, between two strains of the culture that formed her. Describing Jamaica as "a place halfway between Africa and England" (vii), she sees her own writing as an in-between art, which is why *No Telephone to*

Heaven is written half in Standard English and half in Jamaican *patois*. Her concerns both echo those of writers in the African American tradition and indicate subtle differences: "To write as a complete Caribbean writer demands of us retracing the African part of ourselves, reclaiming as our own and as our subject a history sunk under the sea, or scattered as potash in the canefields, or gone to bush, or trapped within a class system notable for its rigidity and for its dependence on color strati-fication...It means re-creating the art forms of our ancestors and speaking in the *patois* forbidden us" (viii–ix). Her return to the politics of language, specifically her "forbidden" *patois*, highlights the complexity of the Afro-Caribbean writer who has immigrated to the United States, where different issues exist.

A key question to ask of these texts involves audience. Kincaid's publications in *The New Yorker* are not intended for an Antiguan audience, and although Cliff published some of her works in less mainstream venues such as *Home Girls* (a black/feminist collective), her major works were published by large American publishing houses, indicating that part of her political aim is to educate those who are not necessarily of her background. In *If I Could Write This in Fire...* she unpacks the complexity of her unique situation, drawing explicit comparisons between American slave plantations and Jamaican sugar mills, but also teasing out the differences between English and American influences on the Caribbean: traditional British colonialism in the form of rigid, disciplinary education as well as neo-colonialism in the form of tourism and the exportation of films and television. She is troubled by her own participation, as a light-skinned Jamaican, in the system of social stratification related to gradations of skin color. She carries Jamaica in her and cannot escape it, yet she doesn't fully romanticize her native land partly because she is aware of the way its tense cultural hybridity presents an unresolved conflict: "No matter how far I travel – how deep the ambivalence I feel about ever returning" (31). As her perspectives branched out from her first two novels, which reflect this ambivalence, her career has gone on to advance the project of highlighting moments of female resistance, including the life of abolitionist Mary Ellen Pleasant in her novel *Free Enterprise* (1993), a work inspired by the work of Toni Morrison, who is a major influence on Cliff.

The Nobel Prize-winning poet and playwright Derek Walcott was born on the small island of St. Lucia. Walcott lived in England and in Trinidad before moving to the United States in 1981. The intensity of his poetry derives from its attention to, and creation of, mythology. His 1990 epic poem *Omeros* (the Greek name for Homer) is his most notable accomplishment. Its primary intent is narrative: it tells the story of a St. Lucia village and its inhabitants who have Greek names like Achille, Helen, Philoctete, and Hector. It also involves the poet himself as he interjects passages about his own life experience in and around Boston. The poem travels across time and space, including Walcott's own experiences as well as an imagined journey on an eighteenth-century slave ship heading from Africa to the New World. The poem's scope is enormous, but part of its central interest comes from Walcott's examination of his own creative process as he conjures his native island and the history behind it from the vantage of "a Brookline of brick and leaf-shaded lanes" (170). His experiences in Boston have conditioned or even helped to create his grand vision:

> Passing the lamplit leaves I knew I was different
> from them as our skins were different in an empire
> that boasted about its hues, in a New England
>
> that had raked the leaves of the tribes into one fire
> on the lawn back of the carport.
>
> *(185)*

The poet invokes his own father, who appears before him in the posh seaside town of Marblehead, north of Boston, and gives him this advice:

> Once you have seen everything and gone everywhere,
> cherish our island for its green simplicities,
> enthrone yourself, if your sheet is a barber-chair,
>
> a sail leaving harbor and a sail coming in,
> the shadows of grape-leaves on sunlit verandahs
> made me content. The sea-swift vanishes in rain,
>
> and yet in its travelling all that the sea-swift does
> it does in a circular pattern. Remember that, son.
>
> *(187–188)*

This circular pattern that the poet's father describes has many resonances: not only the pattern of history and the present blending and recombining, but also the poet's imaginative journeys to Africa, the Caribbean, and the United States.

English is far from the only language spoken in the Caribbean. The ascent of Edwidge Danticat has followed on the heels of the immigration of the second largest immigrant group (after Jamaica) from the Afro-Caribbean: Haitian-Americans. Haiti became known in the late twentieth century as the poorest country in the western hemisphere. Developed countries became even more aware of its poverty in 2010 following a devastating earthquake that left over 100,000 dead and many more destitute. Despite this attention and despite the fact that Haitians have been immigrating to the United States in large numbers since the late twentieth century, many Americans remain ignorant of Haitian history and culture. Danticat's works seek to redress this ignorance.

Danticat has written short stories, novels, and non-fiction. All are characterized by an unstinting examination of the experiences of Haitians and Haitian-Americans. Her vision does not shy away from violence, sometimes disturbing in nature, and it cycles between the personal and the collective. Her 1994 novel *Breath, Eyes, Memory* is the story of Sophie, a girl raised in Haiti by her aunt and grandmother after her mother emigrates to the United States. When she is a young teen, Sophie reluctantly follows her mother to America. She barely speaks to her mother once she arrives, and their relationship remains burdened, largely because Sophie blames her mother for abandoning her. We learn that Sophie's mother was raped. Sophie connects this act of sexual violence to another: the Haitian practice of mothers "testing" their daughters by inserting a finger into their vaginas to ensure that they are virgins.

This practice is horrifying to all who experience it, but it becomes especially traumatic to Sophie in the context of her American experience since it is a practice foreign to the U.S., and thus contributes to her feelings of isolation. She falls in love with an African American man who provides a racial explanation for their belonging together; he says, "I am not American....I am African-American." When Sophie asks him the difference, he responds, "The African. It means that you and I, we are already part of each other" (72). This vital racial connection is violated soon thereafter when her mother "tests" her, lecturing her on the sacredness of the mother–daughter bond. Sophie feels such confusion and guilt over this practice that she assaults her own hymen and severs the bond between herself and her mother so that she can marry her lover. But the scars she creates through this act are not just physical: she develops an eating disorder and extreme sexual anxiety, and she leaves her husband temporarily to return not to her mother in Brooklyn, but to Haiti.

Sophie's damage can be read symbolically as she tries to develop an identity that will allow her to shuttle between the United States and Haiti, but she doesn't manage to do either. In a weak attempt to reconcile with her mother in the presence of her husband, they try to connect African American culture with Haitian identity, specifically through Negro spirituals, which her husband identifies as a universal expression of the African diaspora. Sophie's mother agrees and sings her favorite, which is "Sometimes I Feel Like a Motherless Child." Sophie's mother's trauma from having been raped, coupled with her unexpected pregnancy late in life, causes her to take her own life, and her death may be the only route to healing for Sophie. She returns to Haiti for the funeral and connects Haitian identity with the bond between mothers and daughters; listening to a traditional wake song, she realizes "that it was neither my mother nor my Tante Atie who had given all the mother-and-daughter motifs to all the stories they told and all the songs they sang. It was something that was essentially Haitian. Somehow, early on, our song makers and tale weavers had decided that we were all daughters of this land" (230). Following this logic, daughters who emigrate from Haiti have to deal with issues of cultural separation. One of Danticat's themes is the examination of the difficulty of this separation. In the process, Haitian culture is partly imported into the United States and partly abandoned, as immigrants try to reconcile their collective and individual stories with the African American stories they encounter.

There is a fear underlying this abandonment, as there is in many immigration narratives: that history will be forgotten. Danticat's 1998 novel *The Farming of Bones* tells an important story from Haitian history, a story that is not familiar to many contemporary American readers. The cultural divide between the Dominican Republic and Haiti is profound, based not only on geography, but on race, language, and class. Set in 1937, this novel, narrated by a Haitian woman who works for a

Dominican army officer, centers on the so-called Parsley Massacre, a genocidal event ordered by Dominican Governor Rafael Trujillo. The narrator, Amabelle, is plagued by survivor's guilt and comes to terms with the fact that she "chose a living death because [she is] not brave" (283). Although she survives the slaughter, her soul essentially dies during the horrifying events of 1937. Her burden is to tell the story of her people. Despite her role as storyteller, Amabelle is rendered a woman with no country and no future. She realizes: "Land is something you care about only when you have heirs. All my heirs would be like my ancestors: revenants, shadows, ghosts" (278). This alienation is a function of a traumatic history, and it is the crucial subject of Danticat's growing body of work. It underscores a theme common to all of the writers in this category: there is a difference between moving on from a painful history and forgetting it.

Clever, Irreverent, and Postmodern: "The New Black Aesthetic"

One identifiable group of younger African American novelists has emerged in the last few decades, producing works that are intellectual and ambitious, cool and satirical. Their white counterparts – Jonathan Franzen, Jeffrey Eugenides, Jonathan Lethem, Dave Eggers, Michael Chabon, and Jonathan Safran Foer – do not necessarily form a coherent school, but their works share some common features: intellectual humor, frequent allusions to both pop culture and high culture, and acute attention to detail. The black writers who might be said to participate in a similar tradition have earned popular and critical acclaim through the same attributes, but they have done so while living with the question of the "post-racial," a term which they have to cope with, even if they find it meaningless or ridiculous. In fact, the absurdity of race and racialized thinking is frequently a subject within their works. In contrast to earlier writers, they are more likely to roll their eyes than to issue diatribes.

The first identification of this emerging group came as early as 1989 in an essay by Trey Ellis entitled "The New Black Aesthetic," published in the journal *Callaloo*. He says that this aesthetic "shamelessly borrows and reassembles across both race and class lines" (234). He identifies participants in this New Black Aesthetic as "cultural mulattoes" who "no longer need to deny or suppress any part of our complicated and sometimes contradictory cultural baggage to please either white people or black" (235). This new generation is able to move between white and black communities, is frequently educated both in selective colleges and on the streets, and is inclined toward biting humor about the complexity of their cultural relationship to their nation and to race. They acknowledge, according to Ellis, the importance of the struggles of the Civil Rights era and black nationalists of the 1960s, but they are also inclined to parody the achievements of the older generation as a way of moving beyond them. Ellis recognizes the influence of the poet/novelist Ishmael Reed (Chapter Six), the comedian Richard Pryor, and the film-maker Spike Lee. The sharp-edged humor displayed in the works of these artists had a liberating effect on this generation of writers, who remain concerned with black identity, but not in the traditional ways.

Paul Beatty's first novel *The White Boy Shuffle* (1996) is a textbook example of Ellis's "New Black Aesthetic." Beatty, who initially gained notoriety as a spoken-word poet, has published both fiction and poetry. His 2008 novel *Slumberland* about African American expatriates in Berlin demonstrates the maturation of his aesthetic, but *The White Boy Shuffle* continues to be an important illustration of Ellis's analysis. It is the largely fanciful story of a young man named Gunnar Kaufman who shuffles between white and black worlds as the prototype of the "cultural mulatto" Ellis defines. To wit, his two talents are poetry and basketball. Having grown up in a toney white suburb, he initially feels alienated when he moves to "the 'hood," seeing himself as a sideshow freak: "the whitest Negro in captivity….He says 'whom,' plays Parcheesi, and folks, you won't believe it, but he has absolutely no ass what-so-ever" (52). He struggles to gain street credibility and to mask his stereotypically white attributes while in the black world. Before his basketball talents are discovered, he uses poetry as a kind of weapon: "We'd duel in impromptu verse; tankas at seven paces or sestinas at noon, no use of the words 'love,' 'heart,' and 'soul.' I sent many bards home in shame" (105). This tradition of poetic duels takes the form of the "cipher" in street culture of the 1980s, a public circle of poetic battles that spawned rap music.

Poetry becomes a powerful cultural tool as Gunnar matures, and the novel has much to offer as an illustration of the way such a "cultural mulatto" is able to be bilingual, to modulate between languages not only to assimilate, but also to assert identity. Catalyzed (and confused) by the 1992 Rodney King riots, Gunnar grows into a revolutionary poet whose goal is to expose his followers as hypocrites who speak rapturously about causes without ever embracing them. He leaves California on a basketball scholarship to Boston University, and after visiting every special-interest club there, he accuses a crowd of not being willing to die for a cause: "What we need is some new leaders. Leaders who won't apostatize like cowards. Some niggers who are ready to die!" (200). The crowd chants back, "You! You! You!" (200). His cause becomes, simply, his willingness to die, or to be in control of his own death, and he unwittingly initiates an epidemic of people who commit suicide and write death poems in his honor. In the novel's prologue he is disgusted by the fact that he has so many followers who die misinterpreting his message: he becomes a name on the historical "list of maniacal messiahs who sit in Hell's homeroom answering the Devil's roll call" (2). Poetry has somehow gained a great deal of cultural influence, but when the poet is essentially a nihilist, that influence is a dangerous thing. Ultimately, *The White Boy Shuffle* demonstrates both the value of confronting the stereotypes that inhibit identity and the necessity for establishing a new belief system once they have been destroyed.

Colson Whitehead's works provide a cogent example of the variety of subjects that might appear in African American writing of the twenty-first century. His first novel, *The Intuitionist* (1999), is a postmodern tale in the mode of Thomas Pynchon, focusing on the different schools of thought surrounding elevator inspection in New York City. *Apex Hides the Hurt* (2006) has a similar comic premise, as its unnamed protagonist is called upon as a "nomenclature consultant" to help rename a town. Whitehead ventures into science fiction in *Zone One* (2011), and his autobiographically inspired novel *Sag Harbor* (2009) drew attention because it seemed much more concerned with the throwaway details of 1980s pop culture than with indignity toward racial oppression. Its narrator, Benji, is self-conscious about race as one of a few black teens summering in the white, wealthy Hamptons on Long Island, but this consciousness is rendered with a humor and lightness that would not have been possible in any previous generation. As a child Benji is aware of the way he and his peers disappoint their elders by not being able to identify the "Iconic Figures of Black Nationalism" and he relies on context clues rather than incurring their ire by revealing his ignorance: "The respectful way my mother pronounced *DuBois* told me that the man had uplifted the race" (13). He admits that DuBois's concept of double-consciousness "blew [him] away" (13), and the novel might be read as yet another update of this concept, but Benji is more concerned with TV dinners, ice cream cones, and Coca-Cola than with dwelling on the deep racial divide in America.

John Henry Days (2001), Whitehead's most fully realized work, foregrounds anxiety over the importance or influence of the past. This anxiety is clearly one of the central concerns of a culture in which the term "post-racial" threatens to diminish not only enduring racism in the present, but the horrific realities of the past. The protagonist, J. Sutter, is an opportunistic hack journalist who spends the first pages of the book in pursuit of a discarded receipt so that he can file a bogus expense report. He is on assignment to cover the celebration of John Henry Days, an event in Talcott, West Virginia, the site of the legendary contest between a steam drill and the railroad worker John Henry in the late nineteenth century. Everything about John Henry – from his race to his very existence – is a matter of speculation. His story has been passed down through a famous ballad and through other popular renditions over time. In most versions of the story he is black. He manages to beat the steam drill in a contest, but promptly dies.

J. Sutter feels an unconscious solidarity with John Henry, since he interprets the legend as being about fate, and since he is struggling to define himself in the context of the faceless power of the Information Age just as John Henry struggled against industry. The legendary Henry is born with a hammer in his hand, and proclaims that it will be the death of him. J. Sutter, a diminished version of Henry, also feels that his death is scripted, and he wonders whether his own work has any meaning or nobility, or if he is destined to do the hard work that will make others wealthy. In the novel's first section he chokes on a chunk of roast beef while a boy sings the John Henry ballad at a banquet. He suffers from racial paranoia and believes that he will die in the South while white people watch; he thinks, "too much history gone down here...All these crackers looking up at me, looking up at the tree. Nobody doing nothing, just staring. They know how to watch a nigger die" (79). This motif is repeated throughout the book: one of the junketeers who works with J. recounts the famous story of the Rolling Stones concert at Altamont when a young black man was stabbed in front of the stage by a motorcycle gang member. The incident is racially motivated in this version, and J.'s white colleague says, "we stood in a ring watching" (98–99). He interprets it as "a sacrifice" and compares it to the fate of Crispus Attucks, the first victim (also black) of the Boston Massacre that precipitated the American Revolution.

Like John Henry, all of these black men are framed as sacrificial victims, but the key question is about the meaning of the sacrifice. John Henry's death seems both pointless and inevitable. J., as a youth, watching a film of John Henry in school, wants the teacher to interpret its meaning, but she never does. He wants to ask her the questions that still persist in his adulthood: "Mrs. Goodwin, if he beat the steam engine, why did he have to die? Did he win or lose?" (142). The ambiguity of the John Henry story precipitates a host of questions about historical importance and the relationship between work and identity, especially in a society marked by racial stratification. J. finds the story of John Henry bleak at best, and the proliferation of versions of it and the many stories surrounding it take the reader further and further away from anything like certainty or optimism. When the festival degenerates into violence toward the novel's end, we are not even told the identity of the victims: we can only piece the truth together through patterns. In a sense, it doesn't matter which journalists are shot at the novel's end since sacrifice seems pointless throughout the novel. Its main black characters, J. and Pamela, feel as though they have not been in control of their identities throughout their lives. They are only heroes in the way that John Henry has become a cultural hero to black people. Heroism, like identity in general and sacrifice in particular, is revealed in this book to be a flimsy, unstable concept.

The prolific novelist Percival Everett has gained an increasing following, especially in Europe where he has spent periods of time writing. Everett's relationship to literary fame and to the literary establishment might be described as vexed. His most famous work, the novel *erasure* (2001), is on one level a satire of issues surrounding literary fame, particularly as it pertains to African American writers. In an interview soon after the publication of *erasure* he said, almost hopefully, "I'm not ever going to be a bestselling writer" (Weixlmann, 18). In that same interview he described *erasure* as "a funny, sad book, and I'm sorry I live in a world where I had to write it" (22). That world – our world – is characterized by extraordinary ignorance of the black literary tradition and by rigid, unsophisticated expectations for current black writers fueled by Oprah Winfrey's televised book club and by the classification systems of bookstores. The novel's narrator, a writer named Thelonius Monk Ellison, claims, "Someone interested in African American Studies would have little interest in my books and would be confused by their presence in the [black] section" of the bookstore (28). The only thing "black" about his books, he claims, is "my jacket photograph" (28). Combined with his intellectual aloofness, his refusal to write about the subjects people expect of him has not produced a lucrative career.

Monk would be content to live in relative obscurity while staying true to his art, but the murder of his sister and his mother's descent into dementia demand his financial responsibility. He is infuriated that a popular novelist named Juanita Mae Jenkins (modeled after Zane or Sapphire, discussed later in this chapter) has written a novel called *We's Lives in Da Ghetto* and that a television hostess (clearly modeled on Oprah) has helped it to become a runaway bestseller. He dashes off a pulp novel of his own called *My Pafology* (later renamed *Fuck*) and attributes it to Stagg R. Leigh, echoing the name of the legendary "badman" figure Staggerlee. Its protagonist is named Van Go Jenkins, alluding to the artist Vincent Van Gogh as well as to the reviled author of *We's Lives in Da Ghetto*. Van Go is a grotesque exaggeration of the stereotypical urban black male as portrayed in pop culture: a badly spoken, unemployed, shiftless thug who impregnates multiple women and neglects his offspring. The parody, Monk thinks, should be so evident as to be laughable, and, to make it even more so, he borrows much of the plot, character names, and even some dialogue from *Native Son* (1940).

The joke, however, is on Monk, as his agent actually pitches it to a publisher who wants to publish it and to promote it on the Oprah-like show. Monk cannot believe that anyone, much less powerful publishers and tastemakers, could take *My Pafology* seriously, but it becomes a bestseller and even makes the shortlist for a major literary award. At first Monk tries to enjoy the irony of his situation and compares himself to the character Rinehart in Ralph Ellison's *Invisible Man* (1952) who is able to succeed in society by shifting identity. But this ruse brings him no joy and, in a rare, honest conversation with his mother, he confesses, "I promised myself once that I would not compromise my art" (257). The integrity of his writing is the only thing that has ever truly mattered to Monk, and his fall into the superficial world of popular culture has compromised it, or, following the title, has erased the only thing that ever mattered to him. In a dream-like sequence from the novel's conclusion, Monk stumbles toward a stage, either to receive the award that *My Pafology* has won, or to refuse to accept the award and to admit that he is the book's author. During this sequence a young boy holds up a mirror and Monk sees the face of his alter-ego Stagg R. Leigh, who asks him, "How does it feel to be free of one's illusions?" which is a line from the epilogue to *Invisible Man* (264). He says, aloud, "The answer is *Painful and empty*" (265). In a novel that deeply ponders such subjects as the comforts we seek in the afterlife, the ethics of hiding secrets within a family, and the integrity of art, Monk's response is troubling. Illusions, or lies, can serve to protect or comfort, even as they draw people away from their authentic selves. As a return to the quandary of DuBoisian double-consciousness and *Invisible Man*'s unresolved dilemma, *erasure* is a profound, essential novel, perhaps the most important postmodern work of African American literature in the twenty-first century.

Everett lives in California with his wife Danzy Senna, an author whose production has been spare, but whose 1998 novel *Caucasia* has gained notoriety. All three of Senna's novels and her short story collection deal with the politics of race relations as experienced by mixed-race individuals. *Caucasia* is the story of two sisters, the narrator Birdie and her sister Cole, who are separated when their parents split up. Birdie is closer in color and features to her white mother, and passes as Jewish in their new life. Though the novel advances many themes familiar to readers of twentieth-century African American literature, such as the psychic dangers of "passing" and the lure of invisibility in a racist world, it is also significant in the way it depicts a generational shift. Birdie and Cole's father is a throwback to 1960s-era black power rhetoric, yet he can only deal with race in an abstract way rather than providing guidance for his confused daughters. Their mother is also a sixties radical who once participated in the struggle for racial equality, but who implicitly denies her connections to it as she drags Birdie deeper into white society and away from her black roots. Birdie finally confronts her father late in the novel as he is about to publish his newest study on "the origins of hypocrisy" (390). When she takes him to task for neglecting her when she passed for white, he responds, "there's no such thing as passing. We're all just pretending. Race is a complete illusion, make-believe. It's a costume. We all wear one. You just switched yours at some point" (391). He seems sincere, but his denial of the importance of race fails to account for the fact that it ruined his daughters' childhoods by severing the natural bond between them.

Contemporary Black Drama: Self-consciousness

The radical, experimental, underground theater of the Black Arts Movement yielded to a more mainstream trend at the end of the twentieth century as black play-wrights were driven to represent black historical experience on the stage. As with other genres, black drama in the twenty-first century has spread out in many directions: as Harry Elam writes in his introduction to *The Fire This Time: African American Plays for the Twenty-first Century*, "African American playwrights have equally in form and content transcended previous delineations of race and repre-sentation" (xiii). At the same time, he worries about "crises of direction and politics [that] arise" with this dispersal of something that was once considered a mandate within the black theater: to raise awareness and consciousness about political, social, and economic disparity. Contemporary black drama has proven that it can combine the intensity and playfulness of its predecessors, mixing the earnestness of Lorraine Hansberry and August Wilson, the surreal intensity of Baraka and Ed Bullins, and the postmodern zaniness of George C. Wolfe.

Theater in general in the twenty-first century has to advocate for itself as a genre given the overwhelming cultural influence of film. Black film producers, directors, and screen stars have flourished in recent years while black drama (like poetry) has struggled to be noticed. The actress and playwright Anna Deveare Smith, especially in her work of the 1990s, has helped to keep the genre fresh by converting interviews into dramatic monologues for the stage. Her 1991 *Fires in the Mirror* and 1994 *Twilight: Los Angeles, 1992* attempt to chronicle racially tense civil disturbances in New York and California. In doing so she rejects the notion of "a unifying voice," claiming, "In order to have real unity, all voices would have to be heard or at least represented" (xxv). Her approach to theater is to embody a plurality of voices: "If more of us could actually speak from another point of view, like speaking another language, we could accelerate the flow of ideas" (xxv). Smith's work bridges the democratic impulses of the Black Arts

Movement with a more current emphasis on examining race relations against a broad social backdrop.

Although many African American playwrights have emerged since August Wilson (such as Robert Alexander, Kirsten Greenidge, Thulani Davis, and Lynn Nottage), the prolific and acclaimed Suzan-Lori Parks is worth pausing over as the most important and prominent black voice in contemporary drama. Originally a student of James Baldwin's when he taught in Amherst, Massachusetts in the early 1980s, Parks has earned many accolades, winning a Guggenheim Fellowship, a MacArthur Foundation grant, and the Pulitzer Prize for drama – the first ever awarded to a female African American playwright – for *Top Dog/Underdog* in 2002. She has published a novel and written screenplays, including Spike Lee's *Girl 6* (1996), and has also composed and performed music, but she is primarily known for her accomplishments as a playwright. One of her most startling achievements is *365 Days/365 Plays* (2006), the published record of her attempt to write a brief play each day for a year to be performed across the country simultaneously in grassroots theater festivals.

Parks is difficult to categorize and, for many, to understand, at least on the deeper levels that clearly undergird her work. The concept of erasure, connected to Everett's novel, is germane to Parks's work as it pertains to black history. She is also concerned with the legitimate formation of individual identity, and with the workings of drama, or performance, as the key to that identity. *Top Dog/Underdog* is a play containing many of her themes and a fitting inroad into her work. There are only two characters in *Top Dog/Underdog*: the coyly-named brothers Lincoln and Booth. The conceit that unifies the play is the hustler's card game Three-card Monte. Booth, described in the credits as "the underdog," opens the play practicing a relatively clumsy version of the game in the brothers' apartment. Lincoln returns from his job, which is to impersonate Abraham Lincoln in a local arcade and to allow himself to be mock-assassinated repeatedly.

The play is largely about role-playing, storytelling, and the imagination. The brothers share a number of stories about their collective past and their present lives outside the apartment. Booth's stories are most often about his girlfriend, Grace, who may be dead (if she ever existed at all). Lincoln's stories are about his plans to escape his current situation. He had once been the master of the Three-card Monte game, but had given it up when one of his henchmen was killed, forcing him to meditate on a new dream that he hasn't yet discovered. He tells the story of someone he calls his Best Customer, a recurrent visitor who impersonates John Wilkes Booth and whispers philosophical musings in Lincoln's ear before shooting him, like "Does thuh show stop when no ones watching or does the show go on?" The brothers recall and together deliver one of the Best Customer's most memorable lines: "Yr only yrself...when no ones watching" (34). The play, like much of Parks's work, raises profound questions about identity, and about the complex interrelationship of those who watch and those who perform. These two characters, in many ways, perform the stereotypical role of the contemporary, urban, African American young man, not unlike the parody in Everett's *erasure*: they prefer hustling to wage-earning, they are crude, they come from a broken home, they resort to violence when they feel disempowered, etc. Lincoln, the supposed "top dog," seems weary of this role, and the audience is not likely to find the story of these brothers edifying. And yet, we are implicated as the "someone watching" that expects and perhaps causes these brothers to perform their identities the way they do. The play encourages us to ponder the limited roles available to them.

Black Poetry in the Twenty-first Century: Lift Every Voice and Sing

For black poets, the range of available roles has perhaps never been wider. As a result, the number of black poetic voices has never been greater. The field of African American poetry has become so diverse and richly populated that one barely knows where to begin to discuss it. One place to begin might be the founding of the Dark Room Collective in 1988. Poets Thomas Sayers Ellis and Sharan Strange started a relatively short-lived but important reading series for black poets in Cambridge, Massachusetts, and its members have gone on to become some of the most prominent figures in contemporary black poetry. Their poems are concerned with diverse subjects: consistent with other contemporary genres, they delve into deep questions of identity that often include race, but not as the solitary, defining factor. Cornelius Eady and Toi Derracotte, inspired by the Dark Room Collective, founded Cave Canem in 1996 to recognize and support the work of black poets. As their website says, it is a place for emerging poets to "find sustenance, a safe space to take artistic chances." It also states that its mission is "to remedy the under-representation and isolation of African American poets in MFA programs and writing workshops." It is noteworthy that these poets are associated with formal, academic training, which demonstrates a departure from the street-based or community-based ethos of the Black Arts Movement, and also perhaps represents a departure in contemporary letters between the types of poets who publish their work and those who engage in the Spoken Word tradition (discussed below).

Evie Shockley's 2011 study *Renegade Poetics* is useful in identifying some important contemporary black poets and considering their aesthetics as well as their subjects. She argues: "Just as there are no essential racial characteristics, it is not inevitable that an African American poet will negotiate race in the process of writing. But we should not be surprised to find that so many African American poets do" (196). She also writes, "Criticism of African American poetry too often treats the art as if it can be reduced to antiracist slogans" (197) and troubles the word "accessibility" as the most important feature of black poetry. She holds up Will Alexander as an example of a challenging, complex, and critically neglected poet. Shockley argues that this neglect is partly due to the fact that Alexander's poetry seems divorced from the traditional concerns of African American literature, and yet his poetics are grounded in African belief systems (among others). Her conclusion is valuable, as she attempts to move beyond the imperative set forth by the Black Arts Movement toward collective expression while also acknowledging its importance: "The African American poets of the twenty-first century are writing not in a post-racial moment, but in a moment that is being called 'post-racial' in the face of massive and increasingly violent evidence to the contrary. The meanings of race are more amorphous, and the operation of racism is more difficult to articulate, even for those of us who know it when we see it" (198). Despite her resistance to the term "post-racial," Shockley indicates that definitions of what is or is not considered "racial" need to be revised, expanded, or updated.

Regardless of their subjects and styles, it is clear that black poets have reached a level of recognition higher even than during the Harlem Renaissance. When Maya Angelou read a poem at the inauguration of Bill Clinton in 1993 – the first time a black poet had appeared in this context – she drew attention to the presence of black poetry in a society that had consistently overlooked it for a long time, even after the fiery exhortations of Baraka and his contemporaries. A second black poet, much younger and less prominent than Maya Angelou, Elizabeth Alexander, was selected to read at Barack Obama's second inauguration in 2009. Rita Dove became the first African American to serve as Poet Laureate from 1993–1995, and Natasha Trethewey became the second in 2012. Trethewey also won the Pulitzer Prize for poetry in 2007, and she was joined in this honor by another black poet, Tracy K. Smith, in 2011.

History, particularly as transmitted through family oral history, is a major theme of Trethewey's. The poem "History Lesson" (2000) demonstrates both the subtlety and intensity of her themes. It opens with a description of a photograph of the poet at the age of four, standing on a beach: "My toes dig in, / curl around wet sand. The sun cuts / the rippling Gulf in flashes with each / tidal rush" (4–7). The sun's cutting is augmented by the darting of minnows around the subject's feet "like switch-blades" (8). The violence of this knife imagery is jarring in contrast to the seeming innocence of the four-year-old girl. The scene expands out from the photograph to include the speaker's grandmother who took the picture, then the speaker reveals that it was taken in 1970, "two years after they opened / the rest of this beach to us" (11–12). It brings to mind a parallel image of her grandmother from forty years earlier, standing in a similar outfit, on a beach marked "colored" (15). The personal here yields to the cultural, and the "history lesson" of the title is both for the speaker (who lived through but does not remember the segregated beach) and the reader (who now understands the meaning of the knife imagery in a description of such a serene-seeming image). The poem, like much of Trethewey's work, demonstrates the subtle wounds of history that affect the speaker indirectly, through her family stories rather than through any weight she feels directly.

Harryette Mullen might be considered a representative contemporary black poet in that her work is always surprising and difficult to pin down. Her themes include not only race, but gender and discontentment with consumer society as well. Each volume of poetry, from her first (*Tree Tall Woman* [1981]) through to her most recent (*Urban Tumbleweed* [2013]), is markedly different. What unifies them is a fascination with language and the multiple meanings it can foster when words are artfully arranged. There is also an intoxicating sound quality to her poems, reminiscent of her acknowledged influences Gertrude Stein and Gwendolyn Brooks, as in the following quatrain from her 1995 collection *Muse and Drudge*:

sauce squandering sassy cook
took a gander bumped a pinch of goose
skinned squadron cotillion filled
uptown ballroom with squalid quadrille
(42)

The musical sound qualities of poetry have been intertwined with the black poetic aesthetic at least since the ascendancy of Langston Hughes, but Mullen exploits them to a greater degree than most of her predecessors, paving the way for Spoken Word Poetry (discussed later in this chapter).

Mullen's will to experiment has provided a model for other contemporary black poets who resist traditional form and who even question poetry's status as a unique or separate genre. Such is the case of Thylias Moss, who has developed an elaborate theory of composition she calls Limited Fork Theory, which sees invisible connections between systems. She has coined the word "*poam*" (meaning "product of an act of making" [Rowell, 282]). Such experiments have led to works like her *Slave Moth* (2004), a new narrative of slavery told in verse. *Slave Moth*'s speaker, a fourteen-year-old slave named Varl, is in a position similar to that of Harriet Jacobs in her famous slave narrative (discussed in Chapter Two), resisting the control of her master. Denied the right to write, she secretly stitches her story onto the inside of a garment, literally protecting herself with words. This inventive work adds a fresh perspective to the slave narrative genre by liberating the poetic voice of the slave. The subject of this vital work is language itself: Varl, speaking to her master's wife, says, "Why do you assume that *slave* must mean / just one simple thing? Maybe *slave* is much bigger / than you can imagine" (135). Varl's manipulation of language and the development of her mind produce a fascinating story-in-verse that does much more than simply reiterate accepted wisdom about the era of slavery.

Black poetry has long been influenced by popular music, not just as a conscious model (as in the jazz poetry of Hughes), but also as a product that forms part of the material history of the culture. In the late twentieth and early twenty-first centuries, poetry and music intersect in a few distinct ways. One is evident in a sizable group of poets who are influenced by figures from what might be termed the mature period of jazz (the 1940s through the 1960s). Jazz and blues musicians such as Miles Davis, Thelonius Monk, and especially John Coltrane become culture heroes in these poems. Michael S. Harper is notable in this regard, and is clearly influenced by the Black Arts Movement, which helped to solidify the connection between political and musical culture heroes. In his poem "Here Where Coltrane Is" Harper speaks of Martin Luther King, Jr., Malcolm X, and Coltrane as parallel figures, in consecutive lines. Cornelius Eady also harkens back to musical heroes of the past – Miles Davis, Billie Holliday, Leadbelly – as a way of marking their value and gauging what the culture has lost through their deaths. In his poem "Photo of Miles Davis at Lennies-on-the-Turnpike, 1968," he begins, "New York grows / Slimmer / In his absence" (1–3) and concludes, "Death is one hell / Of a pickpocket" (15–16). Al Young, in "A Dance for Ma Rainey" (the hard-living "Empress of the Blues"), writes, "I'm going to be just like you, Ma / Rainey this Monday morning....I'm going to cry so sweet / & so low / & so dangerous" (1–2, 14–16). Clearly musicians are muses for these poets, and their historical and cultural importance is evident. Young's poem concludes with the hope that Ma Rainey's exuberant but painful life has curtailed the suffering and desperation of later generations of black people:

> Our beautiful brave black people
> Who no longer need to jazz
> or sing to themselves in murderous vibrations
> or play the veins of their strong tender arms
> with needles
> to prove that we're still here.
>
>   *(41–46)*

Tyehimba Jess, Jericho Brown, and others continue to treat the history of black music as a potent subject in more recent work.

Even so, Jess and Brown's generation of music-minded black poets might be less inclined to extol the heroic black jazz and blues heroes of the past and more likely to celebrate the existence of black music itself as central to the black experience. Music still acts as a muse for these poets, even if the life of an individual musician is not the point. Major Jackson, for instance, in "Urban Renewal," nostalgically recalls his youth in which

> Woofers stacked to pillars made a disco of a city block....
> did not that summer crowd bounce in ceremonial fits?
> Ah yes! It was the deejay, and his spinning TECHNICS
> delicately needled a groove, something from James Brown's
> FUNKY PRESIDENT....
> song broken down to a dream of song flows
> from my pen; the measured freedom coming off this page
> was his pillared spell of drums.
>
>   *(1, 9–12, 14–16)*

Popular music and poetry are linked together here and in a number of other poems by younger poets, such as Kyle Dargan's "Microphone Fiend" in which a child fantasizes about becoming a famous rap emcee while taking a shower. The child's mother interrupts the fantasy, but the fantasy is strong enough to withstand reality: "s/he anticipates emceedom like a growth spurt" (25).

Spoken Word, Hip-hop, Rap, and "Hood Fiction"

Dargan's poem alludes to a common dream of fame and wealth for young African Americans in the contemporary world. The rise of rap music and hip-hop culture has been dramatic in recent years. Black popular music has gained acceptance through the twentieth century: blues, soul, and disco informed and changed the trajectory of rock and roll. Hip-hop, though, has come to dominate the contemporary music scene rather than just to inform it or coexist peacefully with it. Hip-hop culture extends to literature, especially through the performative genre of spoken word (or slam) poetry. Despite the influence of the Beat Generation in the 1950s, the Black Arts Movement in the 1960s, and the Nuyorican Poets Café in the 1970s, all of which showcased lively performances of poetry in urban spaces, "poetry" remained a term largely associated with elite, academic settings and print publications. The rise and endurance of poetry slams beginning in the 1980s coincided with the development of rap, which, at least according to legend, is an acronym for "**r**hythm **a**nd **p**oetry."

The definition of what is considered "poetic" deserves some scrutiny in this context. When Gates and McKay published the first *Norton Anthology of African American Literature* in 1997, they debated whether or not to include rap lyrics. There are a handful of rap lyrics in the first edition, and the editors have added two or three rap lyrics with each edition. This modest inclusion is listed not with the rest of contemporary literature, though, but in an introductory section called "The Vernacular Tradition." There is agreement that rap is an important cultural expression that belongs in a black literature anthology, but there is still some question about its status as literature or poetry.

Spoken Word Poetry, the accepted umbrella term for the genre of performed poetry that has developed over the past three decades, provides many examples of important literary artists working in a self-consciously oral medium that favors improvisation and often, as in the case of a poet like Tracie Morris, depends largely on verbal/musical flourishes. Its earliest glimmerings can be seen in the work of Gil Scott-Heron who recorded and wrote prolifically from the early 1970s until his death in 2011. His most renowned work "The Revolution Will Not Be Televised," directly influenced the rap tradition.

Plenty of friction still remains around whether or not to treat Spoken Word and rap lyrics as poetry or to put them into separate categories. Once Spoken Word lyrics are written down and published in a book, as they were in the landmark 1999 book *Listen Up! Spoken Word Poetry*, how do they differ from other published poetry (which is also often read aloud)? When Yale University Press issued *The Anthology of Rap* in 2010 the book met much resistance not just because it put rap lyrics down on paper, but because it attempted to give certain weight to some rap artists while neglecting others. (This is a criticism leveled at any anthology, and *The Anthology of Rap* may have suffered because it was the first major attempt to anthologize rap, even as the genre continued to develop).

There is some disagreement about what the term "hip-hop" finally signifies. Some critics trace two distinct generations of hip-hop culture, the first of which emerged in the mid-1960s and the second in the mid-1980s. In common usage the term often overlaps with "street" or "urban." Its most prominent manifestation is music, but hip-hop is comprised of many other cultural expressions, such as graffiti, fashion, film, dance, and literature. There is, of course, much debate about whether to consider any popular writing as "literature," and that debate cannot be resolved here. If rap lyrics are analyzed as poetry and for their poetic features, they become a text like any other. Certainly great works from the African American literary tradition discussed throughout this book – from Douglass's *Narrative* (1845) through *Native Son* to the poetry of Langston Hughes and the Black Arts Movement – have been popular in nature, and many have struggled consciously against the label of "literature" which connotes (to some) an elitist project. Susan B.A. Somers-Willett writes, "In addition to fostering a countercultural atmosphere and disseminating poetry in unconventional venues, the slam has thrived through the exercise of certain democratic ideals meant to contrast with exclusive academic conventions" (5). At the same time, she is conscious of how the genre has blended with and even been co-opted by hip-hop culture, perhaps at the expense of its countercultural spirit, as hip-hop becomes increasingly mainstream.

Jay-Z's book *Decoded* (2010) is a crucial text at the intersection of a number of these questions. Consistent with the audiovisual culture from which it derives, it is an image-laden book that plays with fonts and other text/image elements the way its author plays with language. Its cover is a stylized Rorschach blot, indicating that it is a book about interpretation. Its primary impulse is to "decode" Jay-Z's lyrics, not fully interpreting them, but unearthing the allusions or "hidden meanings" contained therein. He uses these decodings to tell his story, which is the prototype of many rap stars: from a childhood in the projects where drug-dealing was nearly inevitable, to initial artistic success and recognition, and finally to the level of superstardom where long-desired financial success may threaten political commitment and artistic integrity. Jay-Z doesn't dwell on the last possibility for too long, but there is a definite tension in *Decoded* between pure hustling and artistic commitment, especially as he is trying to argue that rap is poetry, meaning that it should be taken seriously as an art form. He states his intention bluntly: "to make the case that hip-hop lyrics – not just my lyrics, but those of every great MC – are poetry if you look at them closely enough" (235). To *look* at them (as opposed to listen to them) necessitates that they be printed, as they are here, in order to analyze them as we do poetry. At the same time, he knows that he would not be able to publish *Decoded* if he were not an enormously successful and enduring performer: "It's a recurring story in hip-hop, the tension between art and commerce" (128). In short, the big beats and impressive sound of an MC's flow threaten to obscure the thoughtful, intricate, allusive lyrics. He claims to want "to reach as many people as possible – and to get paid" (137), and he doesn't see this tension as a contradiction, but rather a challenge to find a balance. The poetry in rap is what gives it merit and depth, in Jay-Z's eyes, but he doesn't dismiss the popular appeal of rap while arguing for its artistry: "sometimes you just want to dumb out in the club; other times you want to get real and go deep" (129).

Hip-hop novelists like Zane (who has written a great number of popular erotic works), Sapphire, and the rapper and activist Sister Souljah have certainly been influential culturally, and yet their critics do not always see their literary merit. The class divide in the readership of black authors has never been as pronounced as it has been over the past few decades. In addition to the obvious chasm between the three aforementioned popular authors on one hand and clearly literary writers like Colson Whitehead and Percival Everett on the other, there are a host of middlebrow authors like the novelist Terry McMillan, many of whom enjoyed a burst of success through Oprah's televised book club. Works from these three blunt categories (low, middle, high) do not sell to the same audiences, do not have the same rhetorical intent, and do not always speak to one another on friendly terms. The existence of distinctly different types of African American literature, marked by class, popularity, and sophistication, is not unique to the contemporary period, but it is something that cannot be ignored within that period, and it has implications for both the present and future of the African American literary tradition.

Sapphire's novel *PUSH* (1996) is an interesting test case for the implications of this gulf. From a certain vantage point, the novel reads like Everett's parody of popular fiction in *erasure*; it begins, "I was left back when I was twelve because I had a baby for my fahver" (3). The pathos of Claireece Precious Jones's life, rendered in a first-person vernacular meant to reflect the harsh realities of the protagonist's world, is unsparing, but also inspirational in the way she faces and conquers adversity. One could easily dismiss the novel, as Everett's protagonist would, as anti-intellectual and sensational. And yet, the voice and circumstances of Precious connect in some ways to the classics of other lower-class figures from the African American tradition: Hurston's Janie from *Their Eyes Were Watching God* (1937), Wright's Bigger Thomas from *Native Son*, or certainly Walker's Celie from *The Color Purple* (1982), a novel which Precious labors over in school. Following the runaway success of the film version of *PUSH*, (titled *Precious* [2009]), there has been a lengthy critical volume dedicated to the book's literary merit: *Sapphire's Literary Breakthrough: Erotic Literacies, Feminist Pedagogies, Environmental Justice Perspectives*. There is a gap between highbrow/academic and lowbrow/popular in contemporary African American letters, but there are also many attempts to bridge that gap or to ignore it.

Conclusion

But the gap exists, and the question remains as to whether African American literature is a stable, coherent body of work in the twenty-first century. When George C. Wolfe and Percival Everett parody the popular works of the African American tradition, they have to some degree distanced themselves from them, indicating the persistence of the divisions that have been in place since the DuBois/Washington schism a century earlier. "Post-racial" – a term that is not likely to endure given its controversial nature, and given a renewal of racial tension after the unrest that originated in Ferguson, Missouri in 2014 – might be a way of ushering in a meaningful discussion about class, sexuality, regional identity, etc., not as a way of making discussions of race obsolete, but of acknowledging the complexities of "race" in the twenty-first century. It is naïve to describe the United States or its literature as post-racial, but given the diversity of subject matter in contemporary African American writing and the wide variety of factors contributing to the identity of the many writers who are identified as African American today, it is fair to say that "race" does not have exactly the same connotations it once did. For readers of contemporary African American literature, this change necessitates a modification of one's preconceived notions based on established traditions. This is not to say that the traditions no longer exist, but rather that they now point in a plurality of directions, making the field of African American literature more exciting and vibrant than ever before. Langston Hughes's quotation that is the epigraph to the first chapter of this book projects a world in which black artists feel an unprecedented degree of freedom. It may finally have been achieved. The talented artists of today and tomorrow will undoubtedly discover yet more topics and styles we cannot foresee. The best of them will demonstrate a keen awareness of the long struggle that made such free expression possible.

Suggestions for Further Reading

Shockley, Evie. *Renegade Poetics: Black Aesthetics and Formal Innovation in African American Poetry.* Iowa City, IA: University of Iowa Press, 2011. Print.

Somers-Willett, Susan B.A. *The Cultural Poetics of Slam Poetry.* Ann Arbor, MI: University of Michigan Press, 2009. Print.

Stanley, Tarshia L., ed. *Encyclopedia of Hip-Hop Literature.* Westport, CT: Greenwood Press, 2009. Print.

Warren, Kenneth W. *What Was African American Literature?* Cambridge, MA: Harvard University Press, 2011. Print.

Williams, Dana. *Contemporary African American Fiction: New Critical Essays.* Columbus, OH: Ohio State University Press, 2009. Print.

Young, Kevin, ed. *Giant Steps: The New Generation of African American Writers.* New York, NY: Perennial, 2000. Print.

REFERENCES

Ai. "Riot Act, April 29, 1992." *Vice: New and Selected Poems*. New York, NY: Norton and Company, 1999. Print.

Andrews, William L. and Henry Louis Gates, Jr. *Slave Narratives*. New York, NY: Library of America, 2000. Print.

Angelou, Maya. *I Know Why the Caged Bird Sings*. New York, NY: Ballantine Books, 1969. Print.

Appiah, Kwame Anthony. Introduction to *Narrative of the Life of Frederick Douglass, An American Slave & Incidents in the Life of a Slave Girl*. New York, NY: Modern Library, 2000. Print.

Baker, Houston A., Jr. *Blues, Ideology, and Afro-American Literature*. Chicago, IL and London: University of Chicago Press, 1984. Print.

Baldwin, James. *Another Country*. New York, NY: The Dial Press, 1962. Print.

Baldwin, James. *Going to Meet the Man*. New York, NY: The Dial Press, 1965. Print.

Baldwin, James. *Go Tell It on the Mountain*. 1953. New York, NY: Dell, 1980. Print.

Baldwin, James. *Notes of a Native Son*. 1955. Boston, MA: Beacon, 1984. Print.

Baldwin, James. *The Fire Next Time*. 1963. New York, NY: Vintage, 1993. Print.

Baldwin, James. *Blues for Mister Charlie*. 1964. New York, NY: Vintage, 1995. Print.

Bambara, Toni Cade. "My Man Bovanne." *Gorilla, My Love*. 1972. New York, NY: Vintage, 1992. 2–10. Print.

Baraka, Amiri. *Blues People*. New York, NY: William Morrow and Company, 1963. Print.

Baraka, Amiri. "Black Art." *Selected Poetry of Amiri Baraka/LeRoi Jones*. New York, NY: William Morrow and Company, 1979. 106–107. Print.

Baraka, Amiri. "Black Dada Nihilismus." *Selected Poetry of Amiri Baraka/LeRoi Jones*. New York, NY: William Morrow and Company, 1979. 40–42. Print.

Baraka, Amiri. "Look for You Yesterday, Here You Come Today." *Selected Poetry of Amiri Baraka/LeRoi Jones*. New York, NY: William Morrow and Company, 1979. 10–13. Print.

Baraka, Amiri. "A Poem Some People Will Have to Understand." *Selected Poetry of Amiri Baraka/LeRoi Jones*. New York, NY: William Morrow and Company, 1979. 55. Print.

Baraka, Amiri. *The Autobiography of LeRoi Jones.* New York, NY: Freundlich Books, 1984. Print.

Baraka, Amiri. *The Leroi Jones / Amiri Baraka Reader.* Ed. William J. Harris and Amiri Baraka. New York, NY: Thunder's Mouth Press, 1991. Print.

Baraka, Amiri. "Jimmy!" *Eulogies.* New York, NY: Marsilio Publishers, 1996. 91–98. Print.

Baraka, Amiri. *Dutchman and The Slave.* 1964. New York, NY: Harper Perennial, 2001. Print.

Baraka, Amiri. "A Post-Racial Anthology?" *The Poetry Foundation.* Review of *Angles of Ascent,* www.poetryfoundation.org/poetrymagazine/article/245846. Web. May 1, 2013.

Baraka, Amiri and Larry Neal. *Black Fire: An Anthology of Afro-American Writing.* New York, NY: William Morrow and Company, 1968. Print.

Beatty, Paul. *The White Boy Shuffle.* New York, NY: Henry Holt, 1996. Print.

Bernard, Emily. "The New Negro Movement and the Politics of Art." In Graham and Ward, 268–287. Print.

Bone, Robert A. *The Negro Novel in America.* 1958. Revised ed. New Haven, CT: Yale University Press, 1965. Print.

Brooks, Gwendolyn. "The Anniad" and "The Children of the Poor." *Selected Poems.* New York, NY: Harper & Row, 1963. Print.

Brooks, Gwendolyn. "The Last Quatrain of the Ballad of Emmett Till." *The 100 Best African American Poems.* Ed. Nikki Giovanni. Naperville, IL: Sourcebooks, 2010. 72. Print.

Brooks, Gwendolyn. "A Bronzeville Mother Loiters in Mississipi. Meanwhile, a Mississippi Mother Burns Bacon." *Words of Protest, Words of Freedom.* Ed. Jeffrey Lamar Coleman. London: Duke University Press, 2012. 19–23. Print.

Brown, William Wells. *Clotel, or The President's Daughter.* 1853. Ed. Robert S. Levine. Boston, MA: Bedford/St. Martin's, 2000. Print.

Bruce, Dickson D., Jr. *The Origins of African American Literature.* Charlottesville, VA and London: University Press of Virginia, 2001. Print.

Bullins, Ed. *Twelve Plays and Selected Writings.* Ed. Mike Sell. Ann Arbor, MI: University of Michigan Press, 2006. Print.

Bunge, Nancy (ed.). *Conversations with Clarence Major.* Jackson, MS: University Press of Mississippi, 2002. Print.

Butler, Octavia. *Kindred.* 1979. Boston, MA: Beacon Press, 1988. Print.

Carretta, Vincent. "The emergence of an African American literary canon, 1760–1820." In Graham and Ward, 52–65. Print.

Chesnutt, Charles W. *The House Behind the Cedars.* 1900. Ridgewood, NJ: The Gregg Press, 1968. Print.

Chesnutt, Charles W. *Collected Stories of Charles W. Chesnutt.* Ed. William L. Andrews. New York, NY: Penguin, 1992. Print.

Clarke, Cheryl. *After Mecca: Women Poets and the Black Arts Movement.* New Brunswick, NJ: Rutgers University Press, 2005. Print.

Cliff, Michelle. *If I Could Write This in Fire.* Minneapolis, MN: University of Minnesota Press, 2008. Print.

Cook, Martha E. "The Search for Self in Wallace Thurman's *The Blacker the Berry.*" In Ogbar, 140–152. Print.

Corrothers, James D. *The Book of American Negro Poetry.* 1922. Ed. James Weldon Johnson. Revised ed. New York, NY: Harcourt, Brace & World, 1959. 72–79. Print.

Crafts, Hannah. *The Bondwoman's Narrative.* Ed. Henry Louis Gates, Jr. New York, NY: Warner, 2002. Print.

Cullen, Countee. *On These I Stand: An Anthology of the Best Poems of Countee Cullen.* New York, NY: Harper & Row, 1947. Print.

Danticat, Edwidge. *Breath, Eyes, Memory.* New York, NY: Vintage, 1994. Print.

Douglass, Frederick. *Narrative of the Life of Frederick Douglass, An American Slave.* In Andrews and Gates, 267–368. Print.

Dove, Rita. "Courtship." *Thomas and Beulah.* Pittsburgh, PA: Carnegie-Mellon University Press, 1986. 16–17. Print.

Dove, Rita. "Courtship, Diligence." *Thomas and Beulah.* Pittsburgh, PA: Carnegie-Mellon University Press, 1986. 50. Print.

Dove, Rita. "David Walker (1785–1830)." *The Yellow House on the Corner.* Pittsburgh, PA: Carnegie-Mellon University Press, 1989. 34–35. Print.

DuBois, W.E.B. *Writings.* Ed. Nathan Huggins. New York, NY: Library of America, 1986. Print.

DuBois, W.E.B. "Criteria of Negro Art (1926)." *African American Literary Criticism, 1773 to 2000.* Ed. Hazel Arnett Ervin. New York, NY: Twayne, 1999. 39–43. Print.

Dunbar, Paul Laurence. *The Paul Laurence Dunbar Reader.* Ed. Jay Martin and Gossie H. Hudson. New York, NY: Dodd, Mead and Company, 1975. Print.

Elam, Harry, Jr. and Robert Alexander. *The Fire This Time: African American Plays for the 21st Century.* New York, NY: Theatre Communications Group, 2004. Print.

Ellis, Trey. "The New Black Aesthetic." *Callaloo* 38 (Winter, 1989) 233–243. JSTOR.

Ellison, Ralph. *Invisible Man.* 1952. New York, NY: Vintage, 1980. Print.

Ellison, Ralph. *Shadow and Act.* 1964. New York, NY: Quality Paperback, 1994. Print.

Equiano, Olaudah. *The Interesting Narrative of the Life of Olaudah Equiano, or Gustavus Vassa, the African. Written by Himself.* In Andrews and Gates, 35–242. Print.

Ervin, Hazell Arnett (ed.). *African American Literary Criticism, 1773 to 2000.* New York, NY: Twayne, 1999. Print.

Everett, Percival. *erasure.* Minneapolis, MN: Graywolf, 2001. Print.

Fauset, Jessie Redmon. *Plum Bun: A Novel Without a Moral.* 1928. Introduction by Deborah E. McDowell. London: Pandora Press, 1985. Print.

Freeman, Brian. *Civil Sex.* In Elam and Alexander, 91–142. Print.

Fuller, Hoyt. "Introduction: Towards a Black Aesthetic." In Gayle, 3–13. Print.

Gaines, Ernest J. *The Autobiography of Miss Jane Pittman.* New York, NY: The Dial Press, 1971. Print.

Gaines, Ernest J. *A Lesson Before Dying.* New York, NY: Knopf, 1993. Print.

Gates, Henry Louis, Jr. *The Signifying Monkey.* New York, NY: Oxford University Press, 1988. Print.

Gates, Henry Louis, Jr. *Loose Canons.* New York, NY: Oxford University Press, 1992. Print.

Gates, Henry Louis, Jr. *The Trials of Phillis Wheatley.* New York, NY: Basic, 2003. Print.

Gates, Henry Louis, Jr. and Nellie McKay (eds.). *The Norton Anthology of African American Literature,* 2nd edition. New York, NY: Norton and Company, 2004. Print.

Gayle, Addison, Jr. (ed.). *The Black Aesthetic.* New York, NY: Doubleday, 1971. Print.

Gerald, Carolyn F. "The Black Writer and His Role." In Ervin, 129–134. Print.

Giovanni, Nikki. "My House." *My House.* New York, NY: William Morrow and Company, 1972. 67–69. Print.

Graham, Maryemma and Jerry W. Ward (eds.). *The Cambridge History of African American Literature.* Cambridge: Cambridge University Press, 2011. Print.

Griffin, Farah Jasmine. *"Who Set You Flowing?": The African American Migration Narrative.* New York, NY: Oxford University Press, 1995. Print.

Gronniosaw, James Albert Ukawsaw. *A Narrative of the Most Remarkable Particulars in the Life of James Albert Ukawsaw Gronniosaw, an African Prince, as related by Himself.* In Andrews and Gates, 1–34. Print.

Haley, Alex. *Roots.* New York, NY: Doubleday, 1976. Print.

Hammon, Briton. "A Narrative of the Uncommon Sufferings and Surprizing Deliverance of Briton Hammon, a Negro Man..." *Documenting the American South*. http://docsouth.unc.edu/neh/hammon/menu.html.Web. January 10, 2014.

Hansberry, Lorraine. *A Raisin in the Sun*. 1959. New York, NY: Vintage, 1994. Print.

Harper, Frances Ellen Watkins. *Iola Leroy, or Shadows Uplifted*. 1892. Ed. Hollis Robbins. New York, NY: Penguin, 2010. Print.

Harper, Frances Ellen Watkins. "Frances Ellen Watkins Harper." *The New Anthology of American Poetry: Traditions and Revolutions, Beginnings to 1900*. Ed. Steven Gould Axelord, Camille Roman, and Thomas Travisano. New Jersey, NJ: Rutgers University Press, 2012. 481–496. Print.

Harris, Trudier. "History as Fact and Fiction." In Graham and Ward, 451–495. Print.

Hayden, Robert. *Collected Poems*. New York, NY: Liveright, 1985. Print.

Hemphill, Essex. "Heavy Breathing." In Quashie *et al*. 396–408. Print.

Hoving, Isabel. "Michelle Cliff: The Unheard Music." *The Routledge Companion to Anglophone Caribbean Literature*. Ed. Michael A. Bucknor and Alison Donnell. New York, NY: Routledge, 2011. Print.

Howe, Irving. "Black Boys and Native Sons." *A Case Book on Ralph Ellison's Invisible Man*. Ed. Joseph F. Trimmer. New York, NY: Thomas Y. Crowell, 1972. 150–169. Print.

Howells, William Dean. *Mr. Charles W. Chesnutt's Stories*. Virginia, VA: University of Virginia Library, 1995. *EBSCOHost*. Web. Sept 23, 2013.

Huggins, Nathan Irvin. *Harlem Renaissance*. London: Oxford University Press, 1971. Print.

Hughes, Langston. *The Collected Works of Langston Hughes*. Ed. Arnold Rampersad. Vol. 1. Columbia, MO: University of Missouri Press, 2001. Print.

Hughes, Langston. "The Negro Artist and the Racial Mountain." In Lewis, *Portable*, 91–95. Print.

Hurston, Zora Neale. *Their Eyes Were Watching God*. 1937. Ed. Mary Helen Washington. New York, NY: Perennial, 1990. Print.

Jacobs, Harriet. *Incidents in the Life of a Slave Girl*. In Appiah, 115–353. Print.

Jay-Z (Shawn Carter). *Decoded*. New York, NY: Spiegel and Grau, 2011. Print.

Jefferson, Thomas. *Notes on the State of Virginia*. 1785, www.thefederalistpapers.org. Web. June 23, 2014.

Johnson, Charles. *Middle Passage*. New York, NY: Scribners, 1990. Print.

Johnson, Fenton. *The Book of American Negro Poetry*. 1922. Ed. James Weldon Johnson. Revised ed. New York, NY: Harcourt, Brace & World, 1959. 140–146. Print.

Johnson, James Weldon. "Preface to the First Edition." *The Book of American Negro Poetry*. 1922. Ed. James Weldon Johnson. Revised ed. New York, NY: Harcourt, Brace & World, 1959. 9–48. Print.

Johnson, James Weldon. "Lift Every Voice and Sing." *Lift Every Voice and Sing: A Collection of Afro-American Spirituals and Other Songs*. New York, NY: Church Pension Fund, 1981. 111. Print.

Johnson, James Weldon. *The Autobiography of an Ex-Colored Man*. 1912. Ed. Charles Johnson. New York, NY: Library of America, 2011. Print.

Jones, Edward P. *The Known World*. New York, NY: Amistad, 2003. Print.

Kenan, Randall. *Let the Dead Bury Their Dead*. New York, NY: Harcourt Brace Jovanovich, 1992. Print.

Kincaid, Jamaica. *A Small Place*. New York, NY: Plume, 1989. Print.

Kincaid, Jamaica. *Lucy*. New York, NY: Plume, 1990. Print.

King, Lovalerie. *Race, Theft, and Ethics*. Baton Rouge, LA: Louisiana State University Press, 2007. Print.

King, Lovalerie and Shirley Moody-Turner (eds.). *Contemporary African American Literature: The Living Canon*. Bloomington, IN: Indiana University Press, 2013. Print.

King, Martin Luther, Jr. "Letter from Birmingham Jail." *What Country Have I?* Ed. Herbert J. Storing. New York, NY: Saint Martin's Press, 1970. 117–131. Print.

Knight, Etheridge. *The Essential Etheridge Knight*. Pittsburgh, PA: University of Pittsburgh Press, 1986. Print.

Larsen, Nella. *Quicksand* and *Passing*. Ed. Deborah E. McDowell. New Brunswick, NJ: Rutgers University Press, 1986. Print.

Leeming, David. *James Baldwin*. New York, NY: Alfred A. Knopf, 1994. Print.

Leonard, Keith. "'We Wear the Mask': The Making of a Poet." In Graham and Ward, 206–219. Print.

Lewis, David Levering (ed.). *The Portable Harlem Renaissance Reader*. New York, NY: Penguin, 1994. Print.

Locke, Alain. "The New Negro." *The New Negro: Voices of the Harlem Renaissance*. 1922. Ed. Alain Locke. New York, NY: Simon & Schuster, 1992. 3–16. Print.

Lorde, Audre. "Poetry Is Not A Luxury." *Sister Outsider*. Freedom, CA: The Crossing Press, 1984. 110–113. Print.

Lorde, Audre. "Stations." *The Collected Poems of Audre Lorde*. New York, NY: W.W. Norton & Company, 1997. 367–368. Print.

Lorde, Audre. "The Master's Tools Will Never Dismantle the Master's House." *Feminism and 'Race.'* Ed. Kum-Kum Bhavnani. New York, NY: Oxford University Press, 2001. 89–92. Print.

McKay, Claude. *Home to Harlem*. 1928. Foreword by Wayne F. Cooper. Boston, MA: Northeastern University Press, 1987. Print.

McKay, Claude. "If We Must Die." *Complete Poems*. Ed. William J. Maxwell. Chicago, IL: University of Illinois Press, 2008. 177–178. Print.

McNeil, Elizabeth *et al.* (eds.). *Sapphire's Literary Breakthrough: Erotic Literacies, Feminist Pedagogies, Environmental Justice Perspectives*. New York, NY: Palgrave Macmillan, 2012. Print.

Major, Clarence. *Emergency Exit*. New York, NY: Fiction Collective, 1979. Print.

Marable, Manning. *Malcolm X: A Life of Reinvention*. New York, NY: Viking, 2011. Print.

Morrison, Toni. *Song of Solomon*. 1977. New York, NY: Plume, 1987. Print.

Morrison, Toni. *Playing in the Dark: Whiteness and the American Literary Imagination*. New York, NY: Vintage, 1992. Print.

Morrison, Toni. "Recitatif." *Ancestral House: The Black Short Story in The Americas and Europe*. Ed. Charles H. Rowell. New York, NY: Westview, 1995. 422–436. Print.

Morrison, Toni. *Beloved*. 1987. New York, NY: Vintage, 2004. Print.

Morrison, Toni. *Sula*. 1973. New York, NY: Vintage International, 2004. Print.

Morrison, Toni. *The Bluest Eye*. 1970. New York, NY: Vintage International, 2007. Print.

Morrison, Toni. "Rootedness: The Ancestor as Foundation." In Ervin, 198–202. Print.

Moss, Thylias. *Slave Moth*. New York, NY: Persea Books, 2004. Print.

Naylor, Gloria. *The Women of Brewster Place*. 1982. New York, NY: Penguin, 1983. Print.

Naylor, Gloria. *Mama Day*. New York, NY: Ticknor and Fields, 1988. Print.

Neal, Larry. "Malcolm X – An Autobiography." *Hoodoo Hollerin' Bebop Ghosts*. Washington, DC: Howard University Press, 1974. Print.

Nugent, Richard Bruce. "Smoke, Lilies and Jade." In Lewis, *Portable*, 569–583. Print.

Ogbar, Jeffrey. *The Harlem Renaissance Revisited*. Baltimore: The Johns Hopkins University Press, 2010. Print.

Olney, James. "'I Was Born': Slave Narratives, Their Status as Autobiography and as Literature." *Callaloo* 20 (Winter, 1984): 46–73. Print.

Pearson, Hugh. *The Shadow of the Panther: Huey Newton and the Price of Black Power in America.* Boston, MA: Da Capo Press, 1995. Print.

Petry, Ann. *The Street.* 1946. New York, NY: Pyramid, 1961. Print.

Powell, Richard J. "The Blues Aesthetic: Black Culture and Modernism." In Ervin, 289–302. Print.

Quashie, Kevin Everod, Joyce Lausch, and Keith D. Miller (eds.). *New Bones: Contemporary Black Writers in America.* Upper Saddle River, NJ: Prentice Hall, 2001. Print.

Reed, Ishmael. "Neo-HooDoo Manifesto." *Conjure.* Amherst, MA: University of Massachusetts Press, 1972. 20–25. Print.

Reed, Ishmael. *Flight to Canada.* 1976. New York, NY: Simon & Schuster, 1998. Print.

Reed, Ishmael. *Mumbo Jumbo.* 1972. New York, NY: Bard, 1978. Print.

Reed, Ishmael. "Railroad Bill, A Conjure Man." *New and Collected Poems.* Ishmael Reed. New York, NY: Atheneum, 1989. 89–94. Print.

Rowell, Charles Henry (ed.). *Angles of Ascent.* New York, NY: Norton and Company, 2013. Print.

Sanchez, Sonia. "Listenen to Big Black at S.F. State." *The Black Poets.* Ed. Dudley Randall. New York, NY: Random House, 1971. Print.

Sanders, Mark A. "Toward a Modernist Poetics." In Graham and Ward, 220–238. Print.

Schuyler, George S. "The Negro-Art Hokum." 1926. *African American Literary Theory: A Reader.* Ed. Winston Napier. New York, NY: New York University Press, 2000. 24–26. Print.

Senna, Danzy. *Caucasia.* New York, NY: Riverhead, 1998. Print.

Shange, Ntozake. *for colored girls who have considered suicide / when the rainbow is enuf.* 1977. New York, NY: Collier, 1989. Print.

Shockley, Evie. *Renegade Poetics: Black Aesthetics and Formal Innovation in African American Poetry.* Iowa City, IA: University of Iowa Press, 2011. Print.

Smethurst, James. *The Black Arts Movement.* Chapel Hill, NC and London: University of North Carolina Press, 2005. Print.

Smith, Anna Deveare. *Twilight: Los Angeles, 1992.* New York, NY: Anchor, 1994. Print.

Smith, Barbara. "Toward a Black Feminist Criticism." In Ervin, 162–171. Print.

Smith, Welton. "Malcolm." *Penetration.* San Francisco, CA: Journal of Black Poetry Press, 1971. 4. Print.

Smith, Welton. "The Nigga Section." *Penetration.* San Francisco, CA: Journal of Black Poetry Press, 1971. 2–3. Print.

Somers-Willett, Susan B.A. *The Cultural Poetics of Slam Poetry.* Ann Arbor, MI: University of Michigan Press, 2009. Print.

Stepto, Robert. *From Behind the Veil: A Study of Afro-American Narrative.* Urbana, IL: University of Illinois Press, 1979. Print.

Thurman, Wallace. *The Blacker the Berry…* 1929. New York, NY: Macmillan, 1970. Print.

Thurman, Wallace. *Infants of the Spring.* 1932. New York, NY: AMS Press, 1975. Print.

Toomer, Jean. *Cane.* 1923. Ed. Darwin T. Turner. New York, NY: Norton and Company, 1988. Print.

Truth, Sojourner. *Narrative of Sojourner Truth, a Northern Slave, Emancipated from Bodily Servitude by the State of New York, in 1828.* In Andrews and Gates, 567–676. Print.

Turner, Nat. *The Confessions of Nat Turner.* In Andrews and Gates, 243–266. Print.

Walcott, Derek. *Omeros.* New York, NY: Farrar, Strauss, and Giroux, 1990. Print.

Walker, Alice. *The Color Purple.* New York, NY: Simon & Schuster, 1982. Print.

Walker, Alice. "In Search of Our Mothers' Gardens." *In Search of Our Mothers' Gardens: Womanist Prose.* New York, NY: Harcourt Brace Jovanovich, 1992. 231–243. Print.

Walker, Margaret. *For My People.* New Haven, CT: Yale University Press, 1942. Print.

Warren, Kenneth W. *What Was African American Literature?* Cambridge, MA: Harvard University Press, 2011. Print.

Washington, Booker T. *Up From Slavery.* 1901. Ed. William O. Douglass. New York, NY: Doubleday, 1963. Print.

Weixlmann, Joe. *Conversations with Percival Everett.* Jackson, MS: University Press of Mississippi, 2013. Print.

Wells-Burnett, Ida. *A Red Record.* In Gates and McKay, 676–686. Print.

Wheatley, Phillis. *Poems on Various Subjects, Religious and Moral.* www.gutenberg.org/ebooks/409. Web. December 11, 2013.

Whitehead, Colson. *John Henry Days.* New York, NY: Anchor Books, 2002. Print.

Wideman, John Edgar. *Brothers and Keepers.* New York, NY: Holt, Rinehart, and Winston, 1984. Print.

Williams, Dana. *Contemporary African American Fiction: New Critical Essays.* Columbus, OH: Ohio State University Press, 2009. Print.

Wilson, August. *Fences.* New York, NY: Plume, 1986. Print.

Wilson, August. *The Piano Lesson.* New York, NY: Plume, 1990. Print.

Wilson, Harriet E. *Our Nig, or Sketches from the Life of a Free Black.* 1859. Ed. P. Gabrielle Foreman and Reginald H. Pitts. New York, NY: Penguin, 2005. Print.

Wolfe, George C. *The Colored Museum.* New York, NY: Grove Press, 1988. Print.

Wright, Richard. "Blueprint for American Negro Writing." *Richard Wright Reader.* Ed. Ellen Wright and Michel Fabre. New York, NY: Harper & Row, 1978. 36–49. Print.

Wright, Richard. *Native Son.* 1940. New York, NY: Harper Perennial, 1993. Print.

Wright, Richard. *Black Boy.* 1944. Introduction by Jerry W. Ward, Jr. New York, NY: Perennial Classics, 1998. Print.

X, Malcolm. *The Autobiography of Malcolm X.* Ed. Alex Haley. New York, NY: Ballantine Books, 1964. Print.

INDEX